Certainties

and **Doubts**

Anatol Rapoport

Certainties and Doubts

A Philosophy of Life

Montreal/New York/London

Black Rose Books No. DD288
Hardcover ISBN: 1-55164-169-0 (bound)
Paperback ISBN: 1-55164-168-2 (pbk.)

Canadian Cataloguing in Publication Data
Rapoport, Anatol
Certainties and doubts : a philosophy of life

Includes bibliographical references and index.
Hardcover ISBN: 1-55164-169-0 (bound)
Paperback ISBN: 1-55164-168-2 (pbk.)

1. Rapoport, Anatol 2. Social scientists--United States--Biography.
3. Mathematicians--United States--Biography. I. Title.

Q143.R33A3 2000   300'.92   C99-901587-7

Cover design by Associés libres, Montréal

**BLACK
ROSE
BOOKS**

C.P. 1258	2250 Military Road	99 Wallis Road
Succ. Place du Parc	Tonawanda, NY	London, E9 5LN
Montréal, H2W 2R3	14150	England
Canada	USA	UK

To order books in North America:
(phone) 1-800-565-9523 (fax) 1-800-221-9985
In Europe: (phone) London (44) 020 8986-4854 (fax) (44) 020 8533-5821

Our Web Site address: http://www.web.net/blackrosebooks

A publication of the Institute of Policy Alternatives of Montréal (IPAM)
Printed in Canada

The Canada Council | Le Conseil des Arts
for the Arts | du Canada

Table of Contents

To my family, friends and colleagues

Lozovaya, Russia 1914: Author.

Lozovaya, Russia 1910:
Author's parents.

Wolomin, Poland 1921:
Author wearing a Russian *podiovka* (p.30).

Wolomin, Poland 1921: Author second from right;
Shura Raskin on his right (p.26).

Vienna, 1933: Author;
conductor of Wiener Konzert Orchester, Paul Breisach;
author's teacher, Paul Weingarten (p.55).

Chicago 1924: Author (Chapter 3).

Großer Musikvereinssaal, Freitag, den 22. Dezember 1933, halb 8 Uhr abends

Unter dem Protektorat Seiner Exzellenz des amerikanischen Gesandten Mr. George H. Earle

Konzert mit Orchester

Anatol Rapoport

(Klavier)

Mitwirkend: **Das Wiener Konzertorchester**

Dirigent: **Paul Breisach**

Programm:

1. RACHMANINOFF:
Klavierkonzert Nr. 3, D-Moll, opus 30
Allegro ma non tanto. Intermezzo. Adagio Finale. Alla breve

Pause

2. STRAWINSKY:
Konzert für Klavier und Bläserorchester
Largo - Allegro. Larghissimo. Allegro

3. TSCHAIKOWSKY:
Klavierkonzert Nr. 1, B-Moll, opus 23
Andante non troppo e molto maestoso - Allegro con spirito. Andantino simplice. Allegro con fuoco

Klavier: Bösendorfer

Programme of Wiener Konzert Orchester, December 22, 1933 (pp. 156-7).

Berchtesgaden, Bavaria, 1949: Author (right) and Shura Raskin at the ruins of Hitler's villa (p.26).

Fairbanks, Alaska 1942: Author (Chapter 6).

Master class at Gunn School of Music, 1928: Moritz Rosenthal at the piano;
author second from right; to his right, Glenn Dillard Gunn (p.44).

Chicago, 1949: Author and Gwen Goodrich shortly after their marriage.

Chicago, 1951: Committee on Mathematical Biology seminar.
Nicolas Rashevsky (bearded); author on his right; Alfonso Shimbel on author's
right; at the blackboard H.D. Landahl, later president of the Society for
Mathematical Biology; standing, second from right G. Karreman,
later president of the Society of Mathematical Biology (Chapter 7).

Ann Arbor, 1962: Author (Chapter 9).

Toronto, 1971: Author (Chapter 10).

Toronto, 1986: Author.
On blackboard matrix representation of Prisoner's Dilemma (Chapter 10).

Mentors and Celebrities

We are well into the last decade of the second millennium and into the last decade of the twentieth century. And in all likelihood I am in the last decade of my life. Time to take stock.

Measuring time by decades, centuries, and millennia is probably a consequence of a biological accident. We have ten fingers, whence the decimal system. The centuries suggest to many of us roughly the boundaries of recent historical eras. I think of the eighteenth century as lasting from the Treaty of Westphalia to the French Revolution (1648-1789); of the nineteenth as stretching between the French Revolution and the outbreak of the First World War (1789-1914); of the twentieth from then to the break-up of the Soviet Empire (1914-1989).

This way of viewing history is now said to be blatantly Eurocentric like the celebration of the 500th anniversary of Columbus' "discovery" of America. I think this way about recent history, undoubtedly because I am a product of European culture.

I want to tell any one who is interested what I believe (i.e., what I believe to be the case) and why I believe it; and also what I believe in (i.e., what I believe ought to be the case). The basis of *what* I believe is easily recognized. It stems from what is currently regarded as "scientific knowledge," largely a product of European culture. These beliefs coincide to a very large extent with the beliefs of all who rely on the same source. The basis of what I believe in is much more difficult to discern. I suspect that similar beliefs of others have different bases. For instance, I believe that all forms of violence should be eliminated from human affairs, and so do the Dukhobors and the Quakers and Jehovah's Witnesses, and the followers of Gandhi, and the Tolstoyans. But underlying their beliefs is a belief in a personal God, which I do not share. I believe in socialism, and so did Marx and Lenin. But I believe Marx's economic theory is the weakest component of his social philosophy, and I think Lenin's conviction that Marx "discovered the laws of motion of history" was a delusion.

The title of this book suggests different degrees of beliefs I hold about what is and about what ought to be. However, it is not the case that my beliefs about "what is" are all based on certainties, while those about "what ought to be" are ridden with doubts. Both certainties and doubts pervade both areas, and I feel a strong urge to sort them out. In doing so I recall persons who influenced my thinking over more or less prolonged periods—my mentors, so to say—and of persons who made an impact on me at a single encounter. Those were celebrities, outstanding personalities and, in my own eyes, either heroes or villains, in two instances both.

My first mentor was my father, whom I remember in vivid detail since the age of three. Practically all my convictions about "good" and "evil" stem from him. He was a socialist and an atheist, and so am I. He was always gentle and considerate in all relations with others. I have not been, but have always wished I could be. Above all, he was a firm believer in secular enlightenment. His was the faith of the Russian intellectual of the "western" orientation. His ideology was an amalgam of humanist spirituality and old fashioned philosophical materialism. As I search for the foundations of my attitudes, I find the same substrate.

My second mentor was Glenn Dillard Gunn, a piano teacher, who ran a small music school in Chicago, until it folded during the Depression. He was in no way an outstanding musician, certainly not an outstanding pianist. But he was a youthfully enthusiastic lover of music at age 53, an apostle of late romanticism (Berlioz, Liszt, Wagner). He was solidly American, smoked cigars, lived in a suburb, was possibly (though I am not sure) a member of a lodge. But he had studied in Leipzig, spoke fluent German, and engaged me in prolonged conversations about the world of music and musicians during the European *fin de siecle*. He was conscious about living in two worlds. Once he told me about a conversation he had on a train with a business man. To the inevitable question, "What line of business are you in?" he replied, "Try to guess." In naming various "lines of business," Gunn's companion ventured "Banker?" "No, thank you," said Gunn. He chuckled as he told me how he took being taken for a banker as a compliment. Finally, he announced that he was a musician and thoroughly enjoyed the other's astonishment. I was most grateful to this man for the way he freely shared with me his enthusiasms and aversions, for treating me like a friend, for his sincere efforts to teach me everything he knew about music and about piano playing, an experience his predecessor had not provided.

The third person to whom I owe much was Nicolas Rashevsky. He had been a sort of prodigy, who got a doctorate in physics from the University of Kiev at the age of 19 during the civil war in Russia. He married a Caucasian princess, fled from the Bolsheviks, and joined the navy of some war lord. After the Whites were defeated, he fled to Turkey, from there went to Czechoslovakia, then to Germany, finally to America. His first published papers (on the theory of relativity) appeared in *Zeitschrift für Physik* under the name of N. von Raschevsky. I kidded him about the "von", and he gave me some involved explanation, which I don't remember. Like Gunn, he had a precious sense of humour and a prodigious memory. He could quote pages of Russian classics and recite biting satirical poetry by Russian students.

In America Rashevsky went to work for Westinghouse Electric. When the Depression hit, they fired him. He found a niche at the University of Chicago.

There he continued to develop mathematical biophysics, a new field he had founded while still in Pittsburgh. He also founded *The Bulletin of Mathematical Biophysics* (now *The Bulletin of Mathematical Biology*). I worked with him for seven years in Chicago. Although Gunn was thirty seven years older than I and Rashevsky only twelve, my relations with both men were quite similar—a mixture of teacher-student and peer-friend relation, which meant much to me and, I think, also to my mentors.

My fourth mentor was S.I. Hayakawa, a second generation Japanese, who made sense of the ideas of Alfred Korzybski. The same ideas were popularized by Stuart Chase (a member of Roosevelt's Brain Trust) in his book *The Tyranny of Words*, which, like Hayakawa's textbook of college English, *Language in Action*, published in the same year, became a best seller. Hayakawa's exposition of what Korzybski called "general semantics" was much deeper than Chase's. It clarified the basic ideas in Korzybski's magnum opus, *Science and Sanity*, retaining their full strength but trimming away the author's narcissistic posturing and obscure verbiage. I read *Science and Sanity* in Alaska in 1943 and at the time dismissed it as pompous nonsense. But soon afterward I stumbled on Hayakawa's miniature masterpiece and changed my mind. During the twenty years of our collaboration I learned a great deal from him. We became close friends. I met my wife at his house. We parted company when we found ourselves on the opposite sides of the Vietnam War issue.

The first celebrity I met was Rachmaninoff. I was fourteen at the time. We had immigrated to the U.S. from Russia three years earlier. My parents still imagined that a musical career of a youngster was usually launched by his being "discovered" by some great master whose protégé the kid became. Somehow my father managed to get an appointment with the great pianist, and we went to see him in his suite at the Auditorium Hotel in Chicago. A valet or secretary came out into the hall to forewarn us that Rachmaninoff never auditioned any one. So the prospect of being "discovered" was out. Father assured the man that we had no intention of imposing and we were ushered in. I remember the feel of Rachmaninoff's hand, surprisingly soft. He asked what he could do for us. Father explained that according to my teacher I showed great promise and that we hoped to get some idea of where would be the best place to study. Specifically, what was the situation in Russia at that time with respect to musical education?

"Why do you ask me that?" asked Rachmaninoff.

Somewhat flustered, father explained that he thought Rachmaninoff, being Russian, would know.

"No," said Rachmaninoff. "I have had nothing to do with Russia since I left. If you wish me to recommend a teacher, I would suggest Alexander Siloti. He is a man of great integrity and will tell you quite frankly whether it is worth your son's while to pursue a career of a pianist."

There was nothing more to say. We expressed our thanks and left. Siloti was in New York. There was no way for me to study with him any more than for me to go to Russia. My parents ran a grocery store on the Northwest side of

Chicago, paying off a $3000 loan from a friend of my father's, who was in the wholesale grocery business.

My father had come to Chicago in 1906 or 1907 and had made his acquaintance then. But he had stayed only a year. Work in a cigar factory did not appeal to him, and he missed my mother (his cousin). He went back to Russia and married her. When he asked Rachmaninoff about Russia, there was still a shadow of a thought of going back some time, when the wounds of the revolution were healed.

The next celebrity I met was Chaliapin. This was in 1934. At that time I was studying music in Vienna and partly supporting myself by writing a biweekly review of musical events in Vienna for the *Musical Courier*, an American trade publication. So I, along with two or three other journalists, got to interview Chaliapin. He spoke no German, and his French was as bad as mine. Occasionally he would slip into Russian, which I translated for the others. His manner was hearty and jovial. He told an amusing story about how he got around the police censor in some provincial town back in the czarist days. Concert singers were required to submit the texts of the songs to the chief of police who checked for subversive material.

"What's this?" the chief wanted to know pointing to the text of "The Two Grenadiers" (Heine-Schumann). "It says here *v plenu imperator v plenu*. What do you mean—the emperor is in prison?"

"It's not our emperor," Chaliapin replied. "It's the French emperor."

"All right, then," said the chief.

"But because he couldn't read music," Chaliapin continued, "he couldn't see that the song ended with a strain from the *Marseillaise!*"

The Marseillaise was prohibited in czarist Russia.

One of the greatest inventions of the twentieth century, the phonograph, preserved Chaliapin's vocal magic but not his visible personality. I had the great fortune to see as well as hear him in both Gounod's *Faust* and in Boito's *Mefistofele*, in Boris Godunov, and in *The Barber of Seville* (as Basilio), and in two concerts. The earlier one was in Chicago, I think in 1925. He kept singing pieces demanded by a shouting audience. At one point he sat down at the piano to accompany himself in a sentimental Russian romance (having pushed the piano to the front of the stage). I guess Chaliapin was to my parents' generation what Frank Sinatra was to mine and Elvis Presley to my children's contemporaries.

The same year I met Otto Klemperer when he came to Vienna as guest conductor. I was engaged to play the piano part in a concert version of excerpts from Stravinsky's ballet *Petrushka*. The part has some brilliant piano passages in the second movement suggesting Petrushka's helpless rage. The last time I had heard the piece a colleague of mine played the piano part and was invited by the conductor (I think it was Scherchen) to take a bow. I looked forward to the same distinction.

I had played a piano arrangement of the "Danse Russe," which occurs in the first movement. So there was no reason to worry even though the entrance is exposed. Still I trembled during the rehearsal, anticipating a cue. There was no cue. After the little "question mark" phrases accompanying the Charlatan's weird gestures (to make the puppets come alive) and a momentary silence, the piano bursts into the "Danse Russe" on the beat. I plunged in and sailed through.

I assumed that I would get no cue for my entrance in the second movement. As the entrance approached, I again put my hands on the keys and looked at Klemperer waiting for the beat. Suddenly he looked at me. It was not an inviting look; he frowned or scowled, it seemed to me. I froze and missed the beat. Klemperer put down the baton and addressed me.

"Why don't you come in, piano?"

Today, sixty five years later, I can still feel Klemperer's sarcasm and abuse as he made me go through the passage, cutting me off at the brilliant cadenza, where he had nothing to do.

After the rehearsal a member of the *Philharmoniker* took me aside and spoke kindly to me. "You should imagine yourself conducting the piece," he told me, "then imagine the piano coming in and yourself at the piano. Go through this several times, and you will be all right. Don't mind Klemperer. He is like that with every one."

The performance went very well. But Klemperer never looked at me once and didn't invite me to take a bow.

The contemporary scientists I admired were Albert Einstein, Bertrand Russell, Norbert Wiener, Linus Pauling, and Leo Szilard—all of them peace advocates. Of these I met only Wiener and Szilard. I do have a letter from Bertrand Russell which I cherish and plan to bequeath to one of my children, whoever wants it most. It is an invitation to join a committee investigating war crimes in Southeast Asia.

Besides Wiener and Szilard, I met John von Neumann and Edward Teller. The memory of the meeting with Von Neumann is ambivalently pleasant; of the one with Teller unambivalently unpleasant.

Rashevsky sent me to Princeton to see Von Neumann. With the change of administration at the University of Chicago in 1953, the position of Rashevsky's Committee on Mathematical Biology (which I had joined in 1947) became precarious. The new chancellor had little use for work that in those days was regarded as esoteric. I was to ask Von Neumann for support in case the Committee was subjected to a "review" (put on the hit list).

Von Neumann was most courteous, attentive, and sympathetic. He said he believed the extension of mathematical methods to the biological and social sciences would produce dramatic advances. He was well acquainted with Rashevsky's work and even with my modest contribution to the evolution of peck order in chickens. We went on to talk about the philosophy of mathematics, and he surprised me by saying he believed that mathematics was ultimately rooted in experience. I had always believed that although mathematical thinking was originally generated by experience with practical problems (counting, measuring) and empirical verification of its generalizations, it came to full fruition only after the umbilical cord to empirical cognition was cut. I accepted wholeheartedly Bertrand Russell's definition of mathematics as a system of propositions in which one never knows what one is talking about nor whether what one is saying is true. It turned out, however, that Von Neumann meant "inner experience." This cleared up for me something I had wondered about, namely, why the mathematicians who challenged Hilbert's formalism were called "intuitionists." Many years later I recalled that conversation when I became interested in V.A. Lefebvre's mathematical model of the human psyche.

Altogether I was most favourably impressed by Von Neumann. I, along with many others, had always regarded him as the most creative and versatile mathematician of our century. Now I saw him as an enthusiast and an excellent conversationalist. All the greater was the shock I experienced when I found out that he seriously and persistently advocated a preventive war against the Soviet Union.

I recalled my disappointment with Klemperer. I had found it relatively easy to reconcile my admiration for him as a musician with being repelled by his personality. But I couldn't reconcile my impression of Von Neumann as a human being with my image of him as a hawk. In my early adolescence I was strongly impressed by Pushkin's mini-tragedy, *Mozart and Salieri* (only five pages long). It is based on a rumor widespread in Pushkin's time that Salieri poisoned Mozart. The second scene of the play takes place in a private dining room of an inn, where the two are having dinner. Mozart complains of a depression brought on by a commission given by a stranger to compose a requiem, a premonition of Mozart's own death. Salieri tries to cheer him up by suggesting that he reread *The Marriage of Figaro*. Mozart recalls that Salieri knew Beaumarchais and asks him whether he believes the rumor that Beaumarchais poisoned some one. Salieri replies that this is hardly likely, because Beaumarchais had a great sense of humour. Mozart agrees. "Besides," Mozart points out, "he was a genius, like you and I, and I don't think genius and crime are compatible." Salieri's tragedy is now revealed. Left alone after Mozart, whom he had just poisoned, leaves, he realizes that his crime is conclusive proof that he, Salieri, cannot be a genius.

I don't think of human accomplishments in romantic terms; so I can't give serious consideration to the question whether Einstein or Von Neumann or any one else was or was not a "genius." But in some sense the question concerning compatibility of intellectual power or artistic excellence with personal values does make sense to me. I find myself undisturbed by cognitive dissonance in the case of Otto Klemperer or Richard Wagner, whom I regard as great musicians but whose personal manners appall me. But I was disturbed in the case of Newton and Von Neumann. Newton, as director of the mint, sent counterfeiters to the gallows. Von Neumann was a fanatic cold warrior. I don't try to suppress one or the other evaluation. But to hold both images in focus is for me much more difficult in the case of a scientist than in the case of an artist.

In the case of Edward Teller, there was no need to hold on to two incompatible images. My image of him as a scientist (or rather as a corrupter of science) fitted my image of him as a person. In 1965 I chaired a session at the meeting of the American Association for the Advancement of Science. The theme was civil defence. The hawks were all for it; the doves were against it. The hawks talked technology. I remember, in particular Eugene Wigner's magnificent plan of putting the entire country underground—a blue print for a model megapolis (ironically amounting to a commune) to insure the emergence of a free society blinking in the sunlight after the nuclear holocaust. The doves argued that massive civil defence measures were destabilizing because they were consistent with preparations for a first strike (in anticipation of a retaliatory attack).

I was unequivocally on the side of the doves but took a sort of self-congratulatory pride in acting out the role of an impartial moderator. I recognized the partisans of each side in turn and limited my remarks to clarifying some points made. I did call attention to the clash of values underlying the two positions and pointed out that in discussions of policy such clashes were inevitable. The most a scientist can do to satisfy the demands of objectivity is to recognize the sources of his/her possible bias and to disclose them.[1]

After the discussion, Teller came up to me and demanded. "Do you have any sense?" I must have looked flustered or, perhaps, stupid, searching for an answer. "Do you have any sense?" he repeated, "Sense in your head?" And he tapped his forehead apparently to make his meaning clear. I don't remember what I replied. Perhaps I was too flustered to say anything.

Looking Back

In retrospect I see my mentors shaping my intellectual and libidinal commitments. I mentioned my encounters with celebrities not because they were significant in affecting my interests and attitudes but because they revealed to me my longings, commitments, and insights. Rachmaninoff and Chaliapin made me realize what Russia, or rather my idealized image of it, meant to me in my adolescence and youth. Klemperer's rudeness was an impressive negative example of how not to act in a position of authority. Szilard and Wiener reinforced my idea of a scientist responsible to humanity. Von Neumann's obsession showed me that the sharpest intellect for which the most intricate analysis is a normal vehicle of thought can be reduced to thinking in crude cliches. When I met Teller, I thought of a conversation I had with Wiener on a plane about his book, *God and the Golem, Inc.*, which turned out to be his last. It dealt with the role of sorcery in human affairs. Wiener pointed to what he regarded as the essence of sin in the Black Mass: "…using the magic of modern automation to further personal profit or let loose the apocalyptic terrors of nuclear warfare." By a memorable coincidence I heard of Wiener's death on the day I was finishing a review of the book.[2] The Jekyll-Hyde image of science has haunted me ever since.

NOTES

1. Moderator's Remarks: Civil Defense. *AAA Symposium*. Volume 12, Washington, D.C. American Academy for the Advancement of Science, 1966.

2. *God and Golem, Inc.: A Comment on Certain Points where Cybernetics Impinges on Religion.* Cambridge, Mass.: MIT Press, 1964. In *The Bulletin of Atomic Scientists*, May, 1965.

Childhood

2

My parents belonged to a generation of Russian Jews who in their youth rejected religion and with it Jewish cultural traditions. They spoke Russian rather than Yiddish among themselves, aspired to a professional career, and, above all, to a university education.

To enroll in a university one needed a "certificate of maturity," that is, a secondary school diploma, and to get into a gymnasium (secondary school) was difficult. The quota for Jews, if I am not mistaken, was 3%. There was, however, another way of getting the certificate of maturity, namely by studying "externally," that is on one's own. One could take an examination at any time covering any number of gymnasium classes. Passing an examination covering all eight classes entitled one to the certificate. The problem of getting admitted to a university, however, remained. The same quota applied.

Although this path to the university was difficult, it was well marked. One knew at all times where one stood—so many examinations passed, so many to go. One also knew what one had to know and how this knowledge was to be obtained. It was all contained in standardized textbooks. There was arithmetic, algebra, geometry, and trigonometry. There was Russian, Latin, French, and German. There were four textbooks on geography to be absorbed in prescribed order: (1) general, (2) Asia, Africa, America, Australia, (3) Europe, (4) Russia. There was history, ancient, medieval, and modern. There was a textbook on natural science (*prirodovedenie*) covering physics, chemistry, botany, zoology, anatomy, and physiology. Answers to examination questions were all contained in those textbooks. If one could reproduce them, one passed.

Since a large part of the examination was oral, it could not be entirely objective. It was a simple matter to get a student flustered if the examiners were so inclined. Nevertheless, the examinations provided a chance to get the coveted certificate of maturity and so a point of support for further struggle in the pursuit of a university education and of a professional career. So one memorized the Latin declensions and conjugations, the names and locations of rivers, mountain ranges, islands, and peninsulas. My mother used to reminisce about those gruelling years of cramming by rattling off the peninsulas of North America counterclockwise (as was required): Alaska, California, Yucatan, Florida, Labrador. I remember her telling me that she was long under the impression that Florida and Labrador were very much alike, because they were pronounced in the same breath. There was also a list of capes in small print, but those were optional.

I also remember my mother's stories of how she studied ancient history. She was about fifteen when she left home to go to Kiev "to study." I am not sure where she got support. Her family lived in severe poverty at the time. Perhaps she stayed with some relatives. She could not get into a gymnasium, so she studied "externally." Two elderly maidens (both gymnasium teachers), probably impressed by the young girl's determination to get an education, offered to tutor her free of charge, that is to say, to hear her recite the assigned lessons. One time mother recited a lesson about Greek mythology.

"A fierce dog guarded the gate of Hades. He was called Kerberus."

"Cerberus, my dear," one of the ladies gently corrected her.

"In my book it says Kerberus," my mother replied bravely.

"Let me see. Why so it is. But this is an old edition."

It probably was. My mother picked it up in a flea market. "I still don't know," mother used to conclude the story, "whether it was Kerberus or Cerberus that guarded the gate of Hades. Anyway I never found out nor thought I needed to know where or what this Hades was."

Mother's sojourn in Kiev was interrupted by illness. She returned to Cherkassy, a town on the Dniepr where her family lived and doggedly continued her "studies." She was the eldest of seven children. The others emulated her example. All had the same aspiration to get an *obrazovanie* (an education) and to become professionals. Professional status would remove the residence restrictions imposed on Jews in czarist Russia. They dreamt of living in Kharkov or Kiev or even Moscow or Petersburg. Three of my mother's sisters and one brother "made" it to the gymnasium and after the revolution to university. All became physicians. Medicine was about the only profession they had any conception about. Mother, however, married her cousin a few years after he returned from America, and I came fourteen months later.

Russian elementary schools in those days did not provide an adequate preparation for the gymnasium. Parents who hoped that their children would get an education engaged tutors, mostly young people who themselves aspired to professional careers, often university students. My mother had resigned herself to the life of a housewife. but father was determined to enter university. They both made their livelihood as tutors.

I was not quite three when I learned the Russian alphabet from blocks. In those days there was no reticence about making known the intellectual achievements of one's children; so the often repeated family anecdotes have remained in my memory. At times I even think I recall the following incident.

I was walking around the waiting room of a rail road station and pointing out letters of the alphabet in the public notices. (Or rather I must have been carried, since the notices were surely above my eye level.) There was one letter I could not find—the *izhitsa*, the last letter of the Russian alphabet before it was abolished in the spelling reform of 1918 along with other phonetically superfluous letters. As far as I know, the *izhitsa* occurred in only one word meaning "myrrh" (the aromatic oil mentioned in the Bible). It stands to reason that this one word in which the *izhitsa* occurred did not appear in any of the notices posted in a railway station. I was told that my failure to find the *izhitsa* made my cry.

I must have learned to read and write in my fifth year. Before that I used to like to pretend to write. I remember vividly how one boy tutored by either my father or my mother looked at my scrawls and told me they were not real writing. I replied that I was writing German. Thereupon they produced a German capital J and said, "Now here is a German letter."

I know I could write before I was five, because I remembered writing letters to my father (dictated by my mother), when he was away in 1915. He went away to escape the draft. Along with all young men, father had to report for military service every year. He got deferred status each time, because he deliberately starved himself for several weeks before each physical examination. A year after World War I broke out, men with deferred status started to be induced to replace the heavy casualties. When the proclamation announcing the extension of the draft was about to be posted throughout our town, the town printer, an acquaintance of ours, informed us of the order the day before. Father immediately packed and left for Baku, which at that time was still immune to the draft. (The Moslem population of the Caucasus was regarded as unreliable in a war against Turkey, Germany's ally.)

We lived in Lozovaya, the town where I was born, a railway junction on the line from Moscow to the Crimea. When father left, we moved in with my mother's parents just across the street. My formal education (I was taught by my mother) started at that time. Russian children were taught to read by spelling out syllables and putting them together. Russian lends itself well to this method, since most of the syllables are consonants followed by vowels (:as in Italian and Japanese). For instance in learning to read "mama," the Russian child used to recite (perhaps still does, for all I know): "Em-a-ma; em-a-ma: mama." Or else, "el-o-lo; sha-a-sha; deh-ee-dee; loshadee." (Horses)

I was taught to write by tracing the letters along the dotted lines on specially ruled paper. I looked forward to starting arithmetic. Mother told me that soon she would get a *zadachnik* (a problem book). When it finally appeared, the title puzzled me. I expected to see *Zadachnik*. Instead it was called *Sbornik Arifmeticheskikh Zadach* (A Compendium of Arithmetic Problems). In retrospect the formidable title seems wholly inappropriate for the level of instruction, but it reflects the solemnity with which the education process was regarded.

I still remember the first problem in the Sbornik: Mother gave her boy an apple. Later she gave him another apple. How many apples did mother give her boy? Evidently the book was meant to be used for several years. Toward the end it contained problems of this sort: A merchant bought 40 arshins of black and blue serge. Black serge cost 1.20 rubles the arshin; blue serge 1.80 rubles. He paid 54 rubles for the lot. How many arshins of each kind of cloth did the merchant buy?

Mother's youngest sister, about thirteen or fourteen at that time was my favourite aunt in my grandparents' house. She wore the uniform of a gymnasium student—a black pinafore over a brown dress. I remember her cramming Russian history.

"Our ancestors," she recited from the test, "were called Slavs. Several tribes tried to found states, but those were soon conquered or absorbed into more powerful states. Only the great Russian state grew strong and survived to our day as the Russian empire."

And further down: "Emissaries were sent to Rus (a Viking tribe). 'Our land is rich and plentiful,' the emissaries said to Rus, 'but there is no order in it. Come be our princes and rule over us.' A chieftain named Rurik and his two brothers consented. This was in 862."

My young aunt's ancient history book had pictures. I remember the sphinx, still buried up to her neck. (That was before she was dug up.) The natural science book also had pictures, pretty ones of flowers and two scary ones—one in colour of the human muscular system and one of the human skeleton.

I had a little library of my own consisting of Russian folk tales. Each was a separate booklet of a few pages, costing, I think, a kopek. Before I learned to read, they were read to me. Of course I had favourites, which I asked to be read again and again and so memorized them. I was often asked to recite the stories, which I was far from reluctant to do being anything but shy. I think that my intense love for the Russian language stems from those old tales, all in the eloquent idiom of the Russian peasant, quite unlike the monosyllabic readers of today. I think memorization of textbooks defeats the supposed aim of education (enlightenment); but memorization of artistic literature (with which Russian folk tales merge) is gratifying and salubrious. When I went to high school in America in the 1920s, the youngsters were still required to memorize poems or passages from classics. Most American youngsters I knew resented this, but I enjoyed it. I was glad to add Macbeth's soliloquy and passages from Edmund Burke's speech on reconciliation with American colonies in my repertoire, which at the time included several fables of Krylov, Lermontov's "Borodino" and "Lullaby," and magnificent passages from Pushkin's "Bronze Horseman."

Baku

In early spring 1916 my mother once said to me, "Soon we shall go far, far away—to the Caucasus." From then on she would talk to me about that country, about the huge mountains (I had never seen a hill), about the sea (I had never seen a river), about people wearing strange dress and speaking strange languages. Finally she said, "And you know what?" "What?" "You mustn't tell any one. Promise?" "I promise." "Word of honour?" "Word of honour."

"Papa is there!"

We went in March. As mother promised, it was quite warm, and father was there to meet us.

Childhood memories are vivid and lasting. I still remember the address in Baku—101 Bondarnaya. I remember being carried. I remember father pointing to the house across the street and saying, "There is 90." I saw the number—white on a blue background over a gate. "And here is 101." The number was on a lantern.

Among my memories of Baku, one of the most prominent is the absence of mountains—a disappointment. I did see the Caucasian range from the train far to the south. I had memorized the names of the great peaks—Kazbek, Elbrus, Ararat, but I never saw them. The sea, however, was there as promised. I was even taken for a boat ride and got seasick. I loved it nevertheless. I have loved the sea ever since.

I remember the stench of the oil refineries and complete absence of greenery except in the city parks. The one to which I was taken to play (roll my hoop) was called Parapet. Another, which I thought was more beautiful, was called (if I can trust my memory) Balkansky. To this park father sometimes took me early in the morning. We sat on a bench in a shady path. He studied for the final examinations—for all eight classes of gymnasium, that is, for the certificate of maturity. He passed the examination, which took several days, receiving "4" in seven subjects, "5" in three, and "3" in three. "5" was the highest mark; "3" was passing.

The population of Baku included Armenians and people who at that time were called indiscriminately "Tatars" (today they are called Azeris). The labourers (the poorest) were Tatars. Some were porters. They carried padding on their backs for lugging heavy burdens. (I still don't know why they didn't use wheelbarrows.) If I recall correctly, they were called *ambaly*. I was afraid of them. Somehow I got the idea that they kidnapped children and carried them off on their padded backs.

The other vivid memory is about the opera. I was taken to three operas. The first was Glinka's *A Life for the Tsar*, with which an opera season in Russia always opened. Of that I remember the choruses and of the scene where a young boy (sung by a soprano) sings "Otoprite!" (Open!) at the gate of a monastery. The next was *La Traviata*, of which I remember most vividly the dying scene, where Violetta speaks instead of singing. The third was Rigoletto, of which I remember quite a bit, particularly the hunchback's queer costume and Sparafucile's sinister bass.

Beyond Reading, Writing and Arithmetic

In late fall mother and I went back to Lozovaya. Father stayed on in Baku. In winter I started taking piano lessons with Anna Andreyevna Krupenia, a refugee from the war zone. Grandpa, who prospered during the war, had bought an old grand piano for his younger son, who played by ear and taught me two tunes. One was a polka, played mostly on the black keys; the other a revolutionary funeral march, composed, I think, to commemorate the massacre of demonstrating workers in St. Petersburg in January, 1905.

On our first visit, Anna Andreyevna listened solemnly to my polka and funeral march and said she would take me as a pupil. Then she showed me how I must hold my hands. The thumb should not dangle below the keyboard, she said; it should rest on the keys along with the other fingers, because, she said, it was a finger like the others. Then she showed me how to play the C major scale with the right hand and with the left hand. She explained that since the scale has eight notes, and I have only five fingers, it is necessary to pass the thumb under the third finger on the F, so as to make the five fingers suffice for playing the eight notes. In coming back, the third finger has to be passed over the thumb on the E, so as to finish with the thumb. With the left hand the procedure is reversed, since the left hand is a mirror image of the right. (She let me see the reflection of my hands in a mirror.) I was to practice playing one octave of the scale with each hand separately and to play it for her at the next lesson. I fond all this fascinating. There was logic about it and there was a goal—to play the scale up and down without a mistake.

Twice a week I was taken to Anna Andreyevna, and each time she taught me something new, and I looked forward to it. After a few lessons I was introduced to printed music, first the treble clef, then the bass clef. I was taught to play little patterns, first with each hand separately, then with both hands together. The "text" was Bayer's "School." Besides there were the exercises of Hannon—the same pattern repeated on successively ascending or descending sets of five notes in various permutations. In time, I was told, I would play "pieces." I looked forward to "pieces" with trepidation. My first book of "pieces" was a French album called *L'enfant pianist*, consisting of ditties, some folk songs, and some snatches from "classics," that is, tunes from well known compositions or from opera arias, one from *La Traviata* (*"Libiano ne' lilem clici"*), one from *Rigoletto* (*"La donna e mobile"*), both of which I remembered from Baku, one from *Pearl Fishers,* my father's favourite.

The school subjects now included history ("Our ancestors were called Slavs…"), geography (our world is round…), *Prirodovedenie* (nature study) would come later, mother told me, when papa came home. I learned to read gothic print, then roman.

Grandpa showed me the Hebrew letters. Hebrew is written without vowels. Some prayer looks, however, are printed with diacritical marks representing vowel sounds underneath the consonants (perhaps for the semi-literate or for children). Grandpa taught me to read Hebrew words by spelling them out syllable by syllable, just as Russian children learn to read. He did not know much Hebrew nor much about religion. Grandma was much more pious than he. Grandpa spoke Ukrainian to me. Grandma spoke to me in halting Russian. I spoke only Russian, but I picked up an understanding of Ukrainian from grandpa and from country girls who helped with the housework and an understanding of Yiddish from my grandparents' conversations with their children.

I had an appetite for words. I suppose I listened intently to conversations and learned that way. I wanted to learn new words, but wanted to avoid showing my ignorance. So I resorted to a stratagem. Instead of asking what a word meant, I asked what is the difference between something and something else, hoping in this way to learn two new words at once. I remember asking some one what the difference was between "minimum" and "notary public." "Don't you mean between 'minimum' and 'maximum'?" I was asked. "No, I mean between 'minimum' and 'notary public'," I insisted.

During the fall and winter of 1916-1917 I became aware of the war. Postcards came from Uncle Misha (now a prisoner of war) via the Red Cross. On the address side I read *kuda?* (where to?) and *komu?* (to whom?). On the message side were a few words in Russian from Uncle Misha. Going the other way were parcels with cookies baked by grandma. Phrases like "before the war" and "when the war is over" occurred frequently in conversations. I remember making a contraption out of broomsticks and boxes, which, I explained, was a long distance gun. The projectile would take two years to reach "the front" and would put an end to the war.

Several refugees from the war zone came to our town. Anna Andreyevna was one. She did very well teaching middle class Jewish children. I still have a group photograph, where I see myself sitting between her and a little girl I was fond of. I also see my favourite aunt as a teenager. She lived to over ninety.

Other refugees did not do so well as Anna Andreyevna. The Jews were billeted with Jewish families. For a while we had a young couple with a baby. Some prisoners of war were also billeted to private homes. We had one from Austria. Naturally, he, too was Jewish and was treated by grandma as one of the family. She used to say that this would insure good treatment of her son in Austria.

One day Uncle Borya, Misha's younger brother, a gymnasium student, who had taught me the polka and the funeral march, came home excitedly waving a newspaper, shouting, "Franz Joseph is dead!" I knew who Franz Joseph was from conversations and asked whether that meant that the war was over. Adults smiled condescendingly.

Revolution and Tolstoy

One day grandpa said to me. "The tsar abdicated in favour of his brother." But grandma intervened. "Don't talk politics to the child," she said in Yiddish, thinking I didn't understand.

It was mother who introduced me to "politics." On May 1, 1917 she pinned a red ribbon on my Russian shirt with an embroidered collar and told me to announce at morning tea, "I am a Social Democrat Bolshevik." In answer to my questions, she explained that there were Social Democrat Bolsheviks and Social Democrat Mensheviks and Social Revolutionaries and that we were Bolsheviks, because Bolsheviks wanted to end the war. She also told me about the coming elections to the Constituent Assembly. The whole family except grandpa and grandma went to a mass outdoor meeting celebrating the First of May, the first legal celebration of international labour solidarity in Russia. I was raised on some one's shoulders to see the speakers. A brass band kept playing the *Marseillaise*. I learned the Russian version: "Let us denounce the old world! Let us shake its dust from our feet! We need no golden idol…We shall join our starving brothers, etc." And there was the rousing refrain, "Arise, working people!"

In summer, when university classes ended, papa joined us. He had been admitted as a student in the faculty of law at the University in Rostov-on-the-Don. It was actually the University of Warsaw, evacuated when the Germans seized Poland. He was busy teaching evening classes ("liquidating illiteracy"). He also spoke at meetings. Once I asked him how one made a speech. He said, first of all one must have something to say. If one does, one simply says it. The answer struck me as eminently sensible. I decided to try it. I got together some dozen kids, put them in two rows and addressed them. I told them the grown-ups kept "organizing" (I was not sure what it meant); so we, kids should also organize. I don't recall what else I told them, except that I raised the issue of lack of apples in the market.

That summer I was introduced to the public library. The librarian showed me the shelf with children's books. The books were numbered serially. I took Number 1. I no longer remember what it was about. It couldn't have been very interesting. When I returned it, I took Number 2. It, too, was uninteresting, and I returned it without having finished it. I recall wondering whether it was proper for me to take Number 3 without having finished Number 2. Somehow the librarian became aware of my predicament and explained that I could take any book, not necessarily in serial order, and that I could examine it to decide whether I wanted to read it. So I examined several and chose one about bees. It was great, especially the slogan, "All for one, one for all!" that the bees repeated as they went thorough their adventures.

The visits to the library and the music lessons were interrupted when I came down with typhoid fever along with my mother and Uncle Borya (who had taught me to play the black key polka and the funeral march). My father and grandma nursed all three of us. The treatment was starvation. For six weeks we had nothing but heavily sweetened tea. During convalescence we ate a great deal. I remember being ravenously hungry all the time. I had always been a poor eater and was thin. That fall I became fat. And all of a sudden the appetite was gone, and I was thin again.

The lessons resumed, including music lessons, and now I had an additional interest in reading. But the library was now closed. I knew almost all the folk tales by heart. I occasionally opened some books of my parents' library. Judging by the space they occupied in the room where my mother and I slept, it must have contained about a hundred volumes. Most of the books were nineteenth century Russian classics—Pushkin, Gogol, Turgeniev, Dostoevsky, Tolstoy, Chekhov. I also remember two volumes of Karl Marx and two of Max Nordau. Somehow I got the impression and Karl Marx and Max Nordau were related, probably because Marks and Max sounded alike and they had similar covers—imitated marble. I asked questions about what all those books were about but don't remember what my mother said about them except on one occasion. She said I might try to read the stories in Volumes 15 and 16 of Tolstoy's works. This I did.

Volume 15 contained an elementary reader, which Tolstoy prepared when he organized a school on his estate for village children. It also contained arithmetic lessons, a special attraction for me. I remember especially that numbers could be written not only the way I learned to write them but also in roman numerals. There were also pictures of numbers represented on the abacus. I learned to use the abacus, which became a necessary adjunct in my games of "Thousand" (a simple card game of the melding family) with my grandfather.

There were also simple science lessons. I remember one about the sun. The sun gives us light and warmth, it said. I already knew that. But what I did not know and what fascinated me was that the sun's warmth was also "locked" in things. We burn wood in our ovens, Tolstoy said (wood was the principal fuel of the Russian peasant). The warmth that comes from the fire is really the warmth put into the wood by the sun, since it was the sun that raised the trees. We eat bread. The sun grew the grain; so the warmth of the sun is in bread. We eat meat. The animals were raised on grain and grass, and these were raised by the sun. The sun is the source of all life. It all seemed wonderful.

There was a story told by a traveler. He stopped at a country inn and was attacked by the bed bugs as soon as he put out the candle. Assuming they came from the walls, he moved his bed to the middle of the room. That didn't help. He saw the bugs crawling along the floor and up the legs of the bed. Then he had what he thought was a brilliant idea. He asked for four buckets, put water in them and put the legs of the bed in the buckets. "I outsmarted you," he said to the bugs as he was falling asleep apparently undisturbed. But soon he felt a bite. Sure enough there was a bed bug in his bed. How in the world did they get to him? Then he saw. The bugs crawled up the wall to the ceiling, then crawled along the ceiling till they were above him and dropped down on him. (*Si non e vero, e ben trovato.*) A description of the sense of smell of non-humans followed. I remember one piece of information that made a deep impression on me: a bed bug can smell a human being at a distance of hundreds of thousands of bed bug paces. I tried to imagine what this would mean in human terms. Relativity of size was brought home to me.

Chemistry, too was introduced by a dramatic story. A woman was drawing water from a well. The bucket fell off the hook. She asked a neighbour to restore it. He laughed and said, "You lost it, so you get it. However, I will let you down."

He tied a board to the end of the rope; the woman sat on it, and he slowly lowered her down the well, asking now and then, "Enough?" She would reply, "Just a bit more." But once there was no reply. He looked down and saw the woman with her head in the water. Alarmed he called others and had himself lowered. He, too, fell off. A crowd gathered. One young peasant tied himself to the board and asked to be let down. The others all watched. Suddenly he collapsed. Being tied, he didn't fall off and was pulled up. The village school teacher explained that the air in the well was bad and that no one should try to go down. The last man to go was revived, but the woman and the first man were not.

The "bad air," the explanation went on, is called carbon dioxide. We breathe oxygen and exhale carbon dioxide. Carbon dioxide is heavier than air. This is why it concentrates in low places. There was carbon dioxide near the water surface of the well. The gas itself is not poisonous, but it is useless for breathing. Breathing it instead of air, which contains oxygen, causes suffocation. There are some caves, where carbon dioxide is concentrated near the ground. The air above it is all right. So a man walking into the cave is safe, but a dog will suffocate. Once in a war between the English and the Hindus, the Hindus captured several hundred Englishmen and locked them in closed quarters without ventilation. By the time the doors were opened, most of them were dead.

Volume 16 was altogether different. It contained stories Tolstoy wrote in the last decade of his life when he demonstratively stopped writing "literature" and devoted himself to preaching what he believed to be the real message of Jesus.

The first story I read was entitled "Where Love Is, There God Is." It was about a cobbler who lived in a basement. When he was widowed, he was left with a little boy who was his pride and delight. But the boy went down with a "fever" and died. The cobbler went through a deep depression. A pilgrim who spent the night with him advised him to read the Gospels.

Once when he read longer than usual, he fell asleep over the book and heard a voice in his dream. "Martin! Look through the window tomorrow. I shall come." Through his basement window the cobbler could see only the feet of the people who passed, but he recognized them by their foot wear, since most of it had gone through his hands. Still now and then some strange pair of boots passed by, and he bent over to see who it was, laughing at himself for expecting to see Jesus Christ.

During the day he had three experiences. In the morning he saw the old janitor clearing snow and panting exhausted. He called him in and let him warm himself with some tea. At noon, he invited in a woman with a baby who was in some sort of trouble and gave her dinner. In the late afternoon he intervened when he saw a woman beating an urchin who had tried to steal an apple from her basket. He made peace between the two, then gave the boy the apple promising to pay for it. After that he had a long conversation with the woman about Christ's teaching and she forgot to ask for the money.

The day was over, and evidently Jesus failed to come. But as Martin dozed off over the Gospels, the people he had helped appeared to him one by one. Each said, "Don't you recognize me, Martin? It is I." Waking up he read on the page in front of him:

Inasmuch as ye have done it unto one of the least of these, my brethren, ye have done it unto me. (Matthew 25, 40.)

The story dominated my reflections during the "Christian" phase of my childhood, which lasted through the winter of 1917-1918. I was "converted" to Tolstoy's Christianity by the simplified version of the Gospels that Tolstoy prepared for children. There was nothing there about virgin birth, nor about the trinity, nor about the redemption of sins through blood sacrifice, nor about the transfiguration of bread and wine into the body and blood of Christ. Jesus was presented as a son of a carpenter who pondered on how one should live. The needs of the body seemed to be at cross purposes with how God wanted us to live. Should one, then, kill the body? No, this could not be the answer, for otherwise God would not have given us life. Finally the correct answer occurred to Jesus: one must live in the body, but one must serve God, not the body. This made sense to me. I was most impressed by the parables: simple stories illustrating the ethical imperatives by events in every day life.

Crimea

In contrast to the February Revolution, which I remember vividly in connection with what the adults talked about, the only thing I remember about the October Revolution was that I had to learn the new orthography. Father left again to start his second year at the university in Rostov. In March mother and I moved to Crimea, where we stayed until we left Russia. Later father joined us, again after escaping the draft, this time decreed by General Krasnov, a Don Cossack war lord, who organized an anti-Bolshevik force in northern Caucasus.

We lived in Feodosia on the eastern coast of the peninsula. My social environment changed radically. In grandfather's house I was the only child among big people. In Feodosia we lived in an apartment complex surrounding a large court yard, where a dozen children, ranging from three-year-olds to teenagers, formed a genuine community, stratified, of course, according to age. Among them were two cousins of mine, Volodya, a year younger, whom I dominated, and Sonya, five years older, whom I adored.

It was Sonya who started me on foreign literature widely read by Russian children in translation: fairy tales and adventure romances. Andersen, Lagerloff, Defoe, Stevenson, Verne, Kipling, Twain. Some of these I didn't start reading until I was about nine; but Sonya told me the stories in her own wildly imaginative way. She also drew well and aspired to become an artist. She spent all her life teaching art in elementary schools.

Christianity was forgotten. The heroes of the stories were anything but martyrs. Adventures were interwoven with fighting, and fighting led to victories. To be sure, some of the stories projected moral lessons. *Pinocchio* did. There was another widely read translation from Italian entitled *The Heart*. The characters were all school boys. Each chapter was about an incident that involved some moral problem. One boy, in particular, Garonne, was a paragon of virtue and wisdom, as well as a master of conflict resolution. Once a month the teacher read a story connected with events of the Risorgimento, in which acts of heroism or good citizenship were depicted. I remember one story in which a boy searches for his father (missing in the war against Austria). The search takes him all the way to Argentina. I sympathized with the boy, because I felt my own father's frequent absences keenly. On the whole, however, I was not impressed with *The Heart* and its harping moral lessons. I mentioned my misgivings to Sonya, and she said *The Heart* was sentimental drivel, which settled the matter.

The events of 1918-21 crowded out what remained of my Tolstoyan Christianity. The most conspicuous adults I saw in Feodosia were armed men. In the summer of 1918, Crimea was occupied by the Germans. A number of them kept house in an arbour in the middle of the court yard of our apartment complex. They impressed us children by their foreign speech and by their chores—cooking their meals on Primus stoves, cleaning their rifles, and polishing their bayonets. Sonya said (possibly imagined) that they also carried hand grenades and described their action.

After the Germans left in fall, "power" in Feodosia kept changing hands. At times it was the Bolsheviks, at times the Don Cossacks. After Denikin's White Guard Army was routed, Crimea was ruled by General Wrangel, the last of the war lords. His regime was supported by Russia's erstwhile allies. Feodosia harbour was dotted with English, French, and Italian warships. Soon the kids learned to recognize destroyers, cruisers, and mine sweepers. There was awed talk about "dreadnoughts," but I don't remember even seeing one. The streets were often crowded with sailors. They all wore sailor suits and looked like little boys. (I, too, had worn a sailor suit when I was little.) They all spoke foreign languages. A young girl neighbour of ours, once brought home an Italian. Paolo Martello was his name. I remember him going through hammering motions when he introduced himself (martello=hammer). Father, who at the time was with us, tried to converse with him in Latin, how successfully I don't remember. But I remember how the Italian explained with sweeping body gestures that the Mediterranean was usually calm, but that the Adriatic could be very rough.

The ships carried guns, and the kids learned to recognize them and to talk about twelve-inchers and sixteen-inchers. All of us discussed the ongoing war and quarrelled about who was stronger, braver, cleverer—the Reds or the Whites. I don't recall that the issues of the war were ever discussed. The contending armies were for us contestants, nothing else. In the same way we discussed the relative merits of the wrestlers who appeared in the ongoing circus. They all had fancy names: Jaguar, Titan, the Black Mask (who remained masked until he was defeated). We rooted for one or the other. In the same way we discussed the relative merits, that is, the prowess of the English and the French, both of whom, we agreed, were incomparably superior to the Russians. I recall one boy about my age supporting the championship of the English by citing incidents from the French and Indian Wars about which we had read in Fennimore Cooper's *The Last of the Mohicans*. I championed the French, citing instances from Schiller's *The Maid of Orleans*, which I read in Zhukovsky's translation. Zhukovsky, incidentally, was my favourite poet at the time. He is noted primarily for his translations, among them of the *Odyssey*. To this day, I regard his translation of Goethe's *Erlkönig* superior to the original. Eventually, I switched my allegiance to the English. The British sailors played soccer in the lot adjoining the building where we lived on Italian Street. We kids thought they were wonderful. We waited eagerly for a ball to go wild and ran to fetch it and get a nod of approval from a sailor.

Once an American freighter docked. My parents and I went to the harbour to see it. Father shouted in English to some on the deck, "Is there any one among you from Chicago?" I suppose he had a faint hope that he might send a message to his mother or to an elder brother who had emigrated before World War I. But the man on deck did not reply.

All the kids, including me, thought that the world outside of Russia was brighter, certainly richer, more "advanced" than Russia. That world was represented by military might. Most of us rooted for the Whites, whom the English and the French helped to fight the Reds. This loyalty was reinforced by dramatic cartoon posters plastered all over the city showing Bolshevism as a terrible dragon coiled around "the heart of Russia" and being attacked by a Herculean horseman brandishing a sword. My cousin Sonya, however, who was for me the ultimate authority on all matters, despised the Whites. She said the Reds would come soon and would drive them out, and then the English and the French and the Rumanians, and the Greeks would turn tail and go back to their own countries where they belonged.

In the meantime, however, life under the Whites flourished. There was plenty of everything: brisk trade, inflated currency, above all "culture." A considerable portion of the intellectual and artistic world fled south from advancing Bolshevik armies and were bottled up in the Crimean cities. I remember hearing Smirnov, the Russian rival of Caruso, in concert. As he was singing encore after encore, the audience split into two camps. Some kept calling for Lensky's aria from *Eugene Onegin*, others for *"La donna e mobile"* from *Rigoletto*. Smirnov's accompanist played a solo, a composition of his own that he called "Faust." It was very loud and did not make much sense to me. But his jerky mannerisms impressed me. I started to imitate him when I played the piano until my mother told me to stop it. (Anna Andreyevna had also come to Feodosia, and I resumed lessons.) I also had lessons in French and English. French didn't take, but I did get a smattering of English and impressed the kids by talking to the sailors.

The theatre flourished. I remember Schiller's *Robbers*; also a play called *Satan*, a sort of amalgam of Goethe and Sholom Aleikhem. There was a prologue in which Satan bets with God that he can corrupt a righteous man. The man is a pious Jew of whom God is very proud. Satan takes the shape of a business man who worms his way into the victim's confidence and persuades him to buy a lottery ticket. At first the pious Jew objects: "If I win all that money, some one must lose it." Satan explains that this is not so, that people risk only small amounts and no one will really lose much money. So the Jew buys a ticket and wins a fortune. He comes to hate the life of luxury, but is compelled to do what is expected of him. He engages in large scale business operations, and Satan sees to it that he is forced into bankruptcy. I don't remember how he gets redeemed in the end.

I mention this play to illustrate the prevailing attitude toward money in Russia. It was unambivalently negative. To love money, to aspire to riches was disgraceful, sinful, self-defeating. The attitude is reflected in the simplest folk tales and in the deeply insightful novels of Dostoyevsky. Many years later I saw a performance of an adaptation of Sholom Aleikhem's story, "The Big Win." It was a time when antisemitism in the Soviet Union was rampant and hardly anything associated with Jewish culture appeared in public life. But this play was performed in one of Moscow's theatres. The plot revolves around a poor tailor who wins 150,000 rubles in a lottery and the unhappiness the fortune brings him. I remember, in particular, his gnawing hunger for work, which he expresses by a gesture depicting cutting cloth with scissors.

Crimea under the White occupation had also a frightening side. Once father was arrested and questioned about alleged contacts with political prisoners. He attributed his release to a frank acknowledgement of his socialist sympathies. He pointed out that democratic socialists were persecuted by the Bolsheviks as cruelly as the monarchists; so he could not possibly collaborate with them. Apparently the interrogator believed him.

Another incident was more frightening. Once a colonel knocked on the door of our ground floor apartment and demanded, "Where is my laundry?" My mother's astonishment only infuriated him. He began to rant, whipping himself into frenzy. Finally he summed the situation up: "If I don't get my laundry by two o'clock, a shake-up will start from this place and will spread throughout the city. You people know what this will mean!" There was no mistake whom he meant by "you people." Although Wrangel's forces, unlike Denikin's (his predecessor's in the South) were not particularly noted for pogroms, one could never tell.

A clue to the absurd situation was provided by the young woman across the hall, the one who had introduced us to Paolo Martello, the Italian sailor. She was a seamstress. She said a soldier, evidently the colonel's orderly, had brought her some shirts to be mended. She remembered that he had a large bundle with him, which may have been the missing laundry that he took to some washer woman in the vicinity. Possibly he misinformed the colonel about where the laundry was dropped off. A search revealed the washer woman, who wondered why the laundry was not picked up. My mother took it, paid for it, and asked a youngster to deliver it to the colonel who lived in the same building. Months later, when the Reds were already in the city, father saw the colonel in the yard chopping wood. Somehow the man, now in civilian dress, knew who my father was. He came up to him and demanded with a note of defiance, "I suppose you will turn me in, won't you? I have no money to give you, but I have a few things you may be interested in." Father assured him that he had no intention of turning him in. They met frequently in the yard chopping wood and exchanged cordial good mornings until the colonel disappeared.

We knew his fate. Practically all the officers, the bulk of Wrangel's army, who did not get on the evacuation ships bound for Turkey, were rounded up, taken in parties of twenty or thirty to the hills around the city and machine-gunned. The farmers including my uncle and aunt (Sonya's and Volodya's parents) could hear their screams.

The Reds occupied the city on a bright November morning. We saw their cavalry riding past our windows. Five of them, Kazan Tatars, were billeted with us. They all camped in the living room. They were decent fellows and shared their rations with us. One of them could play piano a little. He played tunes on the black keys, which form a pentatomic scale. We felt safe while they were with us. They were from the 30th (Siberian) Division, which had a reputation for discipline and correctness toward the civilian population. After a couple of weeks they were replaced by the Ninth Division, evidently quite different. It was the command of this division that was responsible for the atrocities.

Father went to work as the secretary of the local board of education, citing his status of university student as qualification. His "salary" was a pound and a quarter of black bread per day: a half pound for him (a worker), a half pound for me (a child), and a quarter pound for mother, neither worker nor child. Mother had managed to tuck away a few pounds of barley. Aside from that there were occasional hand-outs. I remember, in particular, a jar of jam, two eggs and a slab of mutton. Some of the hand-outs were useless. Once cans of shoe polish were passed out - anything that happened to remain in the emptied stores.

In the spring of 1921 the N.E.P. (New Economic Policy) was introduced and the Ukrainian markets were full of produce. There was nothing in Crimea, however, Crimea was being punished for being the last stronghold of the Whites. All foodstuff that the authorities could scrape up were shipped in box cars bearing the inscriptions "A GIFT FROM RED CRIMEA."

Exodus

In April, 1921 father was granted a month's leave. We went to my grandparents. We travelled nine days in a box car to get to Lozovaya, a distance of about 300 kilometres. The box car was not as bad as it sounds. It was fixed up with sleeping platforms and equipped with a pot-bellied stove, on which we cooked our food. Peasants brought bread, potatoes, chickens to the train and traded them for things that we had brought along for that purpose. Two or three families occupied the box car. We formed a closely-knit community sharing everything and engaged in interminable conversations as befits Russian intellectuals.

The journey took so long, because the engine had to be changed at every major station. Generally there were none available; so we stayed on a siding for two or three days. Sometimes I woke at night and felt we were moving. But we were just being switched from one siding to another. The engine burned wood. At times expeditions were organized to find wood. The engine was too weak to climb grades; so every one had to get out to push. At the whistle of the engine every one strained to get the train moving. Once it started, the effort could be relaxed. When the top of the incline was reached, the engine whistled again; every one jumped back into or onto the cars. I say "into or onto," because not one travelled inside cars. Many rode on the roof or on brake platforms or even on buffers.

Food was plentiful in Lozovaya, and we ate ravenously, just as after the bout with typhoid fever. When the month was up, mother declared that we were not going back. Instead we went to a *mestechko*[1] on the Polish border, where my uncle Misha (the one who had been a prisoner of war) lived with his wife and baby daughter.

The war with Poland was over, and borders were drawn, but "Soviet power" had not yet been extended to the border regions. In particular, the *mestechko* Satanov was in a sort of no-man's-land, officially in Ukraine (the Soviet Union had not yet been formed) but apparently without "authorities." The townspeople were mostly Jewish; the people in the adjoining countryside Ukrainian farmers. There was lively trade, but I have no idea what was traded for food, perhaps the products of the local artisans—cobblers, tailors, locksmiths. There were two currencies: Polish marks (the predecessors of the *zloty*) and old tsarist twenty-five ruble notes with a picture of Catherine II, the only tsarist currency that was accepted. For some reason these notes were accepted only in perfect mint condition, which was strange, because new notes were more likely to be counterfeit. As for marks, they were accepted in any condition. I don't know what we lived on. Possibly father gave Russian and English lessons to people who foresaw changes in their lives. I understood Yidish but did not speak it. Jewish kids kept passing the word around about me *er ret rissish* (he speaks Russian). They did not actually shun me but close contact was never established. My playmates were Ukrainian boys.

My only Jewish friend was the six-year-old son of the people we lodged with. I taught him to speak, then to read Russian. His name was Shimon. I called him Shima. I showed him the Cyrillic letter Ш (sha), which stands for the "sh" sound and looks much like the Hebrew letter ש (shin), which stands for the same sound. He already knew the Hebrew alphabet. Then I showed him the Cyrillic letter и which stands for the "ee" sound and taught him to say "shee" when he saw the Ш followed by the и letter. Next I taught him to read "ма" to make "mama" and finally to combine Ши with "ма" to make "Shi-ma,"[a] which, to his delight, spelled his name. In Hebrew school they taught him to read in the same way–syllable by syllable, the way Russian children were taught. In a few weeks he could read Russian.

The purpose of coming to Satanov was to find a way of getting out of the country and getting in touch with our relatives in Chicago, who would help us immigrate. But by the time the plan crystallized, an "authority" was established in Satanov. Guards were placed on the bridge across the river Sbruch, the border with Poland. It was decided that at first mother would cross (bribing the guard) and get to Warsaw, where there was an agency that assisted Jewish emigrants. Through them she could contact Uncle Mendel, father's elder brother in Chicago, and we would start the process of emigrating to America.

We heard nothing from mother for three months. There was still no postal service. Messages were brought over by smugglers. Finally, a note came from mother saying that she was just across the river. She wrote that everything was set. Uncle Mendel sent affidavits to be filled out. It remained to wait for a visa, which would be sent to the American consul in Warsaw. But it was too risky for mother to try to cross the border. She might not make it, and we would be stuck. We should somehow try to cross and join her on the other side.

Father got in touch with a smuggler who promised to take us across. We moved in with a family living in a hovel on the river bank, where the smuggler was supposed to contact us when the opportunity to cross arose. For about a week nothing happened. Father must have got desperate. One day he suggested that I might try to get across alone. The river was frozen. I was to take a pair of skates and join the children skating near the other bank, then slip away and find mother. I suppose father thought he might have a better chance of crossing alone or else he wanted me to join mother in case he could not cross.

I took the skates and started across the river in bright sunshine in full view of the bridge, heading for the group of boys skating on the other side. A guard shouted at me from the bridge and it seemed to me that he aimed his rifle at me, though I may have imagined it. I remember turning back and climbing over a fence.

The vigil in the hovel continued. One night father woke me and told me to dress. The smuggler was there accompanied by a Red Army man, who said he would take us across the ice. If we were caught, he told us, he would say that he arrested us and was taking us to the guard station. Whatever happened, he said, he had to be in the clear. We paid him, and he told us to follow him.

As we went over the ice, I remember carrying an extra pair of shoes and drooping one. I didn't bother to pick it up. The only thing that existed for me was the other bank, a rather steep one. We reached it. Some one came down the slope and gave me his hand. He took us to a hut where mother met us. I remember my father sobbing, when mother told him that his mother in America had died two months ago.

We got into a wagon and were driven to a railway station. On the way a Polish soldier stopped us. Crossing the border was prohibited by both sides. Crossers were supposed to be arrested and taken back where they came from. Father had Polish marks, which he kept giving to the soldier until he waved us on.

We were lucky. A train came within minutes of our arrival at the station. We got on and got to Lvov, where we spent a few days before moving on to Warsaw.

We lodged with a Jewish family on Twarda Street (in the old ghetto). The apartment was on the fourth floor of a large tenement house. There were two rooms, (a dining room and a bedroom), a kitchen, and a toilet. The inhabitants were the two pairs of parents, our host's old mother, and three children besides myself—a girl in her teens, another girl my age (10) and a boy of 8. Our host couple slept in the dining room. In the bedroom I slept with the boy in one bed, my parents in another; the two girls slept in the third bed. The old woman slept in the kitchen. The children were in school six days a week; so during the day I was mostly on my own. I read a lot. (Russian books were available in private lending libraries.) I studied English.

When the children came home from school, we all had dinner. Then the children did their homework. Then we played, making up plots of stories we acted out. I got along splendidly with the two younger children, Andzia and Pawelek. I learned Polish. I had hoped to establish a relationship with the elder one (whose name I don't remember, except that it was derived from "dove") similar to my relationship with my cousin Sonya. She did not dismiss me, but she was too busy with her homework and with household chores.

Eleven years later I came to Warsaw to give a recital and felt a strong urge to look these people up. I remembered the address: Twarda 23, Apartment 48. No one answered the bell. I knocked on the door of the apartment below. The same neighbour opened the door. I recognized him by the cataract on his eye. I said who I was.

"Rapoport!" he exclaimed. "Is it possible? You are so young!"

He took me for my father.

Yes, he could tell me about the Frombergs. They moved to the country, where they managed some one's summer resort. The children were in the city, but he had only the elder daughter's address.

I went to see her. She was married. She had emigrated to the United States, but had a wretched time there during the Depression and came back. She seemed genuinely delighted to see me. She talked much about her brother, who was a student, but evaded my questions about Andzia. Finally she told me Andzia was in the Communist underground. I could meet her but only on the street. She would arrange it.

We met on a busy street. I wanted to tell her about myself, but she asked no questions, and I felt uneasy talking about myself before asking her about herself. And this I promised her sister I wouldn't do. So the meeting was perfunctory. I pecked her on the cheek, and she caught a street car. Unless these people managed to escape to the Soviet Union, they all must have perished a few years later.

In Warsaw I saw my fourth opera, Gounod's *Faust*. I was profoundly impressed, and until I was introduced to Wagner five years later, it remained my favourite. In retrospect it seems to me that I was thrilled by the dramatic portrayal of the satanic. Later I was fascinated by the universality of the *comedia del arte* trinity: the passionate frustrated lover, the tantalizing beauty, the object of his passion, and the mocker Harlequin.

My first serious piano teacher was an ardent romanticist. He regarded Liszt's music superior to Bach's. And Liszt, too, seems to have been obsessed by the *comedia del arte* trinity. His *Faust* symphony is in three movements, representing Faust, Gretchen and Mephisto. The thematic material of the last movement is a sort of sarcastic distortion of that of the first. That Symphony was the first orchestral score I studied (at age fifteen). In fact, to get a real "feel" of it, I patiently copied it.

My harrowing experience with Klemperer was also connected with this theme, since Petrushka, the Ballerina and the Moor are the Russian equivalents of Pierrot, Columbine and Harlequin. I suppose that all these experiences have remained exceptionally vivid memories partly because they were resonant with some romantic streak in my make-up.

In the spring, because of some regulation governing refugees, we had to move out of the city. We stayed in Wolomin, a small town, now a suburb of Warsaw. I remember two other refugee families, the Raskins and the Richters. Both had boys of my age. I still have a photograph of me and three boys with our arms around each other's shoulders. I don't remember the third one. Misha Richter crossed the ocean with us.[2] The Raskins settled in Belgium. During the war the Germans rounded up all the Jews they could find. The Raskins were being transported probably to an extermination camp. My friend Shura somehow managed to escape from the train and survived. When the Americans came, he was recruited by the OSS.

Shortly after Gwen and I were married (in 1949), we went to Europe, and I found Shura Raskin in Munich. He was then working for some agency concerned with surviving Jews. He took us to see the ruins of Hitler's villa near Berchtesgaden. After that I tried to continue contact with Shura without success. My guess is that he was working for the CIA and wanted to avoid contact with the people who told me about him, because they were communists. I was told about this by friends of my parents, who had been with us in Wolomin.

Life in Wolomin was waiting for the visa. Father went to Warsaw once or twice a week to inquire and to buy delicatessen. Some money came from America and a large parcel of clothes for the three of us, those for me being too large. (I was eleven but looked like an American seven-year-old.) This went on until July. Then it was all over. Father came back from the city with jars of jam, cans of sardines, etc. On each package he had scribbled "The visa came!" In two or three days we were on the way: Warsaw; Paris (a day of sight seeing), Le Havre; seven days in a dorm for third class passengers, the French liner "Paris"; seven days of rough crossing; the Statue of Liberty; Ellis Island; three days by rail to Chicago (stranded in Buffalo because of a railway strike).

As we were rolling into Chicago, father told us to note the numbered streets which marked the local stations of the Illinois Central: 63rd Street, 59th Street, 55th Street…The numbers kept decreasing. Father said we would arrive at 12th Street. And so we did: end of journey.

NOTES

1. In western Ukraine Jews lived mostly in little towns (distinguished from villages where peasants lived) called *mestechkos*. They are the locale of most of Sholom Aleikhem's stories.
2. His cartoons appeared in *The New Yorker*. I looked him up once, and we reminisced about life in Wolomin.

America

3

All of father's "American" siblings and their children gathered at the home of Uncle Mendel. After much kissing and embracing, father introduced me to a very tall young man and asked whether I knew who he was. When I identified him as Uncle Niuma (Benjamin), he hugged me and made much fuss over me. I recognized him because he had come to Russia when I was three. He had come to register for military service because he did not want to lose his Russian citizenship. I remembered him fondly. He used to crack jokes and sing American songs, such as "Any little girl who is a nice little girl is the right little girl for me." Once an airplane flew over Lozovaya, and he pointed it out to me. In Chicago we became close. He was the only one of father's siblings who spoke fluent Russian.

Father went to work almost immediately. His first job was on the night shift in a printing shop. Soon after that Uncle Niuma got father a job as a milkman (he himself was a milkman). It was a night job. That is, he went to work about 2 A. M. delivering milk by horse and wagon until morning. Then he made collections until afternoon. It was hard work, but it was a union job and paid well—$36 per week. It was August. I had another month till school began. We lived two weeks at Uncle Mendel's, then moved to Uncle Niuma's for two weeks.

Uncle Niuma had a Russian library and a "Victrola" (as record players were called in those days). In 1922 recordings were predominantly of three kinds: jazz, ethnic songs, and arias from operas. These were made famous by the opera stars of the day—Caruso, Galli Curci, Tito Ruffo, Chaliapin. Uncle Niuma had a photo of the "peerless three"—Caruso, Ruffo, Chaliapin—sitting around a table. Chaliapin, like the Moscow Art Theatre, was a legend in my family. My parents often talked about him, although they never heard him until we came to America. They repeated stories about him. One was about how some young people in a provincial town came to him at his hotel to complain that they had looked forward to hearing him for years but that tickets were all sold out. Chaliapin offered to sing for them then and there. The windows were open, and a crowd gathered in front of the hotel as he sang.

The first Chaliapin record Niuma put on for us was "The Song of the Flea." In his Russian library there were memoirs of Andreyev, one of which was about Chaliapin singing "The Song of the Flea," each verse accompanied by the supposed effect on the audience when the real Mephisto sang it to German burgers in the fifteenth century. At first they are amused. What nonsense! A flea gets to be a favourite in Court! But gradually they become uneasy. The mood becomes threatening. The palace is infested with fleas. They bite every one including the queen and her ladies-in-waiting. The courtiers dare not scratch, let alone slap the insects. Finally, the jovial singer, now revealed as the devil, thunders, "But we crush them!!!" Andreyev imagines how the burgers must have panicked. He imagines how one of them says to his corpulent wife in bed, "You know, darling, I think I saw the devil today."

The other legend, the Moscow Art Theatre, became reality in 1923. The troupe came to Chicago—the original company including Stanislavsky and Olga Knipper, Chekhov's widow. They played five pieces: Gorky's *Lower Depths*, Chekhov's *The Cherry Orchard, Three Sisters, Ivanov*, and *Uncle Vanya*. The following year they came again and played ten pieces: in addition to the first five Alexei Tolstoy's *Czar Feodor Ivanovich*, Ibsen's *The Enemy of the People*, two comedies by Ostrovsky, and some excerpts from *The Brothers Karamazov*. The first year we three went to see all five; the second year the other five and The Lower Depths again—eleven performances in all. The tickets cost three dollars each, that is, $99. I believe the money was borrowed and paid off in instalments. Another $100 was borrowed to buy an old decrepit upright piano.

I had gone through elementary school during the first year and now went to high school. I got top marks in Latin and algebra, but at first average marks in English and in "physiology." What was called "physiology" was elementary nature study—about how hydrogen and oxygen combine to make water and about how germs cause disease. All this was old stuff for me, but I had difficulty in copying drawings of flowers and of the intestinal tract from textbooks, which had to be done in ink. (Inkwells were built into the desks and filled from a large bottle by pupils entrusted with that job.)

I also did poorly in art class. My first assignment was to make a cityscape by pasting pictures of houses into a pattern. I made a mess of it and got a failing mark. I did somewhat better on the second assignment. We were to make posters illustrating a nutritive alphabet, the letters and their referents. Each had a slogan. A is for "Apple," B is for "Butter,"...E is for "Excellent, Edible Egg," etc. My letter was U, and the slogan jingle was "U is for us, pepper, mustard, and pickles. We're no good at all except to give tickles." I thought this was silly, but there was no way of getting around it. I knew I wasn't going to be an artist, but I was determined to get a passing mark in Freehand Drawing. I painted three anthropoid figures representing "Pepper, Mustard, and Pickles" holding hands and singing (words and notes depicting "Yes, we have no food value" on a balloon), "Yes, we have no food value!" I was terribly ashamed of it, but the teacher liked it and I passed.

My other nemesis was gym. Although I started to grow rapidly, I was still small for my age. To pass gym, one had to make a six-foot standing broad jump and clear twenty feet in three running leaps. I barely managed the latter but never the standing jump. I made up for it by passing swimming. We had swimming lessons every other Monday, and I loved it. I was also permitted to go to the pool during a free period, a privilege I made frequent use of. Swimming reminded me of the sea and of Crimea, for which I was homesick.

I also took piano lessons. My teacher was a distinguished looking white-haired Scot, Mr. Hunter, who went to his pupils' homes. He charged $2 for a 45 minute lesson. I had two lessons per week. I learned several pieces by Edward Macdowell. I suppose Mr. Hunter felt that children in America should be introduced to an American composer. Among Macdowell's compositions were "To a Wild Rose" (an artless melody), "From an Indian Lodge" (imitating "Indian idiom"), "A Scotch Poem" (depicting waves breaking against rocks at the foot of a castle, where an imprisoned maiden was pining). Later Mr. Hunter introduced me to a volume of Haydn, Mozart, and Beethoven. I had played one of Beethoven's "easy sonatas" (op. 49); now I learned one of the "real ones" (op. 2, No. 1). I also learned a Haydn sonata in D major and one of Mozart's in F major. This was my first contact with serious piano playing, but I had not yet heard a concert pianist.

Appreciation of virtuosity and aspiration to it shaped to a considerable degree the values that became dominant in my life. What impressed me most about the Moscow Art Theatre was the versatility of the actors—their ability to put on personalities that were almost opposites. Stanislavsky, who played the cynic Satin in *The Lower Depths*, also played the sentimental aging bachelor Gayev in *The Cherry Orchard*. Kachalov, who played the decrepit baron in *The Lower Depths*, played the dynamic Dr. Stockman in *The Enemy of the People*. Olga Knipper, who played a prostitute in Gorky's play, played the grande dame in *The Cherry Orchard*. Most astonishing was the transformation of Vishnevsky, who played the pedantic teacher of Latin in *The Three Sisters* and the overbearing Machiavellian Boris Godunov in *Czar Feodor Ivanovich*.

For the first four years in the U.S. aside from the books required in book reports in high school, I read only Russian literature. I went through all of Gogol, most of Chekhov and Kuprin and Andreyev. I could not find my favourite poet Zhukovsky, the champion of German romanticism, but I read through all of Pushkin and Lermontov.

I tried to talk to my older cousins about Russian poetry and short stories, about the Moscow Art Theatre and about Chaliapin. They admired my enthusiasm but could not share it.

During those first years there was still talk between my parents and me about the possibility of going back to Russia some day. I doubt whether my parents were serious about this. Possibly they wanted to allay my own feelings of pseudo-homesickness. I say pseudo-homesickness, because I really never lived in the Russia I knew from books.

Once these feelings almost got me in trouble. This was during our first year, when I was still in elementary school. Our neighbourhood was a mixture of Jewish and Polish immigrants. Many of the kids, like me, had just come.

Practically all the rest were second generation East Europeans. This was often brought up by the teachers. I remember one in particular, a Mrs. Garren. She did not conceal her political opinions. Once she discussed the Japanese Exclusion Act. She asked all the children who were either born in the "Old Country" or whose parents came from there to raise their hands. Practically every one did. She went on to say that they were very welcome in America and that she was sure they would all become good Americans. Then she asked whether they knew of people who were not welcome in America. No one knew. She explained that the "Japs" weren't. She said they could never become good Americans. Besides, she said, they wanted to "take over" at least California, always buying up the best farm land and pushing Americans out.

An issue of the school magazine written mostly by the kids and produced by eighth graders in the school printing shop, appeared at the end of each semester. Mrs. Garren asked me to write a piece for it to be entitled "How and Why I Came to America." I wrote about our life in Crimea, about how hungry we were after the Bolsheviks came, how we traveled by box car, how we crossed the border on ice. I also described our sightseeing taxi ride in Paris and the tough ocean crossing.

Mrs Garren said all this was fine, and now I should finish the piece by telling how I liked America.

"But I don't like America," I said. "I would like to go back to Russia some day."

Mrs. Garren looked strangely at me. "You better let your parents help you with this," she said.

At home my parents told me I shouldn't have said what I said. They told me how to finish the piece, which I did. Mrs. Garren liked the ending, and the piece was published—my first piece in print.

My next publication three years later (1926) was a short story in *The Magazine World*, a monthly literary journal devoted to efforts of high school students. My story was entitled "The Podiovka," which, I explained, was a Russian overcoat, the kind one sees on Russians wearing national dress. I got it when we were still in Crimea and had not yet outgrown it. When it got cold in November 1922, I proudly put it on and went off to school anticipating general admiration and my explanations about its origins.

A mob of kids gathered around me yelling, "Look! He's wearing a girl's coat!" They yelled and jumped around me until the bell rang, and the same thing happened during the outdoor recess. I remember my feelings distinctly. I was not humiliated. I told at home what happened, and my parents talked about getting something more suitable and questioned me about what the other kids were wearing. But I would hear nothing about it. I was determined to continue wearing the podiovka. By and by the sensation wore off. The kids paid no more attention to me. One Saturday morning on the way to the neighbourhood library, some strange kid, evidently taking me for a girl, accosted me with the jibe, "Boy's shoes!" I hit him, and he ran off yelling.

My third year high school English teacher, who had encouraged me to send the story to *The Magazine World*, was very proud of me when the piece was published. I was asked to read the story in other English classes and was told that I was cut out for a literary career. It was then that I started to read English and American literature aside from what was required for book reports.

Music, however, remained my primary concern. Mr. Hunter taught me for about a year. Then he told my parents that I ought to try out for a scholarship in a music school. There were three "serious" music schools in Chicago, The Chicago Musical College, The Chicago College of Music, and the Busch Conservatory. Mr. Hunter suggested the first, whose president was Herbert Witherspoon, a retired bass of the Metropolitan Opera, who had sung Wagnerian roles and whose pictures as Gurmenanz, the Landgraf, Henry the Fowler, etc., appeared in my *Victor Book of the Opera* that I kept re-reading.

On the staff of Chicago Musical College was a Russian pianist, Moissaye Boguslavky, who played occasional recitals in Chicago and was regularly heard on the radio. Mr. Hunter said I could not hope to win a scholarship with Mr. Boguslavsky, but his wife was also on the faculty. I might have a chance of getting a scholarship with her and, perhaps, through her attract the attention of her illustrious husband.

I tried out in September, 1924. The judges were behind a screen to insure impartiality. I remember an attack of nervousness, but I got through my piece without mishap—Macdowell's elflike little thing called "Shadow Dance" in F sharp minor. It had some filigree passages of which I was quite proud. There was rejoicing at home when I was informed that I got the scholarship with Mrs. Edna Boguslavsky.

I was thirteen. After two years on the milk wagon, father couldn't take it any longer. Delivering meant a trip of often three flights up the back stairs every few minutes with a half dozen quart milk bottles. Often there was a note in the empty bottle asking for butter or cottage cheese, which meant an extra trip if he did not have enough in his basket. Collecting meant cajoling harassed women besides spending some time of day with them to keep good will.

An opportunity arose in the shape of a paper route in Oak Park, a western suburb of Chicago. Oak Park consisted of neat little bungalows, which, in comparison with the shabby apartment buildings of the Northwest Side, seemed to us like palaces. The streets were immaculate and there was no stench of rotting garbage in the alleys. However, we did not move to Oak Park. We moved to Berwyn, a working class suburb to the south of Roosevelt Road (formerly 12th Street). We rented an attic flat in a frame house heated by a stove. It was, however, roomier than our two small basement rooms on Oakley Boulevard on the Northwest Side.

A paper route was a newspaper delivery concession. The deliveries were made by boys, who gathered about 6 A. M., received their papers, folded them, and threw them on the porches of the bungalows. The boys gathered again after school to deliver the afternoon papers. My parents went around making collections—60 cents per month for the two-cent papers (*Chicago Tribune* and *Daily News*), 90 cents for the three-cent Hearst paper. Also the German *Abendpost* was delivered. The business required practically no initial capital, and the list of subscribers grew rapidly as the suburb grew during the boom years.

When it got cold, some of the boys did not show up in the morning. This precipitated a flood of complaints. ("Say, how come we didn't get our paper this morning?") There were some cancellations, and my parents panicked. They had a vision of every one quitting. Life became hectic. Father would race around on a bicycle delivering the undelivered papers and apologizing. Mother insisted on getting out while we could. The concession was sold for less than we paid for it. (The man who bought it sold it later for five times the amount he paid.) We moved back to Chicago's Northwest Side, and father went back on the milk wagon. I went back to Tuley High School, where I had spent the first year.

The few months in Berwyn made an impact. It was my first experience with school mates who were not children of Jewish immigrants. Morton High School was in Cicero, a suburb east of Berwyn, dominated by a bootlegging mob. The school was two miles away, and until the snow came, I went there on roller skates. I went only half days, because I now practised piano three hours every day. This was the condition under which Boguslavsky took me on as his student when Mrs. Boguslavsky suddenly died. So father went to see Mr. Church, the principal of Morton High School, who was courteous and understanding. It was arranged that I would go to school only mornings and do my homework at home instead of during designated study periods.

Later, when we moved back to Chicago, father tried to arrange a similar schedule at my old school, but he was rebuffed by Mr. Fisk, the seventy-year-old principal. Mr. Fisk showed him a closet full of musical instruments and explained that they were just rusting away—a waste of taxpayers' money. They were supplied to the school for a band or an orchestra or something, but Mr. Fisk would have nothing to do with such nonsense.

"You don't want your son to be a musician," Mr. Fisk told father. "That's no way to get ahead."

In Berwyn, as long as weather permitted, I enjoyed the two-mile roller skate ride to school and back. And I enjoyed practising. School was easy. I knew all the mathematics they taught in the second year (father had taught me all that back in Satanov). I learned some bits of American history. I made good progress in English and read Caesar's *Gallic Wars*. I had no social life. The kids all lived in Cicero and were much too rough for me. One advantage at Morton was that I got to go swimming every other day through January. During the Christmas break half the school building including one of the gyms burned down. So we went swimming instead of doing calisthenics or playing ball, alternating with the girls. On Saturdays I went downtown for my music lessons.

Besides the piano lessons, there was harmony, ear training, and music history. The music history lectures were given by Mr. Witherspoon. They were illustrated by records played on a crank-up victrola. The first Wagner I heard was the overture to the *Flying Dutchman*. It made me a Wagner fan for life and made me look down my nose on people who look down their noses on Wagner. Perhaps this was the reason why later in life my admiration of great artists was not diluted by my contempt for their personalities or their politics, even though the stature of great scientists was diminished in my eyes if their values or politics repelled me.

All in all, life during the fall and early winter of 1924-1925 was pretty good except for my disappointment in Mr. Boguslavsky. He oscillated between lavish praise and abusive sarcasm. He shouted a great deal: "No, no, no! You play like a mujik!" I had thought he would speak Russian to me, but he actually knew very little Russian. He had come to America as a child and had forgotten the language. I complained at home about his treatment. My parents were sympathetic, but told me that nothing could be done about it. We couldn't afford a teacher of Mr. Boguslavsky's stature; so I had to hang on to the scholarship.

Back in Chicago we moved into a little two-room apartment, much more cheerful than our basement on Oakley Boulevard. Spring came, and soon I had many friends. The street we lived on was only a block long (Alice Place it was called in those days). All the kids on the block formed a pretty friendly community, the boys, that is. There were no girls in it. There was one small empty lot, on which soft ball was played. There was also a baseball-like game played with a rubber ball without a bat. The walls of the apartment building next to the empty lot had a narrow ledge on the bottom against which the ball could be bounced. The "batter" would bounce the ball off the ledge and if it was caught by the fielders, the batter was out. If not, it produced a hit—one base, two base, three base, or home run, depending on where it landed. The kids were fair sharing this place. There was a "committee" that made out schedules on the basis of "reservations." The same wall could also be used as a handball court. My aunt Ruth (father's youngest sister) lived in the apartment building, which was the only one on the block. My cousin Ned, three years my junior, told me proudly of the roller skates derby in which he came in third.

One boy, Eddie, who insisted on being called Swifty, took no part in the games. He was Polish and went to a Catholic school. Word went around that his father beat him. I gathered from conversations that Eddie was a bully who would fight at the slightest provocation. It seems he once challenged all the boys on the block and bloodied some noses, thereby establishing himself in his own eyes as the "boss." But the boy with real authority was another lad, the eldest and tallest. He, too, was Polish. He often settled disputes and discouraged fighting. Swifty surprised me once by asking whether I would coach him in Latin. I said I would, but he didn't pursue the subject. I suspect his parents did not approve.

As I said, girls were not part of the boys' community. I saw them playing hopscotch and jumping rope. After almost three years in America I knew better than to try to establish contact with them.

Here is the way I learned. When school started a month after we came to Chicago, we lived with my Uncle Mendel. (We shifted between him and Uncle

Niuma until we found a place of our own.) Uncle Mendel had four daughters. The eldest, sixteen at the time, was practically an adult. She was a senior in high school. She took piano lessons. But a bond on that basis could not be established. She did not aspire to a concert career. She was going to play the organ in a movie theatre, a union job that paid $60 per week. The next was Estelle, a second year high school student. At first I though she would step into Sonya's place; but she didn't. The youngest was a baby. I liked Sophie, two years my junior. We started to walk to school together. The school was named after Chopin, probably in deference to the large Polish population in the neighbourhood. I told Sophie who Chopin was and played for her a piece I had learned when I studied with Anna Andreyevna, entitled Chopin's Last Chords. The dying Chopin was shown on the cover playing the piano. Sophie was impressed.

We walked to school Russian fashion with arms around each other's shoulders. (The photograph I mentioned earlier shows me with Shura Raskin and Misha Richter with our arms around each other's shoulders.) Shortly mother took me aside and told me that Sophie came home in tears. She was teased by the girls about having a boy friend. The matter had been taken up with Sophie's mother. I was told that it was probably all right to keep walking to school with Sophie but not in an embrace. The situation resolved itself when shortly thereafter we moved away and I was transferred to another school. I kept away from girls on Alice Place.

One warm spring afternoon I went on an errand taking some clothes to the dry cleaners' on Milwaukee Avenue, the main business street in the neighbourhood. Stanley, my seven-year-old protegé, a successor of little Shimon in Satanov, accompanied me. On the way back, crossing Milwaukee Avenue, I was hit by a cab. In crossing I first looked left as I had been taught. But the cab had just passed another car and was almost on the left side of the street. I walked into it and was struck by the left rear fender just above my right hip. A crowd gathered. The cab driver jumped out, picked me up, and drove me to a hospital in the neighbourhood. He kept asking me whether my head hurt.

Stanley in the meantime ran home and rang our bell. He told my father who opened the door that Anatol was just killed. Without saying a word to mother, father ran with Stanley to where it happened. Some one told him where I was taken. He appeared at the hospital just as they finished taking X-rays. We went home in a cab, and I was put to bed.

The same evening a man came who said he was from the Yellow Cab Company. He asked me to tell what happened. Then he turned to father and asked, "What do you expect us to do, Mr. Rapoport?"

Father said he expected the cab company to pay for whatever medical expenses were incurred. The man said that this was reasonable and offered father fifteen dollars. He suggested that father sign a paper accepting this compensation. Father said he could not do it until he knew what the medical expenses would actually be. The man warned us against lawyers. He said they always tell people that they can get hundreds of dollars in a case like this one but these schemes never work. The lawyers just want to make money out of poor people. Father didn't sign.

I was in bed two or three days. Saturday I went down town as usual but told Mr. Boguslavsky that I wasn't prepared because I was laid up and couldn't practise. I told him about the cab company representative's visit and had the satisfaction of watching him pour out his anger on some one other than me. Mr. Boguslavsky said he would put us in touch with a lawyer. When I said we couldn't afford to pay a lawyer, he said we wouldn't have to. He said the lawyer would make the company pay and would take his fee out of what they paid. So we went to see the lawyer recommended by Mr. Boguslavsky. He said he would take up the matter. We heard nothing further until a cheque for $100 arrived from the lawyer. I was told he got $200 from Yellow Cab Company and kept half of it. I don't remember what the medical bills were, but there was plenty of money left after they were paid. The money was put in the bank in my name. I have not known poverty since. By the time I went to Europe in 1929 I was "worth" one thousand dollars.

Adolescence

Father couldn't continue on the milk wagon. His feet hurt. His other elder brother, Uncle Ike, who was a salesman for the Del Monte company (canned fruit), knew several owners of small grocery stores. In those days they were not yet driven out of business by the chain stores. Uncle Ike said a fair living could be made from a grocery. One could be bought for about $3000, most of it representing the stock on hand, the rest "good will," depending on how well the business was doing. An opportunity presented itself. Two young men had a grocery on Chicago Avenue, just west of Oakley Boulevard. The store had been doing well, but it was ruined when word got around that one of the two young men who ran it molested a little girl. It could be bought very cheaply. Besides, there was another plus. An old friend of father's whom he knew when he was in America the first time, was in the wholesale grocery business. He could give us several thousand dollars' worth of stock on credit. It was important, Uncle Ike explained, to have the store well stocked. And if one had the credit, one could keep it well stocked, because canned goods keep. They don't deteriorate like the goods kept in bins or barrels. My father became a storekeeper in June, 1925.

The storeroom behind a partition was turned into living quarters, and we moved in. A dog supposedly went with the premises. She had four newborn puppies. But the men took her and two of the pups, leaving the other two orphaned. I tried to raise them on a bottle. One died, the other survived to become a very lively and friendly little dog, something like a fox terrier. I named her Cookie. She accompanied me when I made deliveries and was generally admired. Soon, however, she came to a sad end. A toddler was rough with her and she snapped at him. The toddler's mother made a fuss, and Cookie was taken to the pound. She was released in a few days but in very bad shape. She died on my hands.

I missed the kids on Alice Place. There was no comparable community in the neighbourhood. Soon, however, I became absorbed in music and forgot everything else.

My relationship with Mr. Boguslavsky deteriorated. My scholarship was extended, but he began to defer lessons from week to week. I would wait at the door of his studio for the preceding student to come out. Mr. Boguslavsky would come out with him or her, sadly shake his head and say, "Sorry, I can't take you this week. Come next Saturday." I stopped coming. I told my parents I would study by myself, and they supported me, probably thinking of their own days as "external" students. Lessons in harmony, counterpoint, etc., however, continued (these were taught in classes).

I discovered a second hand music store, where I picked up the third volume of Beethoven sonatas for ten cents, *The Well Tempered Clavichord* as cheaply and some piano scores of operas—*Faust, Aida, Barber of Seville*—for 30 cents a piece. I discovered that the Chicago Public Library (a handsome authentic looking Renaissance building on Michigan Avenue) had a music room. I discovered orchestral scores and books on orchestration. I discovered the Chicago Symphony Orchestra. Gallery tickets were 50 cents. If you came early enough, you could be among the first to be let in when the door to the gallery entrance opened and could run upstairs to get the choicest seats in the first row right behind the conductor. I practised. I began to give lessons to kids in the neighbourhood for 50 cents, then a dollar. I even took singing lessons from the leading bass in the Chicago Civic Opera chorus, whose wife shopped in our grocery. I played for a Hungarian operetta troupe.

These Hungarians performed in the industrial suburbs of Chicago with large Hungarian populations. They did translations of French and Austrian operettas and some Hungarian ones. They rehearsed in union and lodge halls. The trickiest part of my job was to come in on the right cue. Not knowing a word of Hungarian, I managed somehow to recognize the sounds leading up to the cue. Once I made a mistake at a performance and was severely reprimanded by the director, who was also the comedian and the character actor of the troupe. His wife was the leading lady. Once I visited their home and found to my delight that their two children, a boy and a girl, both read Jules Verne. They read it in Hungarian; so they were kindred spirits, that is, kids who remembered. None of the kids I knew were like that. I kept hoping I could meet some kids who remembered Russian, but I never did. In fact, after we left Russia I never met a Russian speaking child until 1943 in Alaska.

I also took organ lessons, intending to make a living by playing organ in movie houses like my elder cousin. In Chicago electric organs were used even in the shabbiest theatres, successors to nickel shows. Courses in "movie organ" were offered in all music schools. The repertoire of a movie organ player consisted of piano arrangements of songs, marches, waltzes, and such. Some pieces were called "classical," e.g, Tchaikovsky's, Grieg's, Rubinstein's (whose compositions were still played in those days), Chopin's, Massenet's. Some were old salon pieces

("Warrior's Song," "Jacob's Dream"). Some were "ethnic" fragments to be played on occasions when foreigners appeared on the screen (Italians, Mexicans, Russians, Jews). There was also "Indian" music to accompany Indians in Westerns. Finally, there were standard "mood" fragments—*Furioso* to accompany storms, *Mysterioso* to accompany suspense scenes, especially at night, *Amoroso* for love scenes. Each film came with a program listing the sequence of scenes timed to a second together with recommended musical accompaniment. The organist was to arrange the accompanying fragments in proper sequence and switch as the scene on the screen changed. During slapstick comedies or cartoons jazz was played without regard to what was happening except for occasional sound effects, for which special stops were provided on the larger organs. In the large down town theatres a skilful organist was regarded as a valuable adjunct to a film.

The organ was played just like the piano except that the bass of the accompaniment was provided by the pedals. Only the left foot used the pedal keyboard. The right foot was always on the "swell" pedal, which controlled volume. One also learned to manipulate the stops, that is, to mix the imitations of instruments (including *vox humana*). There were stops for special effects: bells, chimes, several kinds of drums. The *vibrato* stop was always to be kept on except in church scenes.

I took lessons in a small music school on the West Side and practised in an ancient mouldy church. All this turned out to be a waste of time. The sound movies killed the profession. I never knew what happened to the hundreds of organs. However, in retrospect I value the experience which put me in touch with popular American culture, until then *terra incognita*. I became aware of the gulf between me and the majority of my school mates and of links between me and a minority.

Once I met my old teacher, the white haired Mr. Hunter on the street. He wanted to know how I was getting on. We had already moved out of the store room in the back of the grocery to a real apartment and had bought (on instalments) a small grand piano. I asked my parents to invite Mr. Hunter to our apartment. (I don't recall what arrangements were made for them to get away from the store; I think we had a young man working for us.) Mr. Hunter listened to me play Brahms's G minor Rhapsody and a Grieg sonata. He told me with as much tact as he could muster that I played poorly. He blamed the organ. He told me what I already knew, namely, that although the piano and organ keyboards looked alike, the instruments had practically nothing in common. In playing the piano everything depends on touch—the range between staccato and legato, the range of dynamics, which on the organ is not controlled by touch. Everything he told me I already knew but tried to ignore, telling myself that many musicians played both organ and piano. But in fact I never liked the organ. Whether the dislike stems from the incompatibility of techniques or from my disdain for the uses to which the organ was put in the movies I don't know; probably both. Even my fondness for Bach does not attenuate that ambivalence. I scandalize purists by expressing my preference for Liszt's, D'Albert's, and Busoni's piano transcriptions of Bach's organ fugues to the originals.

Mr. Hunter said I should forget the organ. There were other ways of making a living in music. He also said I should go to a good teacher. Since I was going to get some sort of certificate from Chicago Musical College at the end of the academic year, I felt I could leave it. Mr. Hunter suggested that I try for a scholarship at the school of music run by Glenn Dillard Gunn. Dr. Gunn (the first person I heard called "Dr." who was not a physician) was the music critic of the *Chicago Herald* and *Examiner* and was generally respected. Mr. Hunter said he was a very conscientious teacher.

I went to see Dr. Gunn in September, 1927. I had graduated from high school in June, spent the summer practising long hours (to the dismay of neighbours, who eventually made the landlord refuse to renew our lease). I played the first prelude and fugue from the *Well Tempered Clavichord* and one of Schumann's *Fantasiestücke*. Dr. Gunn said he liked my playing and that he would recommend me for the Pick scholarship. The scholarship was established by Albert Pick, supplier of hotel equipment, in memory of his son. In a few days I was informed that I got the scholarship.

I spent two years at the Gunn school of music. Gunn was really an inspiring teacher. His interest in music was broad and unabashedly enthusiastic about everything he loved. He told anecdotes about great musicians, offered sweeping judgments about the differences between the Germans, the French, the Russians, and the Italians. He told me how my own ethnic background (a mixture of Russian and Jewish) was (or, rather, ought to be) reflected in my music making. He called my attention to musical imagery. When I was studying Bach's *Chromatic Fantasy and Fugue*, he asked me what the four chromatically ascending notes of the fugue, A-B flat-B-C suggested. I couldn't think of anything. Then he played the opening measures of the prelude to *Tristan and Isolda* emphasizing the ascending chromatic tones G sharp-A-A sharp-B and asked the same question. I still couldn't say.

"Desire," he said.

I had just heard *Tristan*, the first Wagner opera I heard. For years afterward it seemed to me the embodiment of the fundamental function of music—expressing the inexpressible. I was grateful to Gunn. He was an adult, an old man, in fact, in my eyes (53 at the time). Yet he spoke to me, a teenager, about things that were most important to me in a language used among equals. He had strong opinions about everything; yet he was willing to listen to me. He knew German and spoke to me much of Goethe and Heine and Schopenhauer. As I said at the outset, he was one of my early mentors, as was my father, but in an area which did not intersect with my father's, which was socialism.

During these two final years of my adolescence I participated in two local piano contests. I won first prize in one—a grand piano, the sale of which helped finance the first year I spent in Vienna. I was one of three finalists in the second but did not win it.

My preoccupation with socialism began in consequence of conversations with father. Actually these started during the presidential campaign of 1924. The candidates were Calvin Coolidge (Republican), John William Davis (Democrat) and Robert Lafollette (Progressive). Lafollette was supported by the socialists, who ran no candidate in that election. Since 1912 Eugene Debs had been the socialist candidate. In 1920 Debs was in jail for having agitated against the participation of U.S. in Word War I. But now Debs was dead. Lafollette, father explained, was not a socialist, but he would vote for him, if he were a citizen, because he represented the interests of the working man. He told me what those "interests" were. He explained about "surplus value" and about what it means to exploit the labour of others.

About this I had read a great deal in Tolstoy's writings as well as about the evils of war and of the duty to refuse to serve. So I admired Eugene Debs and hoped Lafollette, who, I thought, was also a "sort of socialist," would win. Lafollette carried only his own state, Wisconsin. I wanted to know why, if he, too, represented the working people, working people did not all vote for him. Father explained that most people were influenced by what they read in newspapers and that newspapers were controlled by capitalists. The newspapers distorted socialism, identifying it with Bolshevism. I asked father whether he was not a Bolshevik, and he said no. He said the gulf between socialists and Bolsheviks was wider than between socialists and capitalists. He said socialists were jailed and shot in Russia for opposing Bolshevik dictatorship.

My interest in these matters grew. I think it was in 1925 or 1926 that I heard a debate between Scott Nearing, a prominent American socialist, and some old gentleman, whose name I don't remember. The debate was in Orchestra Hall (where the Chicago Symphony played). The hall was packed. The moderator was Clarence Darrow, who had defended Leopold and Loeb, the teenage thrill killers of their thirteen-year-old cousin and saved them from the gallows. He also participated in the defence of John T. Scopes, a high school teacher, who was prosecuted in Tennessee for teaching evolution. Clarence Darrow was much admired in "left" circles, although in the opening remarks at the debate he professed extreme ambivalence toward both "socialism" and "capitalism."

The theme of the debate was stated in the usual formal way: "Resolved that democracy is impossible under capitalism." Nearing spoke for the affirmative.

"I suppose the best way to begin," Nearing began, "is to define democracy. I define democracy as public control of public affairs."

Over sixty-five years have passed since then, but I still remember these opening remarks. I also remember the opponent's opening remarks.

"I am grateful to Mr. Nearing for defining democracy. I agree entirely with his definition. It remains for me to define capitalism. I define capitalism as private control of private affairs."

I reported these remarks to father, and we had a long discussion about what comes under public and what under private affairs.

About that time I discovered the novels of Upton Sinclair: *Oil, Jimmy Higgins, One Hundred Percent*. They dealt with the class struggle in the U.S.: union busting, the Palmer raids, the vigilantes of California—heady stuff. I spoke of these books to a classmate of mine, who, I knew, liked to read. She said she had not read any of these books, but she read *Babbitt* and didn't particularly like it. I got *Babbit* in the library and discovered Sinclair Lewis with whom my classmate evidently confused Upton Sinclair. I went on to read *Main Street* and *Arrowsmith*. Here I discovered small town America, and this discovery has contributed to my increasing interest in social criticism and its political implications.

My final "conversion" was triggered by the Sacco-Vanzetti case. Niccola Sacco and Bartolomeo Vanzetti were Italian immigrants. They were "anarchists," which, as I found out, meant that they believed in abolishing governments altogether. They were accused of murdering a guard during a hold-up and convicted during the nation-wide red scare. They were condemned to death. As is usual in the U.S., the two men lived on while appeal after appeal was filed and rejected. The case attracted world-wide attention, because of its political implications, possibly because it nurtured a hope of uniting the fractionated Left around a common cause, or, perhaps, because the Dreyfus case in France and the Beilis case in Russia were still living memories.[1] In all these cases sharp lines were drawn between those who identified with power and those who identified with the powerless. I decided I was an anarchist. This, however, did not prevent me from joining the "Yipsels" (Young People's Socialist League) with the idea that I would bring them around to anarchism. We met weekly, discussed world events, read, sold and distributed literature put out by the Socialist Party. During 1928 we were immersed in the presidential campaign. "Our" candidate was Norman Thomas, who became the "chronic" socialist candidate in the next four elections. During a rally my father introduced me to him, and I told the grave gentleman that I was not yet old enough to vote but that in the next election I would be and would vote to re-elect him. He was pleased.

The execution of Sacco and Vanzetti injected sharp and painful emotions into my first participation in politics. The "class struggle" became a passion, manifested in slogans, fiery speeches, awed admiration of martyrs.

There was another aspect of "socialism," which at first I did not recognize as such but which remained an integral part of my ideological commitment to socialism after the "romantic" melodramatic aspects had lost their appeal. The seeds of that other idea were probably implanted by an incident whose connection with politics I did not see at the time.

Keeping a small grocery store in those days meant grueling work—sixteen hours a day seven days a week. The store opened at six and was kept open till ten. Competition was fierce and customers would switch their allegiance if they found the store closed when they needed something. "Big" shopping was done only on Saturdays. For the most part housewives dropped in or sent their children for just one or two items. I remember the cash register recorded the amount of each sale, and I calculated the average, which turned out to be about 30 cents. Both mother and I helped. Father would take a nap during the afternoon hours, when hardly any one came in.

Once (I think it was at father's initiative) several grocers in the neighbourhood met and agreed to close their stores at 7 P.M. on Mondays, Wednesdays, and Fridays and also on Sundays from 1 P.M. to 5 P.M. If every one did it, no one would have a competitive advantage. This agreement was honoured for about three weeks. I remember those summer evenings very well. My parents and I went on bus rides through the city, riding on the open tops of buses, or else on boat rides on Lake Michigan from Municipal Pier to Jackson Park. We had leisurely dinners together. It was wonderful.

Then some one broke the agreement and opened his store. Then another. The whole scheme fell apart, and the covenant was never revived. Father explained that the grocer who started this was like a scab. This brought home to me the idea that pursuit of individual advantage by every one in a community can result in a loss for every one concerned. Years later I read about Adam Smith's "invisible hand"—the regulatory function of the free market—which insures that pursuit of individual advantage by each participant results in collective good. Thinking back to the neighbourhood grocers, I envisage "the invisible back of the hand"—situations in which pursuit of individual advantage by every one results in a collective "bad." Much of my research in the psychology of decision making centred on this effect, illustrating the dichotomy between individual and collective rationality.

Eventually father could not stand the long hours. He sold the store and bought another in Bridgeport, a neighbourhood adjoining the stock yards populated by Poles and Lithuanians. He had paid off his debt to Mr. Katz, his old friend who had helped to set him up in the grocery business, and could pay the full price of the store in Bridgeport.

Now the day was over at 7 P.M. every evening. On Sundays it was closed all day. There was a three room apartment in the rear. But the neighbourhood adjoining the stock yards was dismal. (It was the scene of Upton Sinclair's novel, *The Jungle*.) The Depression struck less than a year later. The priests of both the Polish and the Lithuanian churches urged their flocks to buy only from Christians. On some days not a single customer came into the store.

Finally father quit. The store could not be sold. He took the remaining canned goods and moved to an empty store on Halsted Street, Bridgeport's main thoroughfare. He opened a fruit and vegetable store. He bought an old beat-up pick-up truck and used it to go to the farmer's market on Water Street at the crack of dawn to get his day's supplies of fresh produce cheap. The customers were now transients looking for bargains. The store was busy. Father even had to get help. In three years he was able to sell the store for $3000—a small fortune by our standards.

By that time I was already in Europe. In summer, 1931, father took mother to Europe. We met in Paris, where I was spending the summer learning French and taking courses at the Sorbonne—one on seventeenth century French drama, the other on eighteenth century French painting. My parents spent four months with me, first in Paris, then on a junket through the Riviera and northern Italy, then Vienna—all on the $3000, our total fortune. They never regretted it. Back in Chicago father got a job at a gas station, one of a chain run by an old acquaintance from Crimea. In a few years father became a partner, then president of the company, which meant a steady salary of $100 per week. By conventional standards this was "success." But father often said that he was much happier as a grocer, when he felt he was performing some service, making food conveniently available. As president of a company he felt he was doing nothing useful, because the company was doing nothing useful. There were far more gas stations than were needed. On some busy intersections there was one on every one of the four corners. The company was an "independent" chain, trying to survive in competition with the "majors," that is, the outlets for Standard Oil, Sinclair, Shell, etc. The "independents" sold gas for a half cent less per gallon than the majors. This differential was usually tolerated. Once in a while, however, the independents tried to get a larger competitive edge by lowering the price of gas to a cent below the majors' price. Then the majors retaliated by starting a price war, thereby trying to put the independents out of business. Eventually a "peace conference" was arranged, and a *status quo* was established.

Under socialism, father said, there would be no need for such futile nerve frazzling activity. Things would be produced and sold because they were needed, not because some one wanted to make profits. Prices would correspond to what it cost to produce things. People would be motivated to cooperate rather than to compete. People would value other things besides money. He told me of an incident involving his partner who had run the chain before father took it over. This partner bought a gas station on a busy street on the North Side. In front of the station were four beautiful old elms. Mr. Burakov decided that the elms hid the station from view and prepared to have them cut down. A delegation from the neighbourhood community, a priest among them, begged him not to do so. The elms were cut down anyway. In the world of business, father said, money is a measure of all values. He was not happy in this world. After World War II, he sold the business and retired. He told me about the young man who bought it. In discussing the potential of the business, the young man frankly discussed his situation. He said he needed $15,000 per year to live on and support his family. (It was the equivalent of about $150,000—$200,000 today.) So the question was how much he could count on in excess of that fixed amount "to play with."

"This way of putting it," father said, "reflects an attitude toward life. The meaning of life appears as business. Calvin Coolidge put it well. 'The business of America is business,' he said. And business is a game. Asked about what he does, a business man may say, 'I'm in the insurance game,' or 'I'm in the real estate game.' "

Father often talked to me about his childhood, adolescence, and youth. His greatest regret was that he had to become a businessman. When he ran the grocery, he did not regard himself as a businessman. He felt that he was performing a genuine service in the neighbourhood. Once some boys did some mischief in front of the store, and father talked severely to them. A cop happened to come by. In bawling the boys out the cop said something about having more respect for a "businessman." Father told me he felt ashamed of himself on that occasion.

In the 1930's my favourite American playwright was Clifford Odets, and of his plays I liked *Awake and Sing* best. The character who moved me most was old Jacob, the unemployed Jewish barber, whose most prized possession was two Caruso records, whose religion was Marxism, and whose shrine was a photograph of Sacco and Vanzetti. One of the records was an aria from Bizet's *Pearl Fishers*. It was also my father's favourite aria. He often hummed it and told me how Smirnov (Caruso's Russian rival) sang it lying on the ground. The other record was "O Paradiso" from Meyerbeer's *L'Africaine*. Old Jacob puts it on for the bitterly cynical one-legged war veteran, who is fond of the old man.

"Imagine," says Jacob, "the man looks on the land from the deck of the ship, and what does he see? Utopia!"

It is this same Jacob who in an outburst of despair about his life in America says, "Life should not be printed on dollar bills."

My first contact with an American businessman was with Albert Pick, who financed my scholarship at the Gunn School of Music. Mr. Pick lived in Winnetka, a northern suburb of Chicago in Lake County, in many ways analogous to Westchester County north of New York City. He lived in a palatial home with servants. Shortly after I was introduced to him he invited me to dinner and probed about my background. He was impressed by my story about how we got out of Russia. He was disturbed when I told him that my father "worked for the Bolsheviks" (when he was secretary of the Board of Education in Feodosia). Also when I told him that we left not because we were persecuted by the Bolsheviks but because there was nothing to eat.

"Does your father believe in socialism?" he asked.

I said he did.

"It beats me," Mr. Pick said. "From what you told me, your father must be an educated man. Doesn't he see that socialism is nonsense? If everything is divided up, within a short time, all the money will be distributed exactly as before."

When I told father about this conversation, he asked me what I said to that. I said the conversation was not continued. Father asked me how I would justify socialism if I had to.

I said I would ask by what right the capitalist appropriated part of the value that the worker produced.

Father said, "By right of mutual agreement."

We had a long conversation, which I remember to this day, in the course of which father played the part of devil's advocate defending capitalism.

The other adult with whom I had long, intense conversations was my piano teacher, Glenn Dillard Gunn. The more he talked to me about Europe the more I longed to go there to study. The obvious place to study music was Vienna, the city of Haydn, Mozart, and Beethoven, the trinity of which I thought in the same way as a pious Jew thinks about Abraham, Isaac, and Jacob. For a while Paris and Berlin seemed to be alternatives. Alfred Cortot was in Paris, Arthur Schnabel was in Berlin. But when I went to hear Cortot in Chicago, I did not like him. I had not heard Schnabel. Gunn did not think much of him (romanticist that he was), a prejudice that I "inherited" and did not outgrow till considerably later. The most prominent pianist in Vienna was Moritz Rosenthal, who, Gunn thought was the greatest pianist alive. But my encounter with Rosenthal was unfortunate. He once came as a guest teacher to Gunn's school to conduct a "master class." I played some Chopin preludes and Beethoven's last sonata (op. 111). Rosenthal asked me to describe the first of Chopin's preludes both structurally and from the point of view of emotional content. As I started to do so, he interrupted me.

"Yes, but you are telling me something you have read. I want to know your own interpretation of it."

This was said in front of some fifteen colleagues of mine. I felt humiliated and had nothing to say.

In analyzing the development section of the first movement of op. 111, I pointed out that the theme appeared also in augmentation and was going to mention the use of the main motive of the Fifth Symphony in diminution in the second movement. But Rosenthal was not impressed.

Later Gunn tried to console me by telling me that Rosenthal was rude to every one and told me anecdotes about his feud with Leopold Godowsky and about others who were his enemies. I asked, "Who are his friends?"

Gunn burst out laughing and called me "an impertinent young Jew."

At any rate Rosenthal was out. Another of Viennese prominent pianists was Emil Sauer, like Rosenthal a student of Liszt's; but, as far as I knew, Sauer no longer taught. Anyhow studying with one of the "greats" was not for me. Schnabel charged $25 per lesson. I imagined this was the going rate, which for me was out of the question. However, in Vienna one could study at the State Academy of Music for practically nothing. The piano master class was conducted by Paul Weingarten, a pupil of Sauer's. So I decided to go to Vienna and to apply for admission to the Academy.

Next the problem of financing had to be considered. The proceeds from the sale of the prize piano would take care of the journey and probably of living expenses for a year. Then, I supposed, the Lord would provide, or, perhaps, Mr. Pick.

Pick had already committed himself to support another student of Gunn's, young Saul Dorfman, who was going to Leipzig. So broaching the subject with him was a touchy problem. Nevertheless I did, and he said he would try to get a number of people on the North Shore to support me collectively. Mr. Pick said that success depended not only on one's technical abilities but also on one's personality. Mine was not an engaging personality, he said. I was not responsive to people. I hardly showed appreciation of all the attention those people paid to me, was curt in talking to them. And besides, I looked queer. Why did I not shave off those whiskers?

No one could accuse him of antisemitism, Mr. Pick went on to say. In fact one of the two children he adopted to fill the gap left by the death of his son was Jewish, and he raised him in the Jewish faith in deference to his dead parents. But whiskers made me look like a student in a Jewish theological seminary. Why saddle oneself with this handicap? The upshot of the business was that Mr. Pick undertook to send me $50 per month. He could not afford more, he said, since he already was committed to support the other boy.[2]

Although the elimination of whiskers was not an explicit condition of this arrangement, it was to be understood as such. After considerable soul-searching, I succumbed to the pressure of my parents and shaved off the whiskers. So ended my adolescence.

NOTES

1. Dreyfus (a Jew) was a French army officer who was falsely convicted of spying for Germany and sentenced to life imprisonment on Devil's Island. He was subsequently rehabilitated. Beilis (a Russian Jew), accused of ritual murder was acquitted in a trial that attracted world wide attention.

2. Mr. Pick was true to his word and sent me $50 per month for about eighteen months. The first blows of the Depression made him poor. Eventually he paid a $100,000 debt and restored his fortune by developing a chain of hotels (the Albert Pick Hotels). He was extremely proud of his comeback. I saw him again years later when I came to Miami (where he lived in retirement) to give a recital. He invited me to his home. What struck me at the time was the selectiveness of intellectual capacity. In most ways Mr. Pick was senile. He kept referring to me as "the boy who escaped from Russia" and kept returning to the past showing hardly any knowledge of interest in what was going on in the world. His whole manner changed, however, when, at the request of my father (who played with the idea of investing in an apartment building in Florida), I asked him about the real estate scene in Miami. He game me a detailed picture of it, which, I felt was authentic, even though I understood next to nothing about it. He told me in detail what to tell my father and offered his advice and assistance whenever they might be wanted. I often wonder whether I, too, remain selectively lucid about matters with which I am deeply concerned.

Vienna

4

I came to Vienna in September, 1929 with a letter of introduction to Paul Weingarten, who conducted the piano master class at the *Hochschule für Musik und darstellende Kunst,* the upper division of the *Akademie für Musik.* Weingarten lived in an apartment in the inner city consisting of two large rooms, a kitchen, a bathroom and a vestibule. It was run by an elderly housekeeper who answered the door and led the visitor into the room adjoining the vestibule. There one waited until Weingarten finished with the preceding visitor.

The outer room was crowded with things—plants, china in cupboards with glass doors, bric-a-brac, travel mementoes. Heavy curtains framed very tall windows. It was rather stuffy and smelled of cigar smoke.

The inner room contained two large Bösendorfer grands side by side. Their tops were down and the music racks stood atop of them, so that the sound was rather muffled. The smell of cigar smoke was even stronger here. In the alcove behind a curtain stood a bed. A kitten sometimes emerged from behind the curtain.

Weingarten was a strikingly handsome man in his mid-forties, rather stout with a fine mane of white hair. He spoke halting English. In my halting German I told him I was studying the language and could understand most of what was said. He seemed pleased and from then on we spoke German. He asked me to play and I reproduced some of the Beethoven opus 111. He told me I had a good chance of passing the entrance exams to his master class. Those were the last encouraging words I was to hear from him until the following spring. In contrast to Boguslavsky's abuse, however, his was fairly constructive, that is, explicit enough and accompanied by impressive demonstrations. He persisted until I caught on and he could say (presumably with a clear conscience), "*So, ja!*" He sighed as he said this.

I believe Weingarten was more severe with me than with any one else except perhaps one young man with a club foot and one very plain and very shy girl from Lithuania. Both were Jewish. There was, however, no trace of antisemitism in Weingarten. In fact, he was the son of a prominent Jewish chess master. Nor was there any discernible correlation between his highly unpleasant manner of teaching and the students' abilities. Both the young man and the girl were quite mediocre pianists. I was good.

After I passed the entrance exams, I went to see Josef Marx, who taught harmony, counterpoint and composition. I told him I "had had" all three. He said "So?" and gave me a piece of music paper with seven notes scribbled on it: D, E, F, B flat, A, G, F with a fermata over the F. He told me to harmonize the phrase with four voices as if it were the first phrase of a chorale.

I thought it was easy and handed the paper back to him in a few minutes.

He glanced at it and said, "Not bad. But not good either."

Then he told me to modulate at the piano going from the key of A minor to E flat major. I thought he wanted me to take the shortest path. So I played an A minor chord and followed it by a D minor (the subdominant), then by a B flat major (the relative major), which led naturally into E flat, of which it is the dominant.

"No," he said. "You are not supposed to just play chords. You are supposed to let the voices go where they want to go but nevertheless guide them where you want to go."

And he sat down at the piano and showed me. He improvised "in the style of Bach," he said, going through a dozen keys, each voice going supposedly where "it wanted to go" but guided by him, sometimes diatonically, sometimes chromatically. It was beautiful. Now and then he turned around to make some remark explaining what he was doing.

Suddenly he stopped and dismissed me.

"You may enrol in my counterpoint class," he said. "But you must also audit my harmony class. May be next year you can take composition."

So began my serious musical education.

Weingarten's class met Wednesdays and Saturdays from 3 to 7. Weingarten showed up promptly at 3:30. Every one would stand up and there was silence while he said, "*Guten Tag!*" and proceeded to his chair to the right of the two concert Bösendorfers. During the half hour before he appeared, both pianos were played simultaneously by any who could grab them or who could induce another player to yield. This was called *einspielen* (warming up). Actually one could not hear oneself play because of the other piano, but that did not seem to matter. One felt a compulsion to go over what one was going to play in class. It was considered proper to occupy a piano for einspielen only if one intended to play that day. For this one volunteered when Weingarten said "*Hat jemand was?*" ("Does any one have anything?")

There were two kinds of students: those who wanted to play every time and those who delayed the ordeal as long as possible. So there wasn't much competition for the available time. Five or six students played at each session. There were ten to fifteen in the class, about half of them Austrians, the others from Central and East European countries.

Marx's classes in harmony and counterpoint lasted one hour. He would stretch out leaning back on the piano keyboard putting his legs on two chairs. In this position looking at the ceiling he would dictate. The students sat around a long table and wrote down in their notebooks verbatim what he said. Then he would look at our exercises, comment on them and assign the next exercises. Harmony was standard four part harmony. Counterpoint was at first "*der strenge Satz*" then "*der freie Satz*" (somewhat more liberal rules). I didn't get very far with composition. Marx dismissed my imitations of Liszt rather tactfully (he was a kind man). He thought I would be comfortable in following the footsteps of Russian composers; so he suggested I take Medtner, Glazunov and other minor composers as models. I did get a diploma with a "1" on it the (the highest mark) in composition. I submitted a set of variations on a theme from Carmen (from the first Intermezzo) and answered questions on the range of the trombone and on the form of the last movement of Brahms' Fourth Symphony. But I abandoned all thoughts about becoming a composer.[1]

During my five years in Vienna I was most of the time alone. Except when my parents visited me, I lived in a room rented out by some elderly widow, supplementing her meager pension. Apartments were held in perpetuity and passed on to heirs. Rent control was absolute. So renting out a room took care of a significant part of what the widow lived on. I could use the kitchen to make breakfast and supper. The main meal was at midday. I usually had it at the home of some other widow who had six to ten paying dinner guests. The students had no group social life. I assumed they all spent most of their time practising. Some had partners. I didn't. I practised practically all the time when I was not in class or at a concert or at the opera. Sunday afternoons I played chess with a Soviet student in some cafe, after which we went to a movie. Toward the end of my second year, we became a foursome with two Russian speaking girls, the one from Lithuania (to whom Weingarten was especially cruel) and one from Iran.

Until I started to write for the *Musical Courier* opera and Philharmonic concerts meant standing. (After that I had a press card.) To get a good standing place at the opera, one joined the line about an hour before the doors opened. A good place was in a corner, where one could wedge oneself between the barrier of the standing area and the wall. In that position one could lean both forward on the barrier and backward on the wall. A Wagner opera lasted about five hours. One could sit during the intermissions if one could find a place to sit down in the vestibule.

In those days the standing room area still retained a vestige of imperial Austria. On one side a sign said *Civil*, on the other *Militär*. Evidently civilians were segregated from the military to avoid unpleasantness should a dispute arise about a standing place. Memories of imperial glory were everywhere—in palaces converted to museums, in reminiscences of my landladies, in the plays of Arthur Schnitzler. Maria Theresa was enthroned between the Museum of Natural History and the Historical Museum of Art, surrounded by four generals on horses. Franz Josef was revered by elderly monarchists as a warm compassionate father. I was told about the daily procession accompanying the emperor's carriage along the Mariahilferstrasse, as he rode from the Schönbrunn Palace to his office in the Burg. I was also told about the ceremony of his interment in the Franziskaner Kirche, where the Austrian monarchs are entombed. The hearse stops at the game; an official knocks.

"Who is there?"

"Emperor Franz Josef."

"We know him not."

Another knock.

"Who's there?"

"Franz Josef, Emperor of Austria, King of Hungary and Bohemia, Grand Duke of Styria, Carinthia, and Tyrol, etcetera, etcetera, etcetera..."

"We know him not."

For the third time the official knocks.

"Who's there?"

"Miserable sinner, Franz, servant of God."

"Welcome, Franz!" The gate opens.

Austria was a political battle ground along traditional lines. The Austrian Social Democratic Party was said in jest to be affiliated with the "Second and a Half" International—more militant than the Second but not quite Bolshevik Third. There was a workers' paramilitary organization, *Der republikanische Schutzbund*. Their enemy was the *Heimwehr*, the paramilitary organization of the Right. Memory was still fresh of an armed clash between them in 1927.

The Nazis became prominent after their first big showing in Germany in the elections of 1930 at the start of the Depression. From then on it was a three-way struggle in Austria. Vienna was solidly social-democratic. The countryside was predominantly *Christlichsozial*, sometimes translated "Christian socialist" but actually a party completely dominated by the Church. (Note that in both Austria and Germany "socialist" was not a "growl word," as in America but a "purr word," as Hayakawa would say. The Nazis also called themselves "socialists.")

To me all this was life in the raw. The class struggle was on the front pages of newspapers. On the First of May and on the Twelfth of November the anniversary of the establishment of the *Republik* the city was bedecked with red flags. There was even a Workers' Symphony Orchestra. I heard Richard Strauss conduct one of its concerts.

I read the *Arbeiter Zeitung*, organ of the Social Democratic Party. I also subscribed to *Pravda*. It came by mail with a one kopek stamp picturing a face of a proletarian. (The Soviet Union was still on gold standard.) The diatribes printed in *Pravda* were my first contact with the incipient struggle which was to lead to Stalin's bloody triumphs. The collectivization campaign was just beginning. The peasantry was proclaimed to be divided in three classes. There was the *bedniak*—the poor peasant, whose correct class consciousness enabled him to see the obvious advantages of collectivization. There was the *seredniak*, the middle peasant, who needed persuasion. And there was the *kulak*, the class enemy, the exploiter of landless labourers. The *kulaks* were to be "liquidated as a class." There were enemies also within the Communist Party, hidden ones, the right and "left" deviationists. The "left" ones (but not the right ones) were always put in quotation marks, since "left" was then an honorific terms in Soviet politics. These were always portrayed as "secret allies of the right deviationists."

I discovered a Russian lending library, run by an emigré, and I resumed reading Russian literature, not the classics this time but the Soviet output. I discovered Ilya Ehrenburg, who, before he became a journalist, wrote novels. His first novel made the strongest impression on me. Its hero, Julio Jurenito, is a Mexican intent on destroying European bourgeois civilization, which he regards as a festering sore on the body of humanity. Ehrenburg, writing in the first person, becomes his first disciple. The opening scene of the novel kept haunting me. It seemed like a perfect opening of an opera, featuring a bacchanalia reminiscent of the first act of Tannhäuser. Ehrenburg sits in the Café Rotonde on the Boulevard Montparnasse in Paris waiting for an acquaintance to come by from whom he could borrow six sous for his cup of coffee. The evening crowd appears to him as the hosts of hell engaged in a lascivious orgy. Among them he perceives Satan himself disguised as a young dark skinned man. Ehrenburg is convinced that he is there to collect his soul. Unable to bear the suspense (Jurenito calmly drinks his beer), Ehrenburg approaches him, offering to surrender his passport and his notebook of unpublished verses.

The supposed Satan regards him calmly and says, "I know whom you take me for, but he does not exist."

"But how can that be?" Ehrenburg protests. "What about evil? Where does it come from?"

"There is no such thing."

"But then there is no good either!"

"Correct."

"But what's the meaning of all this?" Ehrenburg exclaims vaguely pointing to the crowd. "What about that fat Spaniard with the nude girl on his lap?"

"The girl has got to feed her youngster. The Spaniard's lips feel like snails, but she's got to kiss him and simulate passion. As for the Spaniard, he's all right for the moment. All his organs are functioning properly. In a few years, they will start deteriorating and he will take to drinking stinking water. Then he will die, and his flesh will start to stink."

"But this is terrible!"

"Can't be helped," says Jurenito. "We are given a furnished house. The most we can do is rearrange the furniture."

Looking back on this exchange (reproduced from memory), I find it difficult to believe that it struck me as a revelation of wisdom and sophistication. But it did. I compared this nihilistic sarcasm with that of Rabelais and Swift.

"But we can destroy the house," says Ehrenburg.

"Yes, we can. Let's look into it."

"A bomb? An infernal machine?"

"Childish nonsense. We shall start from the other end. We shall destroy civilization not by fighting it but by encouraging it, by nurturing its festering sores."

So begins the career of Julio Jurenito, the great agent provocateur, as Ehrenburg calls him. He recruits seven disciples. Ehrenburg, the Jew, is the first. Besides him, we are introduced to an African youngster (the "innocent savage"), a Russian intellectual, who insists on telling the story of his life in a railway carriage according to the hallowed Russian tradition, a French rentier, an American businessman, who supplies houses of prostitution with bibles and condom vending machines, an Italian beggar, who loves revolutions, especially building blockades by overturning street cars, and a German student, who combines Marxism with Fascism. A book of this sort could still be published in the Soviet Union in the 1920's.

Jurenito instigates World War I. He also takes part in the October Revolution, which he thought would lead to the destruction of bourgeois Europe. But when the orgy of destruction subsides and a semblance of order appears, Jurenito gives up and deliberately arranges for his own murder.

As I gather my thoughts, I try to reconstruct the frame of mind I was in over sixty years ago, and I find I can't. The most likely explanation is that I was fascinated by a sort of mephistophelean arrogance that pervades Ehrenburg's first novel. He returns to the same theme in his *D.E. Trust*. An American tycoon grants a two minute audience to any one who wants to propose a worthwhile project. The hero of the novel proposes to destroy Europe. The idea appeals to the tycoon, who regards Europe as a seedy anachronism obstructing progress. A trust with the cover name "Detroit Engineering Co." is formed. But the Soviets decide that D.E. stands for *Dayosh Evropu! Dayosh!* (Hand over!) was the Bolshevik battle cry during the civil war.

Ehrenburg fascinated also with his opposite side, sentimental compassion for the humble and artless. There was a novel about a frail French girl stranded in Russia during the civil war and tragically in love with a severe communist. There was one about a little Jewish tailor, sort of Charlie Chaplin type, pursued by disaster across Europe. There was a novel about the *bezprizornyie*, the homeless children of Moscow. There was one about a "go-getter," who becomes a racketeer during the N.E.P.[2] and comes to a tragic end. Ehrenburg represents the short-lived wave of creativity in Russian post-revolutionary literature produced by sudden cataclysmic change. The outburst was soon stifled. Ehrenburg was one of very few whose survival became a source of embarrassment for him.

Another writer whom I "discovered" during my years in Vienna was H.G. Wells. Along with many other translations from English I had read *The Invisible Man*. Now I discovered *The War of the Worlds, When the Sleeper Awakes, A World Set Free, The First Men in the Moon, The Time Machine*. Here was a continued unveiling of Jules Verne's future spiked with a social message—the promise and the threat of unfettered technology.

I look back on those years as a time of extraordinary rich experience. What was most exhilarating was to roam over a city and to find meaning everywhere. There was nothing like it in Chicago. Western Avenue, for example, is twenty three miles long. It took almost two hours for a street car to traverse it from its southern terminal at 111th street to the northern at Howard Street. There was not a single notable building on it—only used car lots, warehouses, factories and occasional store fronts. There were no people on the street. To see people on the street, one could go down town. But one did not casually go there. One went there on some errand, and then one had to return to the shabby Northwest Side or to even more dismal Bridgeport. In Vienna, roaming at random over the city, I "discovered" a building with a plaque on it saying that it was the site of a house in which Beethoven died. The house where Schubert was born still stood; so did the church where Bruckner played the organ. Freud's apartment in Berggasse 19 was a shrine. People did business in cafes or just sat reading newspapers or playing chess. And of course there were the justly celebrated environs, the Vienna Woods. One took a street car to the edge of the city and wandered over the surrounding hills. There was a chapel on the hill where King Sobieski of Poland prayed before engaging the Turks besieging Vienna in 1683. There was the site in the Seventh Bezirk marking the Turks' nearest approach to the city gates.

As I wandered about the city and over the surrounding hills, I planned my first "wandering" over Europe to be undertaken as soon as classes were over. I bought a rucksack and a long staff. I may have imagined myself as the Wanderer (Wotan in disguise) in the first act of Siegfried.

On July 7, 1930 I started out on foot to Venice. I spent the first night in a field just outside of Baden, a resort town about 30 kilometres south of Vienna and started out again at dawn reaching Wiener Neustadt about noon. I was dead tired, got a room at an inn and slept the rest of the day.

The next day I made it to Semmering, climbing the last 15 kilometres to 1000 metres. Eventually I established a routine: walked from about 5 to 7 A.M., had breakfast, usually a half litre of milk with slices of rye bread thickly smeared with butter and honey. Then I walked with intermittent rests until noon, rested a couple of hours after dinner and put up for supper and bed at an inn. My budget was seven schillings per day (about $1), of which one or two went for lodging, the rest for food. Occasionally in the evening I went to a café hoping to find a chess partner but without success. I wanted very much to talk to people in the manner of Russian intellectuals telling stories of their lives to strangers in railway carriages. But my attempts to get people to philosophize about life failed. I would try to start a conversation on a park bench, but it seldom got beyond a few inconsequential remarks. Told that I was from America, they would express a mild interest, ask me a few questions about it and how I liked Austria.

On the eleventh day I was thrilled by a sign at a fork in the road, which pointed to Yugoslavia in one direction and Italy in the other. I took the right branch and climbed up to Tarvisio on the border. From there the descent began to the Venetian plain. On the seventeenth day I reached Mestre. I found I could not walk into Venice. The bridge in those days was only for the rail road. I took the ferry across and was finally at my destination at the Rialto Bridge.

I must have been conspicuous, since a small crowd of children followed me. I kept asking passers by where I could find "*una osteria non cara*," mistakenly thinking that osteria was the word for "hotel." But it turned out to mean "tavern." Finally an old gentleman who spoke German said something to the children and told me to follow them. They took me to a shabby little hotel.

I wandered all over Venice for three days, saw a lot of Bellinis and Titians, read a lot of brochures, watched the pigeons take off at the sound of the cannon at noon on St. Mark's Square. This thrilled me, since that cannon shot sounds in the third act of Verdi's *Otello*. There was something else about that cannon shot that intrigued me. I noticed that the pigeons started to take off before the shot was heard. I thought of H.G. Wells' *Time Machine* and decided that pigeons could hear something "from the future." Indeed, why not?[3]

On the overnight train ride back I shared the third class compartment with two women from New York who came to visit the "Old Country" after twenty years' absence. They spoke with fondness of imperial Austria, the old kaiser, and so on. I tried to talk to them about the inevitability of historical changes and about socialism as the wave of the future, citing H.G. Wells and Bernard Shaw, but I got nowhere.

It was during my second year that Taras Mykysha joined our piano class. We first got to know each other in Marx's counterpoint class. As usual, before Marx appeared some one used the piano. One time I showed off by imitating Chaliapin singing Pimen's monologue from Boris Godunov. Later Taras asked me where I had learned Russian. I told him. From then on we spent Sunday afternoons and evenings together.

Lida, the girl from Lithuania had a friend, Ruzan, an Armenian girl from Tabriz, Iran, a pianist from another class. Both spoke fluent Russian. Ruzan was beautiful; Lida was plain. I decided that Lida would be "my" girl and felt magnanimous about "letting" Ruzan be Taras's. The entire relationship, however, remained strictly platonic. Time was spent as Russians spend time—in talk. We were of different persuasions. I was an "anarchist," a disciple of Kropotkin, but I supported the Austrian Social Democrats, who, I thought, would eventually see the light. Taras was politically cynical. He caricatured the Soviet stance of uncompromising condemnation of social democracy and, in fact, of every other political position. His sarcasm fascinated me, and at times I tried to imitate it. The girls had little interest in politics. They were concerned with intricacies of human relationships. But Lida was sentimental, while Ruzan was "practical." Subsequently (after World War II) she married Taras. During the war he collaborated with the Germans, who launched him on a concert career. As the Russians approached Vienna, he and Ruzan fled and eventually wound up in Brazil, where Taras died in his early fifties. Lida committed suicide in occupied Lithuania.

Every summer during the years I studied in Europe I explored the continent. In summer, 1931 I was in France. In summer, 1932, my mother came to visit me again, and I proudly showed her Italy. She was a good sport and a devoted tourist. We travelled third class by rail from Venice to Palermo and "did" everything on the way—Florence, Siena, Pisa, Rome, Naples. In 1933 I cycled from Vienna to Barcelona. The U.S. dollar was devalued that summer and I ran out of money. Coming back by rail, I had to take local trains from town to town. They were cheaper than the long distance trains. I also took advantage of a reduced rate for visitors to the lace fair in Milan. To validate the reduction I had to get my ticket stamped at the fair grounds. So in Milan I had to go across the city, a terrible ordeal in the intense heat, since I had not eaten for two days. I got as far as Innsbruck, where Ruzan was vacationing on a farm. I borrowed money from her, then took her to Salzburg, where I was to cover the festival for the Musical Courier. I had a press card; so I took her to all the performances.

My bicycle, which was sent back by rail from Barcelona caught up with me in Salzburg, and I cycled back to Vienna on it. On the way I stopped in Oed, a village in Lower Austria, to see my current landlady's housekeeper, who was visiting her relatives there. The village was in the same situation as Marienthal, described by Paul Lazarsfeld, the first Austrian empirical sociologist. Oed made a devastating impression on me. I was reminded of Lazarsfeld's meticulous description of life in a community with 100% unemployment. The description included comparisons of average walking speeds of men and of women on the street. It turned out that the men walked significantly more slowly than women. The suggested explanation of the difference was that the women had something to do (after all they kept house), while the men had nothing.

Vienna was an improbable mixture of cultural prosperity and economic collapse. The streets were full of beggars. Many of them made music: some played standard instruments, others unusual ones. There was one old man who played the "singing saw," varying the pitch by bending it. Another had several mouth organs mounted on a roller, each in a different key. He twirled the roller (he had no arms) as he modulated from one key to another. A legless man sat on a bridge across the Vienna River in the Stadtpark and played records on a phonograph.

Once I heard Bach's Chaconne from my window. A young bearded man was playing the violin. I made his acquaintance and met with him several times. His name was Josef. He told me of his experiences in the army, where he had a terrible time. He was the bugler of his company. With great satisfaction he told me his cheeky answer to an inspector's question about what his job was. "I take the trumpet and I blow tra-ra." To this day I don't wholly understand why I was so delighted with this prank. Perhaps because it was such a neat way of showing contempt for authority yet immune to punishment. How could the inspector initiate action without himself appearing ridiculous?

In 1938 I ran into Josef in Prague. He had just escaped from occupied Austria. When we were both in our seventies, I heard from him again. He had spent the rest of his life in London. He found out that we both knew a violinist in Chicago and wrote to me about it. These incidents keep bobbing up in my memory and I feel almost a compulsion to relate them. They must in some way be significant, but the significance often escapes me.

My original intention was to stay in Europe if I could establish myself as a musician. With the advent of Naziism, the prospect vanished. Germany with its hundreds of musical establishments (a symphony orchestra and a music school in every town big enough to be on a map) was eliminated. Austria was too small and France too inhospitable. I had played with the idea of going back to Russia, but the news from there was frightening. My cousin Volodya was sent into exile for some remark about collectivization.

Austria went fascist in 1934. The "Christian" government mobilized the *Heimwehr* against the Social Democratic Party. There was some sporadic resistance by the *Republikanischer Schutzbund*. Workers barricaded themselves in Karl Marx Hof, the largest housing development in Vienna built by the Social Democratic city administration. The self-proclaimed dictator Dollfuss placed artillery on the hills northwest of the city and shelled the complex. The two socialist newspapers were shut down, all workers' organizations were disbanded and Dollfuss, a very small man with a face like a cherub's was seen on horseback in newsreels, a ludicrous caricature of the proverbial saviour of a nation. Four months later he was murdered by the Nazis during their own aborted Putsch.

I saw Europe as an exciting scene of action. On the one hand there was participation of the population in high culture and awareness of rich historical heritage, neither of which I sensed in America, at least not in the environment in which I spent my adolescence. On the other hand Europe was a political battle ground and politics was not a matter of capturing the city hall or the White House in a gigantic contest of advertising strategies but an ideological struggle and a class struggle, what I thought politics was supposed to be all about. I wanted to stay in Europe, but I couldn't.

I had a start of sorts in a concert career. I played in Austria, Hungary, Poland and Italy. In my last concert in Vienna I played three concerti with orchestra—Rachmaninoff's Third, Stravinsky's and Tchaikovsky's First. The reviews were impressive and an impresario in New York contacted me. I decided to go back.

What about my original aim of getting a serious musical education? In retrospect it seems to me that it was somewhat subverted by vanity. I envisaged myself primarily as a virtuoso and my ambitions did not differ essentially from those of young people aspiring to careers on the stage as vehicles of becoming centres of attention. To be sure my practising was not all spit and polish. I had an understanding of music and I took Weingarten's admonition seriously to pay attention not only to playing Liszt but also to singers of Schubert's lieder. But it wasn't only a matter of musical feeling (which I didn't lack) but of an altogether different dimension of musicality. I saw no examples of it among my colleagues in Weingarten's class, but I saw some among Marx's students of composition. There was one young man who would reproduce long passages from an orchestral work on the piano having heard it for the first time the evening before. There were some who could read orchestral scores and hear the music in their mind's ear in all its harmonic and instrumental complexity. The sort of musicality made legendary by Mozart and evidenced in our day by a Toscanini or a Richard Strauss was beyond my horizon. It had nothing to do with instrumental or vocal virtuosity, which is a matter of intricate muscle control, quick reaction times and coordination of acoustic receptors and motor effectors. It was more akin to the virtuosity of the mathematician. Years later I heard stories about Von Neumann about how he would instantly see the innermost heart of a formidably complex problem, which immediately suggested the road to solution. I connected these stories to the stories about Toscanini, who would point his baton at the second bassoon and sing his part (from memory) demonstrating the sort of intonation he wanted. I realized while still in Vienna that this sort of virtuosity was beyond my grasp and, as a matter of fact, I did not aspire to it.

In May, 1934 I passed my last exams and left Vienna. I went to London, where I had some business in the European office of the *Musical Courier*, then to New York to make some arrangements with the American impresario, then home to Chicago, where I was welcomed by my parents, uncles, aunts, cousins and boyhood friends, now wonderful young adults.

NOTES

1. My elder son, on the other hand, who studied in the same *Hoschschule* a half century later, became an excellent composer.
2. New Economic Policy (1921-29), when some private enterprise was permitted.
3. Years later I found a more prosaic explanation. The sound is carried by a wave of pressure. The pigeons must feel the front of the wave before we hear the sound.

Transition

5

Relatives and their friends arranged an audience to fill the Studebaker Theatre, where artists who couldn't fill Orchestra Hall performed on Sunday afternoons. There I played a recital in October and was lavishly praised, especially by my old teacher, Glenn Dillard Gunn, who was music critic on the *Chicago Herald and Examiner*. In December I played in Orchestra Hall in a joint recital with Misha Mishakoff, the concert master of the Chicago Symphony Orchestra. The affair was arranged by the Friends of the Soviet Union and featured Russian music.

Shortly afterward I went to New York for the then mandatory debut. During the months of preparation I again lived in a furnished room, as I had lived in Vienna, practising all day. But this time I was lonely. I had a first taste of social life during the few months in Chicago. The youngsters I had known in adolescence were now young men and women. There was a "bunch." There were friendships and romantic attachments. And there was something else I had not known among my colleagues in Vienna: all my young friends were politically engaged.

The political activity I had witnessed in Vienna was a Marxist textbook example of "class struggle," culminating in a shooting battle, lost by the workers, and the establishment of a fascist dictatorship. I had witnessed this bit of history strictly from the side lines, being, of course, in no position to participate in it. And none of the young people I knew (except the violinist who played Bach's Chaconne in the streets) took part in it. All of them lived as I did—alone in furnished rooms. American political life in the thirties was quite different. The New Deal spawned a broad coalition of all kind of people: workers—in fact, not only factory workers but all kinds of people who worked in miserably paying jobs or were altogether unemployed: Negroes (as they were unabashedly called in those days); first and second generation immigrants. They all supported Roosevelt, listened to the Fireside Chats and hated Big Business. I recall a sociological survey reporting a slip of "banking" from first to ninth place in prestige ranking of professions. In the thirties, Glenn Dillard Gunn would not have said, "No, thank you" to the man on the train who mistook him for a banker.

I longed to join in this activity, but I had to concentrate on my "career." In New York, preparing for the debut, I was busy gathering help to arrange for a sizable audience in Town Hall. I made the acquaintance of Leopold Godowsky,

Rosenthal's rival and reputed enemy. I included two rather mediocre pieces of his in my programme, which induced him to come to the recital. Again I had flattering reviews, an especially enthusiastic one in the German paper. But the season was over, and I felt tired and depressed. Without waiting to see whether engagements for the next season would materialize, I went to Mexico.

In Mexico city I started negotiations with a local concert agency. A few days after my arrival, a Mr. Heitler came to see me in the hotel where I stayed. He told me he had heard about me and that he was an impresario and wanted to "sign me up." I asked him just what that entailed. He said he would arrange a private recital for music critics of several Mexican newspapers through the *jefe* of the Fine Arts Department of the Ministry of Education. I told him to go ahead. Following this affair I was invited to play several recitals for various groups—students, soldiers, workers, even children. I was asked to say a few words about the music I played. I memorized my remarks in Spanish. The *jefe* of the Department of Fine Arts was a member of the Communist Party, as were many others in Cardenas's government. If I am not mistaken, all three famous muralists, Riviera, Orozco and Siquieras, were also members.

I stayed in Mexico a year, playing, lecturing (after having learned the language enough to memorize the lectures) and teaching privately and in classes. I even conducted once at a concert commemorating the fiftieth anniversary of Liszt's death.

I gave half of everything I earned to Heitler, who, as far as I knew, managed no one else. I never found out what his background was. He was certainly new to the "music business," as he put it, being completely ignorant of music and musicians. He lived with a woman who had emigrated from Germany some twenty years before. She either owned or managed what had been the palace of Porfirio Diaz, the president of Mexico 1876-1910. The place, broken up into apartments, was shockingly ornate. It was converted into a genteel boarding house. I made my living quarters in a roomy basement. The boarders took their meals together in a dining room with a fifteen foot ceiling on which cherubim and seraphim hovered on an azure background.

The landlady called her friend "Hitler," as did all the Mexicans, who pronounced it "Eetler." He was amused and pleased. From some of Joe's remarks I gathered that he had been in the real estate business in Los Angeles. Why he was living in Mexico remained a mystery. At times I suspected that he was a fugitive from justice.

The landlady's background was also strange. She had wanted to emigrate to the U.S. but evidently had difficulties. She was advised to go to Mexico instead, from where (so she said she was told) one could get to the U.S. by simply crossing a bridge. For some time she wandered over Mexico City asking about the bridge to the U.S. What happened to her then, how she got rich (she owned a huge Rolls Royce driven by a chauffeur) I never found out.

The borders were a mixed lot. Occasionally a representative of an American firm stayed for a few weeks. Some were Mexican government employees. There was a young Swiss widow with a five-year-old son. She had married a Mexican engineer, who had shortly thereafter died of typhus. There was a Panamanian violinist, who, I, gathered, was in the same situation as I. I played a joint recital with him once. There was a government official from Nicaragua. I was astonished when he asked me whether I would consider being the minister of culture in Nicaragua. I never could decide whether he was serious of just whimsical. Conversations at meals were lively and, at times, acerbic. The landlady presided as moderator. As I learned the language, I realized that Joe's Spanish was atrocious, but he was marvelously fluent in it. I felt I was meeting "characters." After five years of solitude in Vienna, it was exhilarating.

I tried to write. I wrote two long short stories in the first person as an observer of events. The central character in one was modeled after an American painter I met in Tlaxcala, the capital of a small province between Mexico City and the Gulf. He was engaged to paint a mural in the post office. I used the locale to write about his relationship with the Mexicans. In the story he is involved in a tragic misunderstanding which leads to his death. I sent the story to *Esquire* magazine, but it was not accepted. I never told the painter about it and don't know how he would have reacted if the story were published.

The other story, entitled "The Cherub" (that was Dollfuss), was about the February, 1934 events in Vienna. The model of the hero was the Ukrainian pianist, Taras Mykysha, whom I cast in the role of an ardent revolutionary. On the day of the putsch he is visiting a worker living in Karl Marx Hof. The apartment complex is besieged by the Heimwehr. Weapons (stockpiled in expectation of the event) are distributed through the apartments, and my hero (now a Tatar named Abdul Khazmin) takes command of a sector of the "front," manning a machine gun mounted at a window. I could not find a publisher for this either.

The president of Mexico was Lazaro Cardenas. I thought of him as a radicalized Roosevelt, that is, the leader of a peaceful revolution of the "common people," aspiring to democracy, enlightenment and a socialist welfare state. That is the way I explained the activities of the Department of Fine Arts, namely, bringing "culture" to the masses. I was impressed by the absence of policed interference in strikes. When a strike was called, a black and red flag, the emblem of Spanish syndicalism, was spread over the gate of each struck plant with just one or two pickets sitting in front of it, often napping beneath their sombreros. Apparently this was sufficient to deter scabs.

The population of Mexico City in 1935 was about one million. Poverty was, of course, conspicuous everywhere, but the general aspect of the city was gay. Frequent fiestas were splashes of colour. The literate ethnic communities, particularly the German and the Russian-Jewish were oriented toward "culture." Strange as it seems, the Russian community, although it consisted chiefly of Soviet emigres, was predominantly pro-Soviet. The anniversary of the October Revolution was marked by dramatic presentations, poetry readings, concerts, lectures and films.

I participated in this life and had a wide acquaintance among the local intelligentsia, the American expatriates and the German and Russian emigres. I don't recall whether I thought much about the future. Joe talked about moving on to Guatemala and from there deeper into Latin America, but nothing concrete developed.

In May I went to Chicago to visit my parents. They posed the question about my future. If I was to become a concert pianist, did I not need to be under contract with an agency that undertook to get me engagements? I told them of my relationship with Heitler. They asked more questions about Joe, questions that troubled me too but which I brushed aside. But my misgivings were reinforced.

When I returned to Mexico City, my apprehensions became reality. Joe was gone. My landlady could not (or, perhaps, would not) tell me anything about him. For a while I held on to the feeble hope that he had gone to Guatemala to arrange for further engagements for me, but the absence of any message or any information about him soon extinguished it. I returned the piano to the lady who let me use it during my stay, packed my few belongings and left for New York.

Again I rented a room on the West side and a piano. I tried to contact some of the people who had "sponsored" me during my first stay. I half-heartedly planned another recital at Town Hall, but I soon realized that this was not a realistic undertaking. The clippings of rave reviews from Mexico made no impression in New York. On my first visit I was "launched" by short recitals in homes of rich people, who could be counted on to mobilize relatives and acquaintances to provide an audience for a public recital. But the people I had known were now busy with other proteges, and our meetings were now lukewarm and embarrassing. I got some dates on the radio. I had a few students. Some agent turned up and talked vaguely about introducing me to Cuba, but I was told by others whom he approached that he was actually looking for night club pianists.

I practised diligently, but most of my concerns were elsewhere. In the fall of 1936 public attention was focused on the presidential campaign and, at least in New York, on the Spanish civil war. The election campaign was the closest approach to the class struggle in an American election. The New Deal coalition included even the Communists, who, although they ran their own candidate, Earl Browder, confined their rhetoric to calling for the defeat of Alf Landon and the "party of big business." In fact, the Communists replaced the Socialists as the principal party of the Left.

These were the days of a "United Front against Fascism," riding the wave of the New Deal and, of course, support of the Soviet Union, now advertised as the leader in the struggle of "progressive humanity" against the forces of barbarism.

I made friends among young Communists and went to their affairs. I learned that Big Business and Fascists were undermining the United Front by infiltrating the labour movement and boring from within. The infiltrators were the numerous "ites," such as Trotzkyites, Lovestonites, etc. I also got to know the

Trotzkyites. They said that Stalin betrayed the Revolution. Their tongues were sharper than those of the Communists. The orthodox Communists demonized the Trotzkyites. The Trotzkyites ridiculed the Communists. I remember two ditties. One, sung to the tune of the refrain of the International went like this:

Let the Trotzkyites sputter; Their barbs won't be felt.
They can have their revolution; We've got Roosevelt.

Another was a parody of the Communists' charge against the Trotzkyites of sabotage.

We build tractors, so that they don't go;
Steel production never was so low,
Because of us and all our friends, We help achieve Herr Hitler's ends.
We're jealous of Stah-LEEN, And that's what makes us all so mean!

It seemed to me that the Communists were crude, while the Trotzkyites were sophisticated. The Communists talked in slogans. The Trotzkyites discoursed knowingly on "theory" and other profound matters. However, in Spain it was the Soviet Union that was said to be helping the workers fight the fascists, and the Trotzkyites who were said to be disrupting the solidarity of the United Front. I held my nose and sided with the Communists.

Against the background of these events my concern with career seemed egocentric and "bourgeois." A significant factor in this change of outlook must have been the fact that I was not making much progress. Moreover, my "lack of charm," to which Albert Pick had called my attention, must have played a significant part. I finally admitted to myself that I did not like the people on whose help I had made myself dependent. Most disturbing was also the recognition that I had to see young musicians like myself as rivals competing for attention and benevolence of people I did not like.

When my parents came to visit me in New York in November and asked how I lived and how I pictured the future, I found myself telling them things that were in the back of my mind but which I had not until then told myself explicitly. I had devoted nine years exclusively to music; but I was only seven years older than the average high school graduate. I decided to switch to another career, returned to Chicago and enrolled at the University as the oldest freshman.

University

Robert Maynard Hutchins became Chancellor of the University of Chicago at age 30. He had strong convictions of what the goals of higher education should be and spoke contemptuously of American universities as "detention homes for the young with professional schools attached." A university, Hutchins kept insisting, should be a community of scholars, generating and sharing ideas and imparting respect and an appetite for them in young people. It wasn't just talk. He translated these conceptions into concrete educational policies. Fraternities and sonorities were discouraged; football was abolished. Professional schools could not be abolished, but the undergraduate programme was radically restructured. There was no "majoring" in anything. Every one had to pass four examinations in what were regarded as four major fields of general knowledge: the physical sciences, the biological sciences, the social sciences and the humanities. Students were required to read the "great books" that supposedly shaped the civilized mind during the last two or three millennia.

Hutchins' comrade-in-arms in this enterprise was Mortimer Adler, professor of philosophy. Adler described the principal function of a university as that of preserving a "liberal" education, explaining that the etymology of the word "liberal" revealed its nature, namely, the education of free men. Professional schools were, by implication, concerned with "servile" education designed to train people to perform various services.

Shortly after I enrolled I had an encounter with Professor Adler. I was invited by the music department to give a series of lecture recitals. My topic was the development of the so called kernel motive, a very short succession of notes around which complete musical structures are built, such as Bach's fugues, Beethoven's symphonies, or Wagner's operas.

Adler taught a course in the philosophy of music, which I attended. I was intrigued by his analysis of Mozart's melodic structures. In Mozart's compositions, a complete melodic "sentence," called a "period," consisted, according to Adler, ideally of all the seven notes of the diatonic scale. A characteristic feature of Mozart's periods was that one of those seven notes was withheld until almost the end of the period. Presumably this created a tension, which was dissolved when the missing tone was heard. As an example, I remember, he cited the first theme of Mozart's piano sonata KV 322. All the seven notes of the F major scale appear in it except the sixth (D), which appears just before the final cadence. Adler made much of this principle as a standard of the aesthetic worth of a melodic line. I cited counterexamples, famous melodic passages of Schubert and Brahms, where, instead of "touching" every note of the scale, the melody dwells on one of them, often the third or the fifth. That led to the argument of whether aesthetic worth should be derived from some a priori standard or whether general aesthetic principles should be deduced from common features (if any) of what we intuitively perceive as beautiful. I raised the question of the extent to which sheer beauty is a sufficient measure of aesthetic worth, referring to the kernel motive as a counter-example.

I recall this incident, because it impressed me as indicative of the sort of atmosphere that was encouraged at the University of Chicago in those days—a sort of resurrection of Platonic symposia. I liked it. I blew up that apparently trivial argument about what made a melody beautiful into a major cultural-ideological issue—the Apollonian (static, finite) ideal of balance, versus the Dionysian (Faustian, dynamic) idea of striving toward the infinite. I introduced this theme into my lectures on the kernel motive, the fundamental unit of architectonic composition. I recalled what Spengler wrote about the affinity between Western music and Western mathematics. I decided to study mathematics, not because I took seriously the old cliche about the correlation between musical and mathematical ability but because I felt that both (Western) music and mathematics were manifestations of the European spirit. In those days, "Eurocentric" was not yet a term of opprobrium, and I had no compunction about adopting what I thought was the European outlook in philosophy, politics and ethics as the basis of my definition of myself and of my aspirations.

A bachelor's degree was conferred on students who passed comprehensive examinations in the four areas (physical sciences, biological sciences, social sciences and humanities) plus an English qualifying exam, all of which could be taken at any time. I passed them in June, 1938 and was admitted to the graduate school.

Europe Again

I spent the summer cycling over Europe, starting in Paris, over Basel, Zurich, across Austria to Vienna, then over Prague to Dresden, Leipsic, Magdeburg and Hamburg to Scandinavia ending in Oslo.

In August, 1938 the Nazis put on an exhibit in Vienna entitled "The Eternal Jew." The history of the Jews in Europe was depicted in imaginative variety from caricature posters (a huge one dominated the entrance to the exhibition halls at the defunct Nordwestbahnhof) to statistical graphs and charts showing the progress of de-Jewification in Germany and Austria and "documentary" films. I remember particularly a series of large portraits of people in several European governments, each marked with the flag of his country and a legend, "Frenchman? No, Jew!" "Dutchman? No Jew!" etc. There was also a portrait of Maxim Litvinov, the Commissar of Foreign Affairs of the Soviet Union. The legend was "Russian? No, Jew!" But there was no Soviet flag accompanying the portrait. There was a film showing the slaughtering of a cow, after which the Jewish ritual slaughterer grinned into the camera. The final caption was *"Haben die Juden auch Menschen geschlachtet?"* ("Did the Jews slaughter people as well?")

I wrote an article on the exhibit, which was published in *The New Masses*, a Communist weekly, under the title "When knives are smeared with Jewish blood," a paraphrased line from the *Horst Wessel Lied* (*Wenn Judenblut vom Messer spritzt*).

Fortunately, I did not take notes on the exhibit, which might have got me in trouble. On the Danish border north of Flensburg, the customs official politely invited me into the back room, where he searched me and paged through my notebook, from which he copied all names and addresses. There were no Germans or Austrians among them except one young Nazi, whom I had met on the road. That summer there were huge crowds of German youths hiking and cycling over Austria. The border between Austria and Germany, closed since the attempted Nazi putsch of 1934, was reopened in March, 1938. There were headlines in the Tyrol papers, "German Youth Wanders over Ostmark!" (So Austria was renamed.) Amusing stories were told about meetings between German and Austrian youngsters, mostly about minor lexical differences and the amusing confusions they caused. Among these travelers was a young man from Munich, whom I met somewhere in Tyrol and with whom I traveled to Vienna. It was he who suggested that we inquire about a youth hostel in Vienna at the office of the NSDAP (National Socialist German Labour Party). He also accompanied me to the antisemitic exhibit and explained the various features to the "visitor from America." It was his name and address that the customs official found in my notebook. I wondered afterward with mixed feelings whether he got in any trouble on this account.

After the search the customs official engaged me in a conversation. He asked me how I liked what I saw in Germany. I was diplomatically evasive. Then he spoke, apparently sincerely and not at all bombastically, about the achievements of the regime. He cited unemployment figures in the U.S. He spoke of the spirit of rejuvenated Germany, of the enthusiasm of the Austrians, who after centuries came back into the fold of greater Germany. And he spoke with affection about the Fuhrer. I listened politely and even nodded once in a while. I found myself liking this mild mannered middle aged man. Nevertheless I sensed immense relief as I rolled into Denmark in the torrent rain. There was an inn a few hundred metres away. I went in and ordered a sumptuous meal. (In North German inns there was sometimes nothing but potatoes to be had.) I fell in love with Scandinavia.

On my return I found a letter offering me a faculty position in a New England music school. I inquired about it, but the position had been filled. In a way, I was glad.

Graduate Student

I spent three and a half years as a graduate student. I still had minor musical engagements and practised on university pianos during the week and at my parents' on weekends. But my chief preoccupation was now with the newly discovered world of science and with what I imagined to be revolutionary activity. I had done very well in all the comprehensive survey courses. But the physical sciences attracted me most, specifically the mathematicized branches. I have always been fond of mathematics. In Satanov father had taught me elementary algebra and geometry and introduced me to incommeasurables. I learned that $\sqrt{2}$ and π could not be expressed either as decimals or fractions, but that they could be approximated to any desired degree by an unending decimal. At first this puzzled me, but at the time I did not give it further thought. The concept of infinity made the first serious impact on me in grade school. We were introduced to decimals and shown how to convert fractions into decimals by the process of long division. The teacher gave us some exercises and went about doing something while we worked. If the denominator of a fraction had only 2's and 5's as factors, the conversion was easy. But then I came across 10/7. I started to divide 10 by 7 and got 1.42857142857142857142...It dawned on me that this was bound to go on for ever. I felt trapped.

The kid behind me called the teacher's attention to my plight.

"Mrs. Beegan," he said (every one heard), "Anatol is crying."

The teacher was solicitous. She asked me what the matter was. I told her.

"You silly boy," she said, "I told you to carry it out to just two places."

"But I want to carry it out all the way," I protested.

"Well, you needn't," said Mrs. Beegan and left me miserable. I brought the problem to my father, who introduced me to the concept of limit, of which he had a vague idea. It wasn't until I took a calculus course at the University that this matter became clear to me.

On another occasion during my second sojourn in New York I had tried to prove the Bridge of Asses Theorem[1] by elementary methods. I succeeded for the case where both bisected angles of the triangle are acute but could not carry out the proof in the general case. The source of the difficulty became clear to me when I took a course in analytic geometry. Altogether mathematical thinking became a source of great satisfaction to me. So I chose mathematics as my field of specialization.

Mathematical physics appealed to me most, but I did not have enough background in physics. I concentrated on algebraic number theory instead. My doctoral dissertation was entitled, "Construction of Non-Abelean Fields of Degree p^2 with prescribed arithmetic." There is a song in the musical, Finian's Rainbow:

If I'm not near the girl I love, I love the girl I'm near;
If I can't fondle the hand I'm fond of, I fondle the hand at hand;
If I don't face the face I fancy, I fancy the face I face.

I interpreted this opportunistic policy in my own way: if I can't solve the problem I have posed, I pose a problem I can solve. In short, I was not proud of my dissertation. It showed no evidence of either profound thought or mathematical virtuosity. But it fulfilled the requirements, and I passed my final orals on Friday, December 5, 1941.

I never returned to algebraic number theory. My interest was in applied mathematics, but, as I said, I did not have sufficient background to do research in mathematical physics. There was, however, another field of application, where bare beginnings had been made, namely, mathematical biophysics. The man who is generally recognized as its founder was Nicolas Rashevsky, a Russian emigre, who came to the University of Chicago after he lost his job with Westinghouse Electric during the Depression.

I met Rashevsky at one of the mathematical seminars or "samovars," as the graduate students called them, because of the antique samovar from which tea was dispensed. I introduced myself to Rashevsky and commented on the extreme weakness of the tea he was drinking. He said he loved tea but was allowed to drink only an "infinitely dilute solution." Then we talked about Tula, the town south of Moscow, where samovars were made, and I switched to Russian which delighted him. He invited me to visit one of his classes. I became a regular auditor. After the war I joined his group, the Committee on Mathematical Biology, where I worked for seven years. My first published paper was a mathematical approach to the phenomena of parasitism and symbiosis, which in another context can be regarded as analogous to conflict and cooperation, a theme that has remained central in everything I wrote in fifty years since then.

"Revolutionary" Activity

In November, 1938 I joined the Communist Party. There were three "leftist" parties on campus which competed as such in student elections: Socialists II, Communists III and Socialists IV. The Roman numerals referred to the Internationals to which the parties imagined themselves to belong: the Second International, the Third International and the Fourth International (founded by Trotzky). I have mentioned my first contact with Communists and with so called fellow travellers in Mexico and in New York. I think a major factor in the orientation of these people was an image of the Soviet Union as a source of power in the coming struggle with fascism already going on in Spain and apparently soon to become global. This was the mentality nurtured by the "United Front" line pervading all Soviet propaganda. Another source was the Soviet film, which made its debut on the world screen with the first Russian sound picture, *The Road to Life*. During my parents' junket in Europe in 1931 it was shown in Vienna, and we went to see it. It was about the *bezprizornye*, the homeless children who lived in the streets of Russian cities in the years after the civil war. Attempts to round them up into orphanages got nowhere. A young man with a profound understanding of the wild kids' mentality succeeded in organizing them into a working commune. Father was deeply impressed. His hostility toward Communism softened. He thought the worst was over and that the country was launched on a programme of building a new life based on devotion to cooperation and common effort. He contrasted *The Road to Life* with the trivialities of Hollywood, the rich panorama of characters (every one of the wild kids was a distinct personality) with the glossy stereotypes of movie heroes and queens peddled in America. In short, he became a fan of the Soviet Union (rationalizing the cruelties of war Communism and civil war as bitter necessity).

In the mid-thirties Soviet films were continually shown in Chicago. There were two films about Lenin—Lenin in October and Lenin in 1918. Lenin was played by Boris Shchukin, The accuracy of the make-up was amazing and the characterization utterly convincing. Here was the Stanislavsky method in the service of "building socialism." Several films about the revolution and the civil war were shown—all grimly realistic. There were also sentimental films, but the sentiments were fresh and touching. There was one about a Tatar youth, who plays the native pipe and is "discovered." He becomes a music student at the Moscow conservatory, then a brilliant flute virtuoso. There was a film about Pushkin's adolescence at the Lyceum and one about Gorky's childhood in the home of his sadistic grandfather. Ostrovky's plays and Chekhov's stories were brilliantly filmed. And there was a film (The Great Citizen) about the beginning of the Trotzkyite opposition in the mid-twenties, showing how the failure in marshaling political support led to its transformation into a conspiracy producing subversion and sabotage. To those who wanted to believe that Soviet Communism was the wave of the future, the interpretation was convincing.

In retrospect, I believe that I, too, was taken in by the scam. But no matter how hard I try, I cannot recreate in myself my state of mind at that time. I cannot say with any assurance that I "really" believed that nonsense. Years later, when I read Tolstoy's *Resurrection*, I thought I discovered a reasonable explanation of what was happening (unnoticed when I read this novel as an adolescent). Tolstoy describes the ritual of the Eucharist with devastating sarcasm and poses the question whether the priest actually believes the cannibalistic hocus-pocus with which it is pervaded. He decides that the priest cannot possibly believe that the bread is turned into Christ's body and the wine into his blood. But he believes that it is necessary to believe it, which is not at all the same thing as actually believing it. Perhaps I found myself in the same position. But this is a simplistic explanation of my actions from 1938 to 1941. I still cannot recreate my state of mind so as to re-experience that time of my life.

The activities of the Communist Party "cell" at the University of Chicago were confined to meetings at the homes of members, mostly faculty people. There was a presentation—summary of current world events with an appropriate "analysis." During local and national election campaigns the party line was transmitted to the cells, specifying whom to support and whom to vilify. Occasionally students were asked to help with distribution of leaflets during strikes. And, of course, there was always the task of recruiting.

Every one had a party name that the recruit was permitted to choose.

"In this respect, the individual party member is completely free to follow his individual inclination," the leader of our cell said smiling condescendingly at my initiation. (The use of the mandatory "him or her" was not known in those days). I became Peter Vickers. Peter was my favourite male name, and Vickers was after Sinclair Lewis's Ann Vickers, whom I admired.

Besides the discussions of world affairs, there was a course on the history of the Communist Party of the Soviet Union, based on a textbook of that name, a collective work said to have been edited by Stalin himself. The crude demagogy and the convoluted gobbledygook of that book must have been apparent to every one. But I suppose every one was convinced (as was the Russian Orthodox priest in Tolstoy's *Resurrection*) that it was "necessary" to believe it.

In the wake of the Hitler-Stalin pact whatever influence the Communists had among the left-leaning American intellectuals largely dissipated. The Soviet Union no longer appeared as a bulwark against fascism, the image peddled in the days of the United Front. There was a feeble attempt to stem the exodus by switching to a "keep America out of war" stance, which became the principal slogan in the 1940 presidential campaign.

To get on the ballot in Illinois 100,000 signatures were required, of which at least 100 were to be gathered from residents in each of the 50 counties. The first requirement was easy to fulfil, the second virtually impossible. The stalwarts did their utmost to whip up enthusiasm for the project. I was to take a group of five comrades to Peoria, an industrial town, where there was some chance of getting 100 signatures.

We were given a sales pitch: "We represent a political party that doesn't want our country to be dragged into the war in Europe. Signing this doesn't mean you intend to vote for our candidate. All it means is that you believe the American people have a choice of saying 'No' to sending our boys to fight for other countries. If you agree, help us put our candidate for president on the ballot."

I was given a shabby old Plymouth belonging to one named Olsen and his driver's license. (That the picture didn't match didn't matter, I was told, they never pay attention to the picture anyway.) Two men, two women and I drove across the state in blistering heat.

We divided up the petitions and a number of streets in a workers' neighbourhood and agreed to meet in an hour. It was awful. The most frequent response through the screen of the kitchen door was "We don't want anything." As often as not, the door was then shut. Other responses were "My husband ain't home" or "Will this get me in trouble?" I got two or three signatures. I think the most any one got was six.

Soon after we started out in another part of the town, we were picked up and taken to a police station. We were photographed and fingerprinted. Then we were locked up separately in foul-smelling cells empty except for a toilet bowl without a seat. I spent the night on the cement floor.

The next morning we were given a talking-to about "making a lot of people awfully unhappy." Our belongings, including the signatures, were returned to us, and we were told to get out of town.

On the way back we passed an outdoor swimming pool with a crowd of noisy youngsters splashing around in it. I had an aching longing to join them.

All the way to Chicago I pondered on the experience trying to bring into focus the source of my misery. It was not the complete impotence of the Communist Party on the American political scene. It was rather a feeling of shame. I had forced myself to do something I hated, namely, to try to sell something. No matter that at the time I really believed in what I was "selling." (Until the German invasion of the Soviet Union, I accepted the isolationist position.) It was vivid throwback to my earlier brush with salesmanship that made me miserable.

Fourteen years previously, when I was looking for a way of earning some money, I had come across an ad addressed to "music students." The place turned out to be a radio shop. The job was to offer people a radio to be installed in their home free of charge for a week. If they liked it, a price would be quoted; otherwise no obligation was involved. For every such installation, I was to receive 50 cents; for every sale $2.50 commission.

"You can start by contacting relatives and friends," the man told me. "They will usually agree (it won't cost them any money). Then we'll give you a territory to work."

Then he briefed me on the sales pitch.

"Tell them you are a music student working your way through music school. People like to help young people who are willing to work hard to get ahead."

I skipped the part about contacting relatives and friends. Instead, I staked out my own territory in a neighbourhood where no one would be likely to know me. It was that awful afternoon that I recalled after the fiasco in Peoria talking through the screen of a kitchen door and hearing, "We don't want any," "My husband ain't home," "No thanks, we've got a radio."

I quit.

Perhaps the idea of quitting the Communist Party occurred to me on the drive from Peoria to Chicago, but I hung on for a year and a half. I quit in December, 1941, not because I was disillusioned but because I was asked to quit. And I was asked, because every one entering the armed forces was asked to quit. Since the invasion of the Soviet Union by the Germans, the Party was supporting the war effort. It was explained that there must be no basis for suspecting Communists of divided loyalty for the duration of the war.

NOTES

1. So called in the Middle Ages, because it stumped mediocre students: Given that the bisectors of two angles of a triangle are equal, to prove the triangle isosceles. Although the proof seems at first sight simple, it is actually quite complex.

War

6

On Friday, December 5, 1941, I passed my doctoral oral exams and went to my parents for the weekend as usual. On Saturdays I taught piano in the suburbs on the North Shore. On Sunday I lay on the living room couch listening to the broadcast of the New York Philharmonic. If I remember correctly, the concert was interrupted between 3 and 4 o'clock to announce the bombing of Pearl Harbor. My parents were out. They went to get some pastries for tea. I broke the news to them. I told them I meant to enlist immediately and got my father's blessing. His pacifism dissolved as quickly as had his anti-Bolshevism several years previously.

The next day I stood in line with hundreds of young men waiting to be interviewed by a navy officer. I was instructed to take a physical examination, which I failed because of nearsightedness. I thought of trying for the other services. But my military career was decided for me by an invitation from Maxwell Field to teach mathematics and physics to aviation cadets.

I went to Montgomery, Alabama and was immediately processed. I lied on my application when I stated I had never been arrested. That is, I said nothing about the incident in Peoria. But my fingerprints were presumably on file, and they were taken again at Maxwell Field. For days I had visions of being exposed and charged with perjury. But nothing happened. The title of Civilian Instructor was conferred on me.

A colleague of mine from the University of Chicago, another newly hatched mathematician, and I found a nice apartment in a suburb of Montgomery, which impressed me with the absence of sidewalks. The colleague had a car, and we drove every morning except Sundays to the base, where we taught six one hour sessions all from the same mimeographed syllabus: 45 minutes lecture, 10 minutes multiple choice quiz, 5 minutes break.

There were 300 multiple choice quizzes to mark each day (six classes of 50 students each with practically 100% attendance). I was especially impressed by the wrong answers given to the following questions.

- A descending parachutist has reached terminal velocity.
(a) The downward force acting on him is greater than the upward force.
(b) The upward force is greater than the downward force.
(c) The forces acting in the opposite directions are equal.

- A horse is pulling with a force of 100 pounds on a rope the other end of which is tied to a tree.
(a) The force acting in the other direction is 100 pounds.
(b) The force acting in the other direction is 0.
(c) The force acting in the opposite direction is 200 pounds.

- Air is passing through a Venturi tube.
(a) Both the velocity of the air and the air pressure are greater in the wide section than in the narrow section.
(b) The velocity is greater in the wide section and the pressure is greater in the narrow section.
(c) The velocity is greater in the narrow section; the pressure in greater in the wide section.

Most cadets marked (a) in the first question, (b) in the second, and (b) in the third. All the answers are wrong. I tried to find the source of the misconceptions, and it seemed to me (and still seems) that I found it. I enjoyed explaining it to the students. They had all memorized the formula expressing Newton's Second Law of motion: F=ma. (The force acting on a body is the product of the body's mass and of the acceleration it undergoes and acts in the direction of the acceleration). Now if the parachutist had reached terminal (i.e., constant) velocity, this means that the acceleration he is undergoing is zero. If we set a=0 in the formula F=ma, the right hand side becomes zero. Consequently the left had side representing the force acting on the parachutist, must also be zero. We know that the force of gravity acts downward. If the resulting force is zero, then the upward force must be equal to the downward force. The upward force is provided by the pressure of the air against the opened parachute.

Having gone through the explanation, I waited for the inevitable question, "If the force acting on him is zero, why is he moving?"

"He is obeying Newton's First Law," I would say. "You remember it. It says that if no force is acting on a body, it will continue either in the state of rest or in uniform motion in a straight line. The parachutist is moving with constant velocity in a straight line."

Then I told them what I most wanted to tell them—about the sources of their misconceptions. I felt I was giving them a sort of psychoanalysis. They thought of force as effort, because that is the way they experienced the application of force. If they wanted to move something, they usually had to push it, say a table across the floor. But as they pushed the table, in one direction, the force of friction was acting in the opposite direction, and if the table moved with constant velocity, the counteracting force was equal to the applied force. But only the force they exerted was felt. That is why the existence of the other force was not recognized.

The problem with the horse illustrates Newton's Third Law: every force is accompanied by an equal and opposite force. If the horse exerts a force of 100 pounds and if no motion results, an equal force must be acting in the opposite direction. Therefore this force is 100 pounds. The error stemmed from the tacit assumption that a tree cannot exert a force (identified with effort).

The wrong answer about the Venturi tube is suggested by a supposedly similar situation. One thinks of the constriction in the tube as something analogous to the narrowing of a road. Traffic moves more slowly when the road narrows down; so one thinks air moves more slowly in the narrow part of the tube. But the same volume of air passes per unit time in all parts of the tube. So if the cross-section is smaller, the velocity must be greater. As for pressure, one thinks of the constriction in the tube as something caused by pinching it, and pinching is associated with applied pressure. But if the velocity of the air is greater in the narrow part, the air must have undergone acceleration in passing from the wider to the narrower part. Thus, some force must have been acting in the direction of the narrow part. This force is reflected in the difference in pressure: greater in the wider part, smaller in the narrower.

There was no time to go from there to theories of cognition or the philosophy of science. But the habit of examining my own beliefs and searching for their sources has remained.

"Newtonian Physics and Aviation Cadets" was the first paper I wrote on this theme. It was published in *ETC.: A Review of General Semantics*, a magazine edited by S.I. Hayakawa, and led to our acquaintance.

The cadets were encouraged to read whatever they came across that dealt with aviation, and the instructors were told to call their attention to any such material. There was an article in *Life* about the history of military aviation with pictures of World War I biplanes, Zeppelins, down to contemporary types. The article ended with a description of "the air war of the future," featuring dog fights in the stratosphere. This was the first time I saw war not as something that was undertaken (justifiably or unjustifiably) in various circumstances but something that existed as an institution which guaranteed careers and produced specialists, inculcated an ethos and nurtured traditions. It was natural for the practitioners of the profession to be interested not only in the history of the institution but also in its future. The professionals also had a conception of "progress" related to their profession in many ways similar to the conception of progress among, say, the practitioners of medicine or of various branches of engineering. How did these conceptions tally with those of people like my father or myself, who regarded war as a disaster and who put their pacifism on hold for the duration. There was no answer to this question, and I simply put it out of my mind.

Life was quite pleasant. The six hours of teaching six days a week was a strain. But it was nice to relax completely afterward, to have dinner in a crowded cafeteria, and to mingle with the gay evening crowds of men in uniform and their girl friends.

In June I was commissioned as a first lieutenant of the U.S. Air Force. The news from the fronts was at first bad, but no one doubted that once the U.S. got going with its immense production volumes, victory was inevitable. Every one believed that victory depended on two things: overwhelming production capacity and being on the right side. For an overwhelming majority of Americans the war was an exhilarating experience. Unemployment evaporated. People had money to spend. The very shortages (which were trivial by world standards) gave people the feeling that they were bravely bearing privations.

The song writers were busy. The songs were supposed to build morale. Some were about girls back home being true to their boy friends in the service: "No fun, no nothing, till my darling comes home!" Or else, "I've looked them over, and lo and behold—they're either too young or too old!" (meaning the men away don't have to worry that the men back home will steal their girl friends). In one song a soldier is writing a letter to his mother: "Dear mom...They treat me all right, but I miss my old bed..." In another a girl comments on her boy friend's passing his physical examination: "He's One-A in the army, and he's A-One in my heart." A soldier explains to his girl friend why he has to go: "I've got to get rough now, so I can be nice to my baby another time."

I remember a song written by the wife of my commanding officer. It had passages like "Oh my, oh me! You're in the infantree!" The idea was to call attention to a branch of the service less glamorized than the air force. Referring to the air force was the line, "They bomb and supply and do what they can; but the hero on land—he wins close at hand!"

When I went on some mission to Chicago, my commanding officer asked me to see Glenn Miller (a well known band leader, then in the entertainment section of the U.S. armed forces) and ask him if he would "push" that song. I went to see Major Miller and showed him the song. He glanced at it and looked at me. We understood each other. I was sorry when I heard that Glenn Miller died in an air crash.

Swallowed up by the euphoric mood of the time, I suppressed my disgust with its vulgarity, as I had suppressed my pacifist convictions. That was the time when the future seemed brightest. Victory would reconcile the United States with the Soviet Union. There would be no more need for ruthlessness and harshness in building socialism. After victory the broadening of the New Deal policies would lead to a welfare state, which to me appeared as the very essence of socialism. American patriotism, which in the early 1920's Upton Sinclair had depicted as union-busting terror (see his *One Hundred Percent*) now appeared as loyalty to humane ideals. Already in the mid-thirties American Communists had adopted the slogan "Communism is twentieth century Americanism!"

When orders came transferring me to Alaska, I was overjoyed. I knew that the transfer had to do with my knowledge of Russian. It was also generally known (in spite of so called secrecy) that there were Russians in Alaska engaged in some sort of joint operation with Americans. I was thrilled and filled with self-importance to see my orders stamped SECRET and remembered to burn them as instructed.

I was given two days' leave in Chicago to say good bye to my parents. From there I went by rail to Minneapolis for some processing, then to Great Falls, Montana for more processing, and from there by plane to Fairbanks. That was the first time I had travelled by air. I sat twisted in the bucket seat of the C-47 cargo plane looking out of the window behind at the thickly forested Canadian landscape. A giant swath was cut through the forest—the Alcan Highway from Edmonton to Fairbanks was being built. I played with the idea of writing a novel opening with the same words as Thomas Mann's *Magic Mountain*: "A simple young man travelled…" I thought of myself as that "simple young man" and of the shattering life experiences that might be awaiting me like those of Hans Castorp's. I thought I might witness the meeting of two worlds and the beginning of their consolidation into one.

The operation in which I was involved was the implementation of lend-lease, supplying allies with war materiel. In Alaska the recipients were the Soviets.

The Russians were given planes of four types. One was the slow but extremely rugged and safe C-47. It carried thirty men and was used to ferry the Russian pilots back from Siberia after they flew the combat planes across from Alaska to the Chukotka Peninsula just across the Bering Strait. The combat planes were pursuit planes, first P-40's, later replaced by P-39's (Aerocobra), which the Russians preferred; the light bomber A-20, used in ground attacks, and the medium bomber B-25.

The planes were flown to Fairbanks by American pilots. There the Russians checked them out and flew them to Nome, the last landing in North America, and from there across the Bering Strait to a place called Welkal, then to Anadyr, Yakutsk, and so on directly to the battles of Stalingrad and Voronezh.

The American pilot who taught the Russians to fly American planes was Nick De Tolly, a Russian-speaking descendant of General Barclay De Tolly, the first Russian commander-in-chief against Napoleon in 1812. In civilian life Nick was an artist in Disney's studio. He told me that he drew the mushrooms that looked like Chinese in "Danse Chinois" from Tchaikovsky's *Nutcracker Suite* in Disney's *Fantasia*.

Nick was an excellent teacher, very tough with his "students" (which they loved) but very adroit in mixing his toughness with good humour. He told me of the difficulties he had to overcome. The Russians were trained to move in jerks as if executing barked commands, "Present arms!", "Roundabout face!" etc. In flying, Nick insisted, one must use smooth "rounded" movements, just the opposite of what the Russians were doing.

"You're a pianist," he said to me once, "so you understand the difference between *staccato* and *legato*. The Russians do everything staccato. Another thing, they transfer something they are proud of to a situation where it doesn't belong. They are proud of making a three-point landing. In a P-39 the three-point landing is a flub."

Both the P-39 and the P-40 had three wheels. In the P-40 two wheels were in front, one behind. It was proper to land this plane on all three wheels at once. A P-39 had a so called tricycle landing gear—two wheels behind, one in front. This plane had to be landed on its two hind wheels, keeping the front wheel up, then slowly lowering it. The Russians insisted on trying a three point landing with the P-39, which bounced several times (made a "goat", as the Russians called this hopping), until they finally learned.

There were two other Russian speaking Americans in Fairbanks. One was a young artillery officer, who was not pleased with his job as liaison officer with the

Russians. (He wanted to command a battery, where he could do what he had been taught, namely, to fire off cannon.) The other was an older civilian, a Russian emigré from San Francisco. He and I were assigned the task of preparing a glossary of aviation terms: English-Russian and Russian-English. For this we had to enlist the help of some Russian English-speaking flyers, who would explain to us what the terms meant by reference to things, relations, and events. Dictionary definitions of many terms were useless because they also had non-technical meanings, which the dictionary listed but which did not correspond to the non-technical meanings of the English terms. Picturesque slang was freely used by the flyers, as by any professionals and served the same function—as an in-group language. For instance, the Russians called the wind shield wiper *dvornik*, which means "janitor." In Russia the janitor of a building does a lot of sweeping. These sessions were the first contact I had with the Russians. I longed to engage them in conversations about ideology, politics, and war aims, about life after "victory," etc. But life at Ladd Field (the Fairbanks air base) was very busy, and I had only fleeting contact with the Russians until I was transferred to Nome.

My main job in Fairbanks was to sit in the control tower and to give the Russians procedure instructions in Russian. They did a lot of practice flying and paid practically no attention to regulations. For example, they flew over the town, which was prohibited. Often something went wrong with the transmission and receiving; so light signals had to be used, to which they paid no attention. Reception was severely distorted by static and interference. It was a mess.

The Russians wanted to have some sort of celebration on the 7th of November, the anniversary of the October Revolution, but they were afraid such an event would rub the Americans the wrong way. They asked me to put out feelers, but I already knew that a joint celebration was planned. The Russians were impressed. The recreation rooms were decorated with crossed Soviet and American flags. Speeches were translated in both languages. There was a concert and much eating and drinking and swearing of eternal friendship.

Toward the end of November I was promoted to captain and transferred to Nome. Winter had already set in. The temperature in Fairbanks often dropped to the point where the Fahrenheit and the Celsius scales coincide -40 degrees below zero. But the cold was bearable because there was no wind. However the planes that had not been winterized were grounded; the lubricating fluid in the landing gear mechanism froze. The operation came to a standstill. The Russians panicked. While I had no direct evidence, I was almost certain that they suspected sabotage. As a matter of fact, I did not discount that possibility. I was somewhat relieved when the Russian commanding officer asked me to interpret at a meeting with his American opposite number. The decision was to try to find a suitable addition to the lubricating fluid to enable it to function at -50 C. Alcohol would not do, because it dissolved the neoprene gaskets of the landing gear mechanism.

There was a chemical laboratory at the University of Alaska on the outskirts of Fairbanks. A Russian engineer and I went there to see what could be done with kerosene. We added various amounts of kerosene to the lubricating fluid, measured the resulting viscosity, and brought the mixture down to -50 C. A particular concentration seemed to give satisfactory results. The Russian remarked, as he held up the test tube:

"Do you realize what is happening in this test tube? The fate of nations is being decided."

He was referring to the Battle of Stalingrad still raging, into which the planes were thrown after crossing Asia at its greatest extent.

Nome

The temperature in Nome seldom dropped below -30 F, but the cold was much worse because the wind always blew. There were only about five hours of daylight, and the planes came only in fair weather. The control tower was reached by a wooden ladder. I would climb up there about 20 minutes before the estimated time of arrival radioed from Fairbanks and would wait for their call: "Allo, allo! Dikaya Koshka!" That meant "wildcat," the code name of the Nome air base. I would reply that I heard him and asked for identification. He would call out the number of planes coming in. I would give landing instructions. They were simple. There were two runways, one running east and west, the other north and south. Since landing had to be against the wind, and since the wind was almost always from the north, I always landed them from the south. That was fortunate. There were hills north of the base. Coming in from the south over the Bering Sea was safer.

Facilities in Nome were primitive. Even the officers' quarters had no plumbing. Everything was built of wood except the prefabricated huts, which served as enlisted men's quarters and as storage warehouses. There was constant anxiety about fire. The officer of the day (on twenty-four hour duty) had to make the rounds of the base every hour through the night to check the precautions. There were only five officers besides the commanding officer, who was exempt from the twenty-four hour duty. Thus, one had to stay up every fifth night. Aside from that there wasn't much to do. A brigade of infantry stationed a few miles from the base was also idle. It had been sent in expectation of a Japanese attack on Alaska. (Two of the Aleutian islands had been already occupied by the Japanese. But after the Battle of Midway in June, 1942 the threat receded.)

Nome was a town of 1500 souls, predominantly Eskimos. It didn't have much to offer in the way of entertainment. There was a movie house, which wasn't much of an attraction, since movies were shown every night at the base. The Russians were fond of westerns. They called the cowboys "American cossacks." There was a café that served things other than spam, predominantly reindeer steaks. There was also a bath house in the form of a few shower stalls in the back of the barber shop. The barber was a descendant of the Russians who lived in Alaska when it was part of the Russian Empire. There were other vestiges of the Russian colony. Salt herrings were sold right out of a barrel. For the Russians they were a welcome supplement to the base fare, which consisted almost exclusively of powdered eggs and spam. The reason was that in the expectation of a Japanese invasion, food stores had been buried, and their location forgotten. Fresh supplies were, to be sure, delivered in the spring, when the harbour was freed of ice; but until then the monotony of the diet was one of the "severe hardships" suffered by American troops outside the United States.

The richest man in Nome was the banker. He lived alone. His wife and little girl lived in the States. The commanding general of the infantry brigade, the commander of the air base, and I were invited several times to have dinner at his home. He talked a great deal about his little girl, who, he said, was exceptionally gifted. He showed me her little piano pieces, published under the title "Six pieces by a little girl." Possibly I was invited because the host wanted my opinion about the pieces. They were all right, and I praised them. I was also asked to play the piano. When conversation turned to politics, the banker, my commanding officer, and the general decried the erosion of American values under the New Deal, and I was rather outspoken in expressing my views.

In addition to my duties as control tower officer and interpreter, I became supply officer of the base. Once I was introduced to a civilian, who, I was told, was to inspect the security provisions at the base. (Eskimos, it was said, were hard to distinguish from Japanese.) I was asked to explain the gasoline delivery system. I showed the visitor the pump house, guarded around the clock, and other installations, showed him the cache of gasoline stored in barrels as a back-up to the pipeline. It occurred to me that he listened without much interest. He did ask questions about the Russians, their attitudes, habits, and behaviour. I told him our relations with the Russians were good and that things were going smoothly.

Soon after the war, I had a telephone call from the banker, who was stopping in Chicago. He invited me to his hotel, saying he had a surprise for me. The surprise was that my commanding officer was also there. He informed me that the civilian who presumably came to examine our security system really came to investigate me. (The infantry general had reported my views expressed in our conversation at the banker's.) On the strength of his report, my promotion to major (recommended by my commanding officer) was blocked.

At our reunion we reminisced about Nome with the nostalgia usual in reunions. The colonel said we were by no means finished there. Soon we would be going up there again, he said, since, as he put it, "Uncle Joe and Uncle Sam are starting to make faces at each other." This was the first time I felt the chill of the Cold War.

I recalled the article on "the air war of the future" in *Life*. I thought of my commanding officer. Colonel was his temporary rank, the result of rapid promotion during the war. Very soon he would be no more than a lieutenant again, at most a captain. If war with the Soviet Union were to break out, he would retain his wartime rank with chances of further promotion because of his experience in the Arctic and his contacts with the Russians.

Ambivalence

We buried ten Russians in Nome (killed in crashes). Two of them had become almost close friends of mine. The friendship was the kind that feeds among Russians on endless conversations, mostly soul-searching. I saw the crash from

the control tower. The plane was being tested after repairs. It took the snow
vehicle several hours to get to the wreck and bring the bodies back. The colonel
told me to ask the Russian commanding officer what kind of service he wanted at
the funeral. I told him that it might not be appropriate to ask this question, since
the official religion in the Soviet Union was atheism. He told me to go ahead and
ask anyway. I told the Russian major that we had a Catholic priest and a
Protestant pastor as chaplains. I explained that there were also Jewish chaplains in
the American armed forces but we didn't have one at the base. Possibly one could
be brought from Fairbanks. To my surprise he said that the Catholic chaplain
should be asked to officiate. So there was a service followed by speeches about the
alliance of freedom loving peoples "cemented in blood."

I thought of this phrase in another connection. After the fourth partition of
Poland in September, 1939, Molotov, then foreign commissar of the Soviet
Union referred in a speech to the "eternal friendship between the German and
the Russian peoples cemented in blood." It took two blows, Molotov said, one by
the German army and one by the Soviet army to destroy Poland, that "monstrous
offspring of the Versailles Treaty."

I remember distinctly being shocked when I read excerpts of that speech
and now I was reminded of it at the funeral of my friends in 1943. But I can't
recall how I rationalized my adjustment to it. The Hitler-Stalin pact was easy
enough to rationalize. Stalin was, apparently playing for time. He was frustrating
the treacherous schemes of England and France to sick Hitler on the Soviet
Union. I imagined Stalin as he was pictured in U.S. Ambassador Davies' film
"Mission to Moscow," explaining to Davies the ABC of global politics,
illustrating his explanations by pointing to places on the globe. I remember also
that my admiration of Stalin outlasted my disappointment with Dialectical
Materialism, the official philosophical dogma of the Soviet Union. In an article
sharply critical of dialectical materialism, I singled out Stalin as a pragmatist, who
did not take the official doctrine seriously.

American ex-communists used to say, "Every one of us has had his
Kronstadt," referring to the event that precipitated a break with the Party. The
first Kronstadt was the brutal suppression of sailors' demonstrations against the
Soviet regime. (Kronstadt was Russia's principal navy base.) Some Communists
left the Party then. Some broke away to follow Trotzky. Some condemned the
Moscow trials of 1936-1937. Many refused to accept the Stalin-Hitler pact. My
"Kronstadt" was the Lysenko affair (of which later).

The eighteen months in Nome marked the zenith of my loyalty to the
Soviet Union, which I regarded as the leader of a "democratic" world to emerge
after the war. I suppose the feeling was not unlike that of many Americans during
the Cold War, who viewed the United States as the leader of "the free world" or
of the "New World Order" after the collapse of the Soviet Union.

In 1943-44 the Nome air base was "developed." Hangars were built as well
as "stateside" officers' quarters with running water, a lounge with arm chairs, and
a bar. At the festive opening pictures were taken of groups of Russians and

Americans in lively interchanges. Again a shadow passed over my enthusiasm. One of the Russians confided to me that these pictures made him uneasy.

"It is, of course, possible to refuse to be photographed," he said, "but we would consider it rude. We would rather take the risk than offend the Americans."

"What risk?" I asked puzzled.

"Who knows how a picture might be used against one, when an occasion arose?"

Years later I realized that his apprehensions were well founded. Practically all Soviet officers who participated in the Spanish civil war, "stemming the tide of fascism," were liquidated upon returning home. The Gulag awaited survivors of German prisoner of war camps. It is not unlikely that my Nome friends (except the ten that died in the crashes) ended up in the same way. The idea was, evidently, to remove possible sources of contagion.

Semantics

It was in Nome that I became interested in the ideas of S.I. Hayakawa's mentor, Alfred Korzybski, who was regarded in academic circles as a crank, a view to which I now take perhaps somewhat unjustified exception. Korzybski's major work, *Science and Sanity* was lent to me by a civilian employed at the infantry base, whom I took out two or three times to the café where they served reindeer steaks. She wanted to know what I thought of the book, in particular why Korzybski kept insisting that "the word is not the thing"? I told her that I found the book pretentious and dull; that it shouldn't take more than a few pages to say what every one knows. I asked her why she was interested in the book. She said she was told it is about how to achieve mental health. She went on to tell me that several people she knew thought the book helped them "find themselves" and among those who praised it was S.I. Hayakawa, author of the best seller *Language in Action*. I had heard about that book when I was still in Montgomery. That the author was Japanese intrigued me.

I came across *Language in Action* by a coincidence vividly remembered. Soon after the Battle of Midway, when the Japanese invasion of Alaska was no longer expected, the infantry brigade left. Some of us from the air base went to the abandoned base to see what could be salvaged. There was a plethora of home made furniture, gasoline barrels converted to various uses, stacks of paperbacks in what used to be the day room. And on a dusty shelf there was a dog-eared copy of *Language in Action*, which I immediately appropriated.

The book was a college English text. It presumed to teach Freshmen how to write. It told them to write about things they knew, and it told them that knowledge comes from contact with things and events not from learning to fit words together. To be sure, knowledge comes through words but only if there are "non-verbal" experiences behind the words. Knowledge that comes through strings of words alone is illusory. (So this is what Korzybski meant when he insisted that "the word was not the thing.")

Hayakawa applied this principle in explaining the teaching of English. He wrote:

> What is the teacher's duty when a child says in class, 'Taters ain't doin' good this year'? Traditionally, teachers of English and speech have seen their first duty as that of correcting the child's grammar, pronunciation, and diction in order to bring those up to literate standards. The teacher with a semantic orientation will give priority to a different task. He will ask the student such questions as, 'What potatoes do you mean? Those on your father's farm or those throughout the county? How do you know? From personal observation? From reports from credible sources?'[1]

I noted the emphasis on the two fundamental questions that constitute the foundation of scientific cognition. "What do you mean?" and "How do you know?" These questions relate both meaning and knowledge ultimately to experiences that people have in common.

I found out that Hayakawa taught at the Illinois Institute of Technology in Chicago. I sent him an article describing my experience in teaching physics to aviation cadets. He wrote that he would be happy to publish it in *ETC.: A Review of General Semantics*. It appeared in the third issue of Volume 1 (1944). This was the beginning of a collaboration that lasted for over twenty years.

Shortly after I received acknowledgment of the article, I went to Chicago on leave and came to 1234 E 56th Street, where Korzybski conducted "seminars." His lecture had started and I took a seat in the back of the room. He demonstrated a gadget that he called the Semantic Differential. He dropped a box of matches to demonstrate the action of gravity. He showed how the spinning of an electric fan blurs the blades into a fuzzy disc. He showed how the number of relationships between pairs of people grows much more rapidly than the number of people. I didn't think these demonstrations were particularly interesting or enlightening.

I recognized Hayakawa from his picture on the jacket of *Language in Action*, sitting up front on the left. After the session I introduced myself. He said he wanted to introduce me to Korzybski, to whom he had spoken about me, and we went to the Master's office. The first thing Korzybski asked me was, "You have read *Science and Sanity*...how many times?"

I said something about re-reading some passages, but Korzybski evidently was not interested in my answer. He kept talking about the same things he talked about in the "seminar." I decided to write him off. But I didn't. The basic idea of what he called "general semantics" stuck with me. My first book, *Science and the Goals of Man*, was based on it. Korzybski never saw the book in print. He died just after he read the galleys and denounced me as a vulgarizer. He had also denounced Hayakawa on the same grounds.

Thirty Men Aboard

The operation in Nome was going smoothly. One dramatic incident, however almost ended in disaster. I often recalled it when I wondered about sources of human motivations including my own.

One winter evening when we were not expecting any arrivals, Operations got a call announcing the approach of a C-47 with thirty Russian pilots aboard. I went up to the control tower and made contact. There was trouble. Only the east-way runway had been cleared of snow. But a strong wind blew, as usual from the north; so landing northward was indicated. But landing on an uncleared runway could drive the plane into a snow bank. To avoid the risk of a crash, I gave instructions to land eastward. It couldn't be done. The strong wind blew the aircraft off the course. The pilot made two or three passes and finally said, "Can't do it. Request permission to land northward."

I had my standard instructions to land planes up-wind. But who would be responsible if it hit a snow bank and crashed? I would. Or would I? I would have acted in accordance with instructions, but would that absolve me from real responsibility for possibly killing 30 people?

"Try westward," I shouted into the microphone. That didn't work either. Finally I said, "Keep circling until further instructions. It won't be long."

The commanding officer had gone to the movies. I contacted the officer of the day and ordered him to find the colonel and bring him into the control tower. The colonel appeared.

I explained the situation and told him I couldn't take the responsibility for landing the plane on the uncleared runway. If he thought this should be done, he should give me the order to permit the plane to land northward. This was done and the plane landed. It did go into a snow bank but suffered only a bent propeller.

In an hour the Russian pilot and I were eating reindeer steak in the cafe in town. He told me that when he landed the altimeter still showed 170 feet above sea level. (Our runways were about 20 feet above sea level.)

"Thirty men aboard," he kept repeating.

I kept thinking of other things. This job of mine—landing planes—had become pretty boring. The wind was practically always from the north; so the landing instructions never varied. I recalled experiencing a feeling of importance giving different instructions and even a sort of grim satisfaction in insisting on the procedure overruling the pilot's request. I recall feeling miserably ashamed of myself afterward. I learned a lot.

Interlude

Toward spring of 1944 I assumed the duties of supply officer. A young Russian emigre from San Francisco had been brought in and took my place as interpreter. There was little to do except take an inventory of the repair shop, and even that was superfluous, because an aviation maintenance battalion had replaced the infantry brigade and had brought their own repair shop. I applied for training at a language school (I wanted to learn Japanese), but my application was turned down. Instead I was transferred to Love Field in Dallas. I arrived there on June 6, the day the Allies landed in France.

There was nothing to do at Love Field. I was supposedly the supply officer of some unit, but my duties were limited to checking whether certain items had been issued and whether the recipients had them, for instance, gas masks, and whether certain items were on proper shelves in proper quantities. Then there were "parades." Thousands of men and women in uniform gathered in open areas in intense heat and stood in formation while the brass walked up and down the lines inspecting them. I was gigged for having failed to polish by belt buckle.

Although I was entitled after my stint "overseas" (Alaska counted as "overseas") to stay in continental U.S. possibly for the duration, I volunteered for another overseas assignment and within a few weeks was shipped out to what was then India and is now Bangladesh. The journey across the Pacific took a month. We embarked from a port near Los Angeles, sailed to Melbourne, zigzagging all the way (eluding torpedoes). We stayed three days in Melbourne but were not allowed to go into the city. We could promenade up and down the dock. From there we went to Bombay. Two destroyers escorted us on the last two days. Actually the U.S. navy was in full command of both the Pacific and the Indian Oceans throughout the last year of the war.

India

I was assigned to an Air Transport Command base near Dacca (now the capital of Bangladesh). My first assignment was to organize a laundry. The clothes were washed by Indian civilians by hand. I was to interview labour contractors and engage one who seemed competent. I had no idea what the standards of competence of a labour contractor were, and surely knew no more about the laundry business.

The first thing that struck me in those interviews was the way the applicants recommended themselves. They said nothing about their experience or qualifications or, for that matter, about the job to be done. Instead, they pointed out how badly they needed the job, that is, how many children they had and so on. This struck me as a violation of a fundamental principle of a market economy. I had been most impressed by the following passage from Adam Smith's *Wealth of Nations*, one of the Great Books we had to read at the University of Chicago in the social sciences survey course:

> It is not from the benevolence of the butcher, the brewer, and the baker that we expect our dinner but from their regard to their own interest. We address ourselves not to their humanity but to their self-love and never talk to them of our own necessities but of their advantages. Nobody but a beggar chooses to depend chiefly on the benevolence of his fellow citizens.[2]

On the other hand, in negotiating wage rates, the contractors followed the dictates of the market. One was apologetic for the rates he was obliged to ask.

"Unfortunately," he pointed out, "these people have an advantage. Over five million of them died in last year's famine. There are fewer of them, and this pushes the rates up."

The famine, too, was a result of market forces. Speculators were able to corner the rice harvest and kept it in storage until the price soared. By then millions could not afford to buy it and starved to death.

We were in the business of flying gasoline "over the Hump" (a stretch of the Himalaya range) into China, supposedly in preparation for an offensive against the Japanese by Chinese armies supported by the U.S. Air Force. At first the gas was transported in C-109's (B-24 bombers converted to tankers). But several of these exploded on take-off as a spark ignited the cargo. Almost immediately after my arrival, my room mate, a young Chinese pilot died in one of these explosions. The C-109's were replaced by C-54's, cargo planes that carried the gas in fifty-five gallon barrels. These were safe, and the operation went smoothly until the Japanese surrendered. However, this gas was never used against them. Instead, Chiang Kai Shek used it against the Communists.

Ours was one of a string of bases in the Assam Valley, each engaged in the same operation. The commanders of these bases were mostly airline executives, experienced in transporting people and things rather than in combat. In fact, the Air Transport Command was a gigantic world air line. The bases were operated like civilian airports with arrival and departure schedules, facsimiles of airport hotels, etc. The analogue of the shopping mall was the Post Exchange (PX), where, in addition to toilet articles, candies, etc., one could buy cameras, sweaters, wrist watches, stationery, and costume jewelry.

More than any other institution they represented a metastasis of the American way of life over the globe. In fact, the GI's referred to the United States as "the Big PX."

Some of my experiences in India seem worthwhile relating. The fact that I often think of them suggests that they made some impact on me but just how is not easy for me to discern.

There was a university in Romna, a spacious slumless suburb of Dacca, where I made contact with some faculty and graduate students, in particular with T. Vijayaragavan, a mathematician of note, whose field was number theory. He was originally from Madras. A number of graduate students met at his home once or twice a week in a sort of seminar. He questioned me about my dissertation and made some profoundly perceptive comments. On one occasion he took me to Madras (I managed to get three days' leave), where I gave a talk on the Galois theory at the university. I was mildly surprised to see two Catholic nuns in the audience.

Vijayaragavan's deep knowledge of number theory contrasted sharply with his primitive conceptions of the physical world. After the war he visited the U.S. My wife and I drove him across the country to from Chicago to San Francisco. We had long rambling conversations in the course of which he surprised me by declaring that he could tell compass directions when he shut his eyes. I tried him, but it didn't work. He did not give up his belief, however. He said he could do it in India. One foggy morning during our trip when we were driving in a canyon above a rapid stream, I called his attention to an illusion: the stream seemed to be flowing uphill.

"Look," I said jokingly, "that stream is flowing uphill."

In all seriousness he asked whether this was a common phenomenon in North America.

As I said, I took only a lukewarm interest in algebraic number theory. I was more strongly attracted to mathematical physics. But Vijayaragavan kindled my interest in that purest branch of the purest of sciences, the field which Godfrey Hardy (one of the greatest in it) glorified especially because he insisted that competence and sophistication in pure mathematics was quite independent of worldly experience or of any other knowledge. It occurred to me that there were just three fields of endeavour where child prodigies made an appearance, namely, music, mathematics, and chess. These were precisely the fields of intellectual activity in which cumulated worldly experience plays no part.

I was invited to give a talk on "Western materialism" at the university of Romna. I was told that when the invitation was proposed to the dean, he asked whether the subject would be discussed "seriously." He was evidently skeptical about Americans' range of intellectual interests. During the discussion I became painfully aware of the gulf that separated Western philosophy of science from speculative philosophy. When this gulf became apparent in the West in the 18th century, science broke away from its parent. In India, apparently, the break never occurred.

I was curious about what Western music meant to the Indians, if anything. I was giving a recital at the base (yes, we had a piano: the "Special Services" that provided entertainment for the GI's saw to that). I arranged to bring two truckloads of faculty and students to the base, but again attempts to find a common language did not get very far. How could relativism be reconciled with universalism in the realm of values?

I became aware of being watched. One of the intelligence officers got drunk at the officers' club and told me that my hobnobbing with the reds in town was well known and would come to light in due time.

Another incident that stuck in my memory was the loss of the "duck," a valuable but in the circumstances a totally superfluous piece of equipment.

A so called jungle camp was established on the shore of the Indian Ocean south of Chittagong, ostensibly for training personnel in survival techniques. Men were supposed to be dropped somewhere in the adjoining jungle and expected to walk out, a sort of boy scouts' training course. My job was to deliver supplies to the camp once or twice a week. There was a stream between the landing strip and the camp. It was dry at low tide and full at high tide. Thus, we had to come in at low tide, so that the truck coming from the camp to pick up the supplies could cross the stream bed.

Shortly after the operation began, the commander of the base gave me a manual in which the tide tables were given for various locations. I looked it over and noticed that the schedules shown for Chittagong (the nearest point to our camp) did not coincide with what I knew, having been to the camp once or twice. I told this to the commander, adding that I could easily estimate the times of the tides for the next several weeks on the basis of previous observations; but he told me to use the manual.

Sure enough, we landed at high tide. We contacted the camp by radio, and they said they would send their duck, which, they said, could cross the stream. This was a welcome opportunity to see the duck in action, for which, as far as I knew, no use had been found.

We all gathered on the bank of the stream to see the duck perform. It plunged in and was promptly carried out to sea. The GI's all jumped off and swam ashore, while the duck floated away into the Indian Ocean. There was much laughter. No trouble was anticipated in "writing off" the amphibian craft. In fact, it had probably been written off already, since the Japanese bombed the landing strip twice, which authorized writing off every piece of equipment in the area. I could imagine the bombing welcomed like rain during a prolonged drought.

Victory

The end of the war came suddenly. I don't know what happened to the stocks of goodies at the Post Exchange. I do know what happened to the military stores. At the insistence of the British, they were destroyed. Tents, blankets, clothes, good quality wrist watches (standard issue to pilots and navigators) were all thrown into piles, soaked with gasoline and burned. Space for transporting them back to the States was unavailable, and the British forbade distribution of these things among the population. I violated this prohibition by giving my alarm clock to my orderly, a ten-year-old boy, who probably saved my life. Cleaning up my basha one morning while I was in the shower, he found a krait in my shoe, killed it, and proudly showed it to me hanging on a limb of a tree. He spoke some English, and I tried to engage him in conversation but without much success. On one occasion, however, we touched on a subject close to politics. When Roosevelt died, he asked me who would succeed him. I told him. "Is Truman Roosevelt's son?" he asked. I thought this was an occasion for introducing political systems as a subject of conversation; but he did not seem particularly interested. Nevertheless, when the time came to say goodbye, and I gave him the clock, he seemed genuinely touched and shed tears.

When the atomic bomb was exploded over Hiroshima, I was asked to give a lecture on atomic energy. I used the occasion to advertise the "practicality" of theories. I pointed out that every advantage has its reverse side, and American "know-how" with its implicit contempt for "theory" is no exception. I asked the officers and men to tell me what they knew about the American geniuses of technology, Thomas Edison and Henry Ford. They knew a lot. I asked them what they knew about Gibbs, perhaps the most outstanding American physicist of the nineteenth century. They knew nothing. I asked them what they knew about Einstein. The most frequent answer I got was that only nine (or eleven or something) people in the world could understand his theory of relativity. I told them about Sinclair Lewis's character in *Arrowsmith*, whose monograph on immunity was read by 9/11 of the people who could understand it, the total number of these people being eleven. Then I told them what Edison said about what he expected from a young man whom he would hire to work in his laboratory in Menlo Park.

"I don't care how much 'theory' they know," he is reported to have said. "What I care about is whether they can tell me offhand what the speed of sound is."

I told them about Henry Ford's famous dismissal of history as "bunk." I quoted Kurt Lewin, the founder of social psychology: "Nothing is as practical as a good theory."

Then I told them about how Einstein came upon the concept of space-time and how starting with that concept he derived the relationship between matter and energy, which pointed to the possibility of converting one into the other. I explained what the equation $E=MC^2$ meant. This was only a day or two after the massacre in Hiroshima, before any one had heard about the "magic formula," the awesome "secret" of the atomic bomb.

A few days later V-J was announced and our C-54's were rerouted from Chunking to Shanghai, from where they flew to Japanese POW camps to evacuate Americans. Priorities were established for evacuating us as well. They were based on "points" calculated from time overseas, age, family situation, etc. I got out in October.

We were flown to Karachi. Over Agra the pilot circled around the Taj Mahal, so that we could say we had seen it. In Karachi we were packed aboard the S.S. Anderson, the same troop ship on which some of us had sailed from California a year before. But this time we didn't have to wear life jackets all the time, and at night all the lights were on. The mood was euphoric.

Home

In New York we were greeted with three toots by every craft in the harbour. We were told this meant "Wel-come-home." A boat load of girls came out at dawn to meet our ship. They were shouting through megaphones, doing cartwheels, and so on. At the pier Red Cross girls met us with coffee and doughnuts.

We were processed, then delivered to the terminal of the Lackawana Railroad in New Jersey. The processing continued at the Great Lakes Naval Station north of Chicago. It went smoothly. Every officer was interviewed and asked whether he wanted to stay in the service. I was offered a promotion to major, but I said thanks, but no thanks.

My parents met me at the exit. Mother had prepared a great Ukrainian borscht with cabbage, beets, and potatoes, but I couldn't do it justice, because I was coming down with the flu.

After a few days on the living room couch, I went to New York to attend a mass meeting at Madison Square Garden. It was part of an effort by the New Deal Democrats to rebuild the coalition of workers, Negroes (as they were then called), ethnic minorities, and intellectuals, which would carry on what was thought to be a grass roots revolution against the concentrated power of Big Business. Danny Kaye presided. Helen Keller made a speech. The attempt sputtered on for a couple of years. The musical Pins and Needles dramatized the unions. Another, Finian's Rainbow, celebrated a vision of opulent prosperity based on peaceful uses of atomic energy and on populist egalitarianism. It featured a dance in a southern locale attended by Whites and Blacks. But no mixed couples danced.

The Cold War came on full strength in 1946, sparked by Churchill's Iron Curtain speech in Fulton, Missouri, the same town where forty-two years later Mikhail Gorbachev was to give it the *coup de grace*.

I still wore my uniform. I was not officially separated from the service until the end of the year, and I thought the uniform would help me find a job. There was no difficulty, however. I got the first job I applied for—instructor of mathematics at the Illinois Institute of Technology, where S.I. Hayakawa was also on the faculty. I joined academe.

NOTES

1. S.I. Hayakawa, *Language in Thought and Action*. Second Edition.
2. Adam Smith, *The Wealth of Nations*. New York: E.P. Dutton, 1910, Volume 1, p. 13.

Chicago

7

"Today is the first day of the rest of your life," says an upbeat homily. This is the way I felt on my first day as college teacher, when I faced forty men, to whom I was engaged to teach differential calculus. They all wore a little yellow lapel pin (the "ruptured duck"), identifying them as war veterans. I, too, wore one. These men were using their opportunity to get a post-secondary education under the (U.S. veterans) GI Bill of Rights. They, too, stood at the beginning of something. I was sure they felt as I did.

I, too, took advantage of the GI Bill and enrolled again at the University of Chicago. I thought I would get another doctorate, perhaps in some biological science. But it turned out the University did not award more than one Ph.D. I took the courses anyway, developing a sort of addiction or a hoarding compulsion. I told myself that hoarding knowledge could not be as reprehensible as hoarding money or power. Money and power were "conservative commodities": the more one gets of them, the less others get. But if A gives B a piece of knowledge, B is enriched while A is not impoverished. Iago called attention to the grim reverse side of this condition: "...he that filches from me my good name robs me of that which not enriches him and makes me poor indeed."[1]

So I felt self-righteous about hoarding knowledge, especially since my longing to impart and disseminate knowledge was so keen.

There was another sense in which I felt that my "return from the wars" was the beginning of "the rest of my life." I got married.

Gwen was a friend of Mrs. Hayakawa (both had been active in the cooperative movement). We first met at a New Year's Eve party at the Hayakawas, at which I was with another woman and she was with another man. I got into a heated political discussion with her escort. During the fifty years of our marriage Gwen often needled me about not remembering her when we met again at the Hayakawas almost a year later on Saturday, December 4, 1948. As soon as I saw her walk into the room, I knew that I would marry her.

Gwen lived in Madison, Wisconsin at the time, working in the School for Workers at the University of Wisconsin. She still kept an apartment with a friend on the Near North Side of Chicago, where she stayed when she came to town. I invited her to the opera on the following Saturday. We saw Eugene Onegin. Her next visit was during the Christmas week. We met again at the Hayakawas on December 26 and every day thereafter. I proposed on New Year's Eve and was accepted. We have gone through the same ritual at 6 P.M. on December 31 every year since then.

Gwen stayed in Madison until summer. We spent our honeymoon (six months after our marriage) cycling from Zurich to Venice. As we pushed from Altdorf up to the Gotthard Pass, I told Gwen about Suvorov's expedition against Napoleon in 1799 (which I remembered from the Russian history lessons of my childhood). That crossing was compared to Hannibal's feat two thousand years before. Just as I was telling the story, we came around a bend and saw a huge carved inscription on a rock in Russian commemorating the expedition.

Gwen joined me at the University of Chicago where she enrolled as a graduate student, worked in the Industrial Relations Program and directed a training program for union officers. We shared a political outlook, a thirst for knowledge, and delight in family life, giving concrete meaning to the ancient Russian proverb, *muzh da zhena—odna satana* (man and wife are one devil). Why devil? I guess just because *zhena, odna, and satana*, all accented on the last syllable, rhyme—another confirmation of the Sapir-Whorf-Korzybski hypothesis: our language does our thinking for us.

Knowledge that interested me most turned out to be knowledge of the second order, as it were: knowledge of self, knowledge of knowledge. How do we know what we know? How can we tell truth from falsehood, from delusion, from nonsense? In short, theories of cognition became central in my preoccupation: general semantics, philosophy of science, psycholinguistics, general system theory. Under Rashevsky's tutelage I explored the range of application of mathematical methods outside the physical sciences: to individual psychology, theories of mass behaviour, description of social structures, inferential statistics (measures of reliability of knowledge), etc.

All these fields have to do with criteria that justify beliefs in what is. Of equal, perhaps greater importance are fields having to do with criteria justifying beliefs in what ought to be: primarily ethics.

Of greatest importance to my way of thinking then and subsequently to this day have been criteria that link the two kinds of belief. The linkage, as I began to see it, is reflected in the four parts of my book on *Semantics* published in 1975: Man and His Language, Symbol and Meaning, From Meaning to Knowledge, From Knowledge to Responsibility.

Another such chain connects normative and descriptive decision theories, that is, theories of how a "rational" actor ought to choose among available alternatives and theories of how real actors choose. Preoccupation with game theory led me to scrutinize the very concept of rationality, in particular, the sharp distinction between individual and collective rationality revealed in the analysis of so called non-zerosum games, in which what some win others do not necessarily lose. The relevance of these findings to the increasingly widely recognized global problems became a constantly recurring theme in my preoccupation and expression.

The most formidable obstacle to the solution of these problems appeared to me to be the Cold War and its ramifications: the nuclear arms race, ideological polarization, the cancer-like spread of war-related institutions through the entire fabric of both superpowers. My book, *The Big Two* (1971) is devoted totally to this theme, which is also a major theme in *Fights, Games, and Debates* (1960), *Strategy and Conscience* (1964), and *The Origins of Violence* (1989).

In what follows I will attempt thumbnail descriptions of several fields of knowledge (or, more properly, speculation) that determined the crystallization of my outlook on the way things are and the way I think they ought to be, which is the principal theme of this book.

My First Paper

Rashevsky's group, eventually called Committee on Mathematical Biology, was housed in a flat of an old house on Drexel Avenue just off the University of Chicago campus. Rashevsky taught a course based on his monograph, *Mathematical Biophysics* and presided at weekly seminars, where members of the group (five or six young men and a young woman) presented papers subsequently published in the *Bulletin of Mathematical Biophysics*. At the time they and Rashevsky were the only contributors. The journal, now called *The Bulletin of Mathematical Biology*, has world stature today.

Soon Rashevsky offered me a part time assistantship with his group, and I accepted, splitting my time between it and my job at the Illinois Institute of Technology. My first task was to proof-read a paper of Rashevsky's entitled "A Problem of Mathematical Biophysics of Interaction of Two or More Individuals Which May Be of Interest in Mathematical Sociology."

The paper gave me an idea. What would happen if each individual pursued his own "interest," and, in doing so, interacted with another, who also pursued his own interest? There are two ways of answering this question. To see "what would happen" one could observe a situation of this sort. Or one could postulate certain principles governing the dynamics of the situation and deduce the implications of these principles. The first method is based on principles of empirical science, putting direct questions to nature, as recommended by Francis Bacon in the seventeenth century. The second method is the method of mathematics, celebrated by Plato and Descartes. In textbook descriptions, "the" scientific method is portrayed as a cycle in which deduction (mathematical derivation) alternates with observations, which either confirm or disconfirm the deduced predictions of "what will happen." Rashevsky was concerned exclusively with deduction, and for that reason the Committee on Mathematical Biology remained on the fringes of the scientific establishment of that time. Alvin Weinberg[2] pleaded with Rashevsky jokingly to let us put on white coats so that we would at least look like "scientists," but Rashevsky would have none of it. He insisted on a special niche for mathematical biology, which, he was convinced, would some day attain a status comparable with that of mathematical physics.

So my aim was to construct a mathematical model of two interacting individuals, each pursuing his own interest. First, the notion of "pursuing one's own interest" had to be defined in a way permitting mathematical deduction. This could be done by identifying the "pursuit of interest" with maximization of some quantity. In economic contexts, this might be maximization of profits by a producer of marketable goods. In a biological context it could be the maximization of fitness (reproductive advantage). From the point of view of the mathematical model builder, the concrete context does not matter. Only the mathematical form of the assumptions matters.

To fix ideas I assumed that each of the individuals produced some nurturing substance that both individuals shared, whereby the amount of "satisfaction" derived by an individual was represented by the difference between two terms. One was a logarithmic function of the amount of nutrient received; the other a linear function of the effort expended.[3] Thus, the respective satisfactions of the two individuals were denoted by $U_1(x,y)$ and $U_2(x,y)$, where x and y are the amounts of nutrient produced by the two individuals respectively.

Each individual adjusted his own effort so as to maximize the utility accruing to him, given a particular level of effort of the other individual. To find the point of equilibrium of the maxima attainable by such adjustments, we set the rates of change of $U_1(x,y)$ and $U_2(x.y)$ with respect of x and y respectively (what the economist calls marginal utilities) equal to zero.

The point (x,y) at which both rates of change of effort vanish represents an equilibrium in the sense that neither individual can increase his satisfaction by either increasing or decreasing his effort, if the other does not.

Two illuminating results can be derived from this model, which represent a sort of "theoretical harvest." By this I mean an understanding of the nature of the phenomenon represented by the model. One result relates to the nature of the equilibrium represented by the point (x,y). The other is an implication of the individuals' independent attempts to maximize their respective satisfactions. Let us consider the nature of the equilibrium first. Physical equilibria are characterized as stable or unstable. A case of a stable equilibrium is represented by a bead resting on the bottom of a hollow hemisphere. If it is displaced, it will move generally downward and will eventually come to rest again on the bottom. An unstable equilibrium is represented by a bead resting on the top of the hemisphere. A slightest displacement will send it rolling down, and it will never come to rest in its original position.

Similar examples of stable and unstable equilibria are observed in a wide variety of situations. The temperature of a match is initially in equilibrium with that of its environment. If the match is rubbed against a rough surface, the temperature will rise. If it rises only slightly, it will return to an equilibrium with the environment when the rubbing stops. But if it rises beyond a certain threshold, the match will ignite and will no longer return to its original state.

Certain body states of living creatures are kept in equilibrium, for example, concentrations of substances in the blood or body temperature of warm-blooded animals. These quantities oscillate around equilibrium states. As long as the oscillations are not too large, the concentrations or the temperatures tend to return to their equilibrium states after disturbance. However, once a deviation becomes sufficiently large, the equilibrium is no longer restored. For example, the organism dies. Death is an irreversible event.

The equilibrium of the system comprising the satisfaction-maximizing individuals can also be stable or unstable. If it is completely unstable, the slightest deviation will be magnified rather than diminished. That is to say, the efforts of one individual will keep increasing, while that of the other will keep decreasing, until the latter will become "parasitic" on the other. Which of the individuals will become the parasite depends on the direction of the initial displacement from the equilibrium.

If this is indeed the case, that is, if parasitism can develop in an arrangement of this sort, the question naturally arises under what conditions this will occur. The mathematical model suggests an answer. The system will be unstable if the product of the portions shared is greater than the product of the portions retained. One may find this result intuitively acceptable and regard it as an indication that the model does capture some aspect of a situation of this sort. The other theoretical spin-off of the model is revealed by the observation that the amounts of satisfaction accruing to the individuals at equilibrium are not the largest that can be attained in this situation. Both individuals can benefit if their efforts are interdependent, for example if each exerts an amount of effort proportional to the amount exerted by the other.

In sum, my first effort at constructing a mathematical model led me to the realization of two principles encountered in a great variety of situations. First, situations involving interactions between individuals pursuing their respective interests can be stable or unstable. In a stable situation some sort of equilibrium can be expected to be attained, in which the system will persist. If it is unstable, the equilibrium, although theoretically possible, will not persist. The system will move away from it and go toward one or another extreme. In the situation depicted above the sharing of a resource "degenerates" into parasitism, whereby which of the individuals became parasitic on the other depended more or less on chance, that is, on the direction in which the system happened to move from the precarious (unstable) equilibrium. Second, it turned out that when each attempts to maximize his own satisfaction, the individuals fail to achieve the levels of satisfaction they could have attained if their efforts were interdependent. In other words, the result pointed to a "cooperative dividend," a concept that was to dominate my thinking about the human condition for the rest of my life.

Mass Behaviour

Another theme around which much of my early work at the University of Chicago revolved was mass behaviour. Rashevsky's interests switched from mathematical biophysics to more general contexts of mathematical biology, and soon afterward to mathematical psychology and sociology, that is, to constructing mathematical models of human behaviour—individual or in the mass. The latter context interested me more, because the phenomenon of mass behaviour appeared to me to resolve the age-old controversy between "determinism" and "free will." Surely there is no "objective" evidence supporting either position. To "prove" determinism of human behaviour one would have to show that the behaviour of an individual can be predicted even if he is aware of the prediction. But unless the individual is constrained, he can always falsify the prediction at least in some contexts. On the other hand, if an individual attempts to demonstrate "free will" by predicting his own behaviour and then fulfilling the prediction, there is no way of refuting the conclusion that his very "prediction" was determined by his state at the time it was made. I had long decided that the controversy was sterile as are a great many "metaphysical" arguments of this sort. It did make sense, however, to investigate conditions under which human behaviour can be predicted more frequently and with greater accuracy. It turns out that human behaviour in the mass can often be predicted much more accurately than the same behaviour performed by an individual.

This principle was amusingly demonstrated in the late 1940's, when television appeared in a large majority of American homes. Within two or three years practically every American household was equipped with TV. It was noticed that during the so called "prime time" hours, water pressure in city mains suddenly dropped for two or three minutes every half hour on the half hour. An explanation readily suggested itself. When the programs changed, people went to the bathroom. It became clear that while every individual had the "free will" to go or not to go to the bathroom, in the mass people's behaviour might be governed by "laws." Moreover, it became clear that such laws are not like the classical deterministic physical laws but rather manifestations of statistical effects. Here, then, I thought, was a basis for mathematicized biological and social sciences.

Epidemics and Rumours

Rashevsky's book, *Mathematical Biology of Social Behaviour* appeared in 1951. In Part I, there were still some allusions to brain functions as determinants of behaviour, but that is as far as "biology" went. The rest of the book was devoted to formal mathematical models, explicitly or implicitly statistical, of the development of social hierarchies, of imitative behaviour, of motivation, imitation, learning, and so on.

I imitated him. In constructing models of spreading epidemics I noted that the spread of information, of rumours, or of fads may follow the same patterns. There was no opportunity to test these conjectures. But that did not worry me. *The Bulletin of Mathematical Biophysics*, edited by Rashevsky, was practically a guaranteed publication outlet. Rashevsky was not a careful editor. He was enthusiastic about spreading the methods of mathematical model building into every nook and cranny of the social sciences, regarding them as generalizations of his mathematical biology, which, in turn, he regarded as a generalization of mathematical biophysics. In this way a gross error in my third paper on interaction between two individuals went unnoticed and became a source of embarrassment to me. And it is hardly a consolation that no one noted the error. This only indicates that hardly any one has ever read the paper carefully.

The first experience with a test of my model of rumour spread was, in a way, traumatic but also, in a way richly instructive. This was the occasion of my first encounter with the post-war American military establishment. Assuming a large population and completely random contacts between its members, I deduced a relationship between the average number of persons contacted by each person hearing the rumour and the ultimate fraction of the population that will have heard the rumour. The process of random contacts turned out to be remarkably effective. It was shown, for example, that if the average number of persons contacted by each transmitter is two, fully 80 percent of the population will eventually have been contacted, and this fraction is virtually independent of the size of the population, which can be arbitrarily large. The same formal model applies to epidemics. In real life epidemics of this magnitude (pandemics) are rare, even though the numbers of persons contacted on the average per transmitter may be quite large. There are several factors that contribute to the limitation of epidemics: immunity, recovery, or death of infected, and, above all, the fact that contacts are not generally completely random. It stands to reason that most people contacted will be in the vicinity of the source, and this substantially reduces the rate of spread of a disease through a population. We can suppose that analogous factors enter the spread of information, behaviour patterns, and the like. I kept working on the problem, attempting to take such factors into account.

Before I got anywhere with it, a well known American sociologist visited me. He told he had got a dramatic confirmation of my "theory" of rumour spread, referring to my model based on random target selection. He did an experiment in a large class, and the results fit the predictions of the "theory" almost perfectly. I tried to explain to my colleague that all he "tested" was the randomness of target selection, not the dynamics of rumour spread. He could have got the same results if he used markers instead of people. But I wasn't sure he knew what I was talking about.

Some time afterwards I received a report of another experiment performed by a team organized for that purpose. The experiment was funded by the Air Force with Air Force personnel taking part.

The cite was a town in Colorado. A piece of information was "planted" in the population, namely, a slogan used to advertise a brand of coffee: "Golden's coffee is as good as gold." A prominent announcement was made in the local paper to the effect that whoever repeated the slogan to an employee of a local market would receive a pound of this coffee while the supply lasted. The idea was to trace the spread of this information. It was assumed that people who became "knowers" would tell their relatives or friends. Accordingly, people who recited the slogan to get their coffee were asked to fill out a questionnaire, in which they were to indicate from whom they got the information and to whom they passed it on.

Why was the Air Force interested in funding an experiment of this sort? The most important reason, I later surmised, must have been that they felt obligated to dispose of moneys allocated to "research," of which there was God's plenty. If the money was not spent within a given period, it had to be returned.

Later the strength of this motivation became apparent in another context, namely, when Congress ordered operations in Cambodia to stop. Just before the deadline several tons of bombs had not yet been exploded. They were dropped on whatever targets were convenient, presumably so as not to let them go to waste. Fifteen thousand civilian casualties were reported.

The local Air Force command did not know much about experimental design, the use of controls, and the like. The rationale of this "investigation" was to see to what extent populations could be informed of whatever the Air Force wanted to inform them about if the usual media (radio, press, etc.) were not functioning, that is, if the spread of information had to depend on word of mouth. In other words, the experiment was to assess the effectiveness of person-to-person communication. But evidently this goal was somehow lost sight of. The local commander decided he was going to give the process a boost. Or, perhaps, he wanted to see how effectively the information could be spread by methods sometimes used by the Air Force, namely, by leaflets dropped from planes. Accordingly, he ordered the town covered with leaflets bringing glad tidings:

WANT TO GET A POUND OF COFFEE FREE?
JUST SAY "GOLDEN'S COFFEE IS AS GOOD AS GOLD AT …
SUPERMARKET.
TELL YOUR FRIENDS THEY CAN DO THE SAME!!

To test the "effectiveness" of this campaign, more questions were added to the questionnaire, such as:

Did you pick up a leaflet? Where did you pick it up? Did you pass it on? If so, to whom? Did you tell any one what was on the leaflet?

As the leaflets were dropped, they were photographed from the plane, presumably to determine how they spread. A man was perched on the roof of a tall building, another on a mountain top overlooking the city to provide additional information on which way the leaflets went. Two cars toured the streets to see where the leaflets fell. The city was divided into districts and the numbers of leaflets that fell in each district recorded.

The report submitted to the sponsor included a section on "theory." Information, the reader was informed, can be transmitted in different forms, e.g., in writing, orally, by visible signals. It can be received first hand, second hand, etc. It can be transmitted accurately or distorted. People are motivated to transmit information in different ways. "Knowers" gain prestige. Desire to share knowledge with others plays a part. According to whether the news is good or bad, information will spread more or less rapidly, etc., etc.

I was shocked. I knew the designer of this "experiment," (the sociologist who had performed the meaningless class room experiment), a warm, good-natured human being, youthful in spirit in spite of advanced years and full of enthusiasm. But apparently he was deluded, seduced somehow. Here was a concrete manifestation of blossoming technolatry (worship of technology) coupled with a sterile formalistic distortion of the so called "scientific method."

The Boulder fiasco brought home to me some sources of perversion of science. One was easy (too easy) access to funds, which encouraged wishful thinking about the significance of one's ideas. But the triviality of much of the research spawned by the availability of steady sources of funding was not what disturbed me most in the beginning of my life in academe. This could be easily rationalized. The projects provided opportunities for academic careers and so for the development of scientific talent where it existed (which might otherwise be extinguished for lack of ways of making a living). What I was most disturbed by was the co-optation of scientific talent by the military, by far the most generous dispenser of research funds. Never mind that the "spread of information" project was a scandalous waste of time and money. Many of the funded projects did much more damage. They led to sensational and far-reaching advances in techniques of mass destruction. They fed a euphoria generated by the sense of power in the self-designated "defence community." Coupled with this self-congratulatory euphoria was a rationalization of science in the service of war, prevalent in the scientific community itself, which spread from the natural to the social sciences.

Science and Values

Soon after I joined Rashevsky's group I came across a pamphlet by George Lundberg, a professor of sociology at the University of Washington, entitled Can Science Save Us? The motto introducing the pamphlet was a citation from *Alice in Wonderland.*

"Please, Puss," she [Alice addressing the Cheshire Cat] began, "can you tell me which way I ought to go from here?"

"That depends," answered the Cat, "on where you want to get to."

Science, argued Lundberg, can't tell us which way we ought to go. It can only tell us how to get where we want to go. Decisions about where we want to go are not scientific decisions. They are political decisions.

I disagreed categorically with this view of science, not to be sure, with Lundberg's view of how science currently functions (in this he was probably not too wide of the mark), but with his view of how science ought to function.

What science ought to be was the theme of my first book, *Science and the Goals of Man.* In this book I came to grips with two issues, which, I believe, should be illuminated from the point of view of the present role of science in human affairs. One is the relativity of values, an issue raised by cultural anthropologists of the American school. The other was the issue raised by Korzybski—the relation between the scientific mode of thinking and sanity.

The relativity of values is clearly related to the issue raised by Lundberg, namely, that the function of science in society must remain strictly instrumental: the question "What is to be done?" can be answered only with reference to the question how given goals are to be achieved. In this way, scientific cognition appears to be irrelevant to questions of ethics or morality. On the other hand, a cardinal principle of scientific cognition can be invoked to support the relativity of values, namely, the theory of relativity. In the light of careful analysis of what happens in the process of observation and measurement, it turns out that even such apparently entirely "objective" data as the distance between two points or the time interval between two events are relative to the frames of reference of different observers if they are in motion with respect to each other.

The main theme in my first book, *Science and the Goals of Man* (1950) was based on the contention that the "relativists," in invoking relativity as a universal principle of cognition and, by implication of internalizing values, did not appreciate the full import of the relativistic paradigm. What the theory of relativity revealed was that *although* space and time intervals are relative to the frames of reference of observers, the so called *space-time*, a four-dimensional construct in which space and time are fused, *is* invariant for all observers. Thus it may be that while parochial value systems differ from each other, they may be reflections of a more general value system common to all humans. For example, the male Christian entering his place of worship removes his hat; the Jew keeps his head covered. Both express reverence but by different gestures. Among Europeans, the colour of mourning is black; among the Chinese white; but the underlying feeling of grief is common to both. Can it be that "relativity of values" can be transcended by the discovery of "ethical invariants," i.e., more general human values, of which those we are directly cognizant of are specific manifestations?

There have been attempts to list such supposedly universal human values. Abraham Maslow once offered such a list.

(1) Every one feels a need to belong. That is, to be a member of a family, a peer group, an organization, a church, in short of a group whose members share the same values or pursue the same goals and hence have feelings of benevolence toward each other, based on giving and receiving support.
(2) Every one feels a need to love some one or something.
(3) Every one needs to have a feeling of self-respect, a feeling that he or she represents something worthy and that this worthiness is appreciated by others.
(4) Every one has a need for growth, that is, expanding one's knowledge and awareness and progressive integration with others.

I agree with every one of these statements. But I have no way of knowing whether this agreement is simply a manifestation of the fact that Maslow and I belong to the same culture or, rather a subculture of what has come to be called "Western" culture. How can one be sure that if one traces the origins of different people's predilections, commitments, convictions, and aversions far enough, one will find that they are specific manifestations of these four basic needs? Or, for that matter, of any other set of general principles that can be justifiably called universal human values?

Attempting to answer this question, I chose for a starting point the assumption that all values stem from conceptions of what is true, what is good, and what is pleasant. The most obvious and, at times, glaring differences among people of different backgrounds are conceptions of what is pleasant. Having reached a certain stage of maturity, we are generally not appalled by observing that what some people regard as delicious, others regard as repulsive. The notion of pleasure extends also to the notion of beauty. Here, perhaps, a conception of some universal aesthetic principle might be justified. But if such a conception turns out to be vacuous, it doesn't seem to matter much. In my estimation the statuette of the goddess of fertility discovered in the Wachau region of Austria, the Venus of Willensdorf, as she has been named, doesn't hold a candle to Venus of Milos; but I can live with this sort of "relativity of values," as easily as with the knowledge that some people in Africa love to eat termites.

Differences in conceptions of what is "good," on the other hand, have had much more serious consequences. These underlie ideologies, and we have witnessed cataclysmic outbursts of violence attributed to clashes between ideologies.

Clashes between adherents of different religions or ideologies have also been attributed to differences of conceptions of what is "true." In fact, in the context of religions or ideologies, conceptions of what is "good" and of what is "true" are frequently confounded.

It seemed to me, therefore, that a recognition of universal standards of either truth or virtue or both could be of help in forestalling conflicts rooted in differences of conceptions of what is "true" or what is "good." Moreover, in view of the awesome destructive power of such conflicts manifested in modern war, it seemed imperative to find ways of preventing them.

Now it appears to me that conceptions of what is "good" are still largely conditioned by people's cultural background. Attempts to transcend these, for example, in numerous declarations of basic human rights or in distilling some general ethical principles supposedly underlying all religions, have become commonplace. But there is no assurance that these distillations are not themselves products of a particular culture. Indeed, they have most frequently been ascribed to the particular "Western" way of thinking and so are no more rooted in some universal principle than rules of etiquette or culinary traditions.

Nevertheless, it seems to me that conceptions of what is "true" can have a common foundation independent of ways of thinking or feeling induced by particular cultures. In fact, science provides such a foundation. The ways of thinking underlying scientific cognition are the same in Indonesia and in Iceland, in Uganda and in Uruguay, in Jordan and in Japan. The relativists can naturally reject this argument out of hand by pointing out that science is a distinct product of Western culture, and the fact that scientific thinking has to some extent penetrated cultures far removed from the Western is a consequence of Western imperialism. I don't agree. I believe that even if the so called "primitive" cultures were carefully nurtured and protected from cultural hegemony of the West, there would be no way, short of absolute intellectual quarantine (which could be imposed only by a ruling elite) of preventing the scientific view of the world from "infecting" any other world view and undermining some of its foundations. Of course, the repartee of the relativists can be immediately anticipated. Reference to a "ruling elite" carries a pejorative connotation and reveals a Western prejudice. What appears as a despotic ruling elite to the Westerner imbued with Western ideas of democracy may appear as a wise, revered leadership to the people of a different culture. And so on. There is no way of resolving this controversy. The most each can do is to state his/her position sincerely and clearly. I have done this.

If this is indeed so, that is, if the adoption of the scientific mode of cognition in forming our conceptions of the world (and of ourselves) is ultimately inevitable, then a basis for resolving conflicts about what is "true" exists. Conflicts about what is "beautiful" or "pleasant" do not threaten humanity with extinction and can be resolved by simply recognizing the relativity of values in these contexts and developing tolerance based on that recognition. On the other hand, conflicts about what is "good" (essentially ideological conflicts) are fraught with danger. In view of the formidable destructive potential of massive organized violence, resolution of such conflicts appears to me to be a matter of survival of the human race. Recognition of the distinctive difference between so called instrumental and so called basic values suggests a way.

Instrumental values are those whose realization is regarded necessary for realization of fundamental values. Fundamental values are not further reducible. The distinction parallels the distinction between theorems and postulates of mathematics. Theorems are proved by reference to theorems proved previously. Infinite regress or circular reasoning is avoided by assuming some propositions to be "true" without proof. The same distinction is made in logic between defined and undefined terms. Terms (names, concepts, etc.) are defined with reference to other terms. Since the number of words in any language is finite, continuing this process will inevitably lead to circular definitions, for example, defining liberty as freedom and freedom as liberty. Thus, in any logically structured reasoning process, undefined terms must be involved which are assumed to be understood in the same way by every one.

As an example of reducing instrumental values to fundamental ones, consider a farmer who is asked why he sows wheat. He might respond by saying that he sows it in order to harvest it. Pushed further, he might reply that harvested wheat will produce grain, grain will produce flour, flour dough, dough bread, and bread will sustain his life. He may be either unwilling or unable to answer the question why he wants to sustain life. Grain, flour, dough, and bread represent instrumental values; life a fundamental one.

Now scientific cognition provides a way of gaining more or less reliable knowledge (at any rate knowledge more reliable than that provided by other forms of cognition) about the extent to which instrumental values function effectively. If sustaining life is a basic value, then a substance that helps cure a disease is an instrumental value. Whether a particular substance is, in fact, of value in curing a disease is something that can be determined by methods developed in science. Again, if one has a notion of a "good" society, then the extent to which different forms of social organization (e.g., democratic, hierarchical, autocratic) produce the "good" society can be assessed (in principle) by applying techniques of analysis, generalization, observation, deduction, etc., all of which are components of scientific cognition. In other words, science provides more or less reliable methods of singling out, testing, and evaluating instrumental values, and in this way provides (in principle) ways of resolving disputes about what is "good" when "good" refers to effectiveness of ways of attaining basic values. Therefore, whether resolution of conflicts about what is "good" are in the last analysis resolvable by application of scientific cognition depends on whether universal basic values exist. The conviction that they do exist is an article of faith. It has the same status as postulates (that neither can nor need to be proved) in mathematics or undefined terms (that neither can nor need to be defined) in logic.

If this conviction is justified, that is, if differences about what is good turn out to be differences of opinion on how the fundamental values can be most effectively nurtured or realized, then scientific cognition (testing the effectiveness of instrumental values) becomes a basis of achieving unity amid diversity, that is taking the step from relativity of values to the recognition of invariant imperatives.

I discussed these matters once again in *Operational Philosophy*, published three years after *Science and the Goals of Man*. Along with scientific cognition, a central theme in both books was a philosophy of language strongly influenced by Alfred Korzybski.

General Semantics

Korzybski's philosophy of language rests on two assumptions. One views language as a specific survival mechanism of the human race; the other views it as a screen between a human being and reality.

Every plant and animal species survives for some time thanks to some sort of adaptation to its environment, which, in turn, determines its "life style." Among animals predators have their sharp claws, which enable them to catch and kill their prey. The animals preyed upon are equipped with fleet feet and a refined sense of smell, which enable them to become aware of predators and to escape them (sometimes). Some animals are expert swimmers, some are expert flyers, some expert runners. Man can do many of the things other animals can do but apparently not as well. He can swim but not as well as a seal; he can run but not as fast as a cheetah. His body is less specialized than that of most other animals. But there is one thing he can do far better than any non-human—talk. We don't call the sounds made by non-humans talking. But they do serve as signals in communication, along with gestures, including exuded odours. So non-humans have languages of sorts. Some bird species have been reported to have "vocabularies" of some hundreds of "words." Nevertheless, non-human languages are severely limited as instruments of communication. Animals can communicate only about "here" and "now." They cannot communicate about something that happened in the past, about something that is expected to happen in the future. They cannot communicate about an event that never happened or about a hypothetical event.

Consider a dog, an animal that can communicate to humans. A dog can "say," "Some one is coming!" He can say something like "I love you" or something like "I'm sorry" (mostly by gestures). He can say something like "Give me some of what you are eating." But no dog can say, "When you were out, some one was trying to break in, but I chased him away with my barking." He cannot say, "Unless you give me a little of what you are eating, I shan't love you any more, and then *you'll* be sorry." All human beings who can talk can say things like that. That is, they can make statements about events removed in space and time, conditional statements, and statements about things that don't exist and about events that never happened. In short, they can lie.

The units of communication used by non-humans are called signals. They have direct relations to the things that they stand for. The units of communication used by humans are called symbols. Their connections to the things that they stand for are conventions. There is no necessary connection between a word and what the word stands for. In English the word for "word" is "word." In French it is "parole." In Russian it is "slovo." None of them is the "proper" way to say "word." Or, if you will, every one of them is equally proper. It is this lack of a natural connection between a word and what the word is supposed to stand for that enables human beings to invent words for hypothetical, not necessarily existing things, events, or relations. The principal idea of Korzybski's earlier book, *Manhood of Humanity*, is that man's symbolic language is his unique survival mechanism. It enables him to transmit knowledge gained by experience to those who did not have the same experiences and so makes possible learning by means other than direct experience. Moreover, it enables man to transmit experienced knowledge to future generations and so to make knowledge accumulate across generations. Korzybski called this process "time-binding."

Apparently time-binding is a unique characteristic of the human species. It immerses man in an environment entirely of his own making—a cultural environment.

The principal idea of Korzybski's only other book, *Science and Sanity*, is that symbolic language is by no means an unmixed blessing. Korzybski sees language as a sort of screen between man and the world in which he lives ("reality"). Man does not perceive reality directly. His conceptions of reality are formed by what he sees on the screen, and the picture on the screen is surely not a complete "map" of reality. In fact, no map can be a complete representation of a territory. Moreover, the picture on the screen need not even correspond to anything in reality. In sum, man forms conceptions of the world about him from what others (and also he himself) tell him about this world.

Sanity, according to Korzybski, is one pole of a spectrum. The other pole is insanity. The spectrum represents gradations between degrees of correspondence between a user's language and reality. The language of science is the language of sanity in the sense that the structure of the language of science corresponds most closely to the structure of reality. The structure of something reflects relations among its parts. For instance, the structure of a map reflects distances between locations and directions of some locations from others. If a map shows Kingston roughly between Toronto and Montreal, its structure corresponds to the structure of the territory it represents. If it shows Toronto between Kingston and Montreal, it is a distortion of reality. The language of science corresponds most closely to reality that it is supposed to represent. Moreover, this map of reality is constantly being revised and updated and so made to correspond ever more closely to reality.

Between the language of science and the language of insanity, is the language that almost every one uses in every day life. The assertions about and descriptions of reality produced in this language are not, as a rule, constantly checked against direct experience (as the assertions and descriptions produced in scientific language are constantly checked by observation and experiment). Thus, a relation exists, according to Korzybski, between science and sanity.

It is now clear why language appears as a mixed blessing. Time-binding, a process generated by symbolic language, results in an accumulation of concepts, knowledge, ideas, attitudes, etc.—a map, whose structure may or may not correspond to the structure of reality it is supposed to represent. Whether it does or not, man "navigates" by this map. He may end up where he wants to get to or get lost in a forest or drown in quicksand or fall off a cliff.

Science and the Goals of Man and *Operational Philosophy* represented a crystallization of my conception of science as primarily a reflection of collective sanity—collective because it relates truth to common experience, a reflection of sanity, because the structure of its language corresponds most accurately to the structure of reality. This conception of science, therefore, contains an ethical component. Identifying awareness of truth with shared experience serves to integrate humankind. All other bases of integration, for instance, institutionalized religions, identification with a national, ethnic, or racial group, have both an integrative and a divisive component. The latter tends to split people into "us" and "them." Integration based on shared scientific cognition is not limited by such a divisive component.

Sanity and the Cold War

As I said, I was a member of the Communist Party from November, 1938 to December, 1941, a fact which I looked forward to stating in public when, as I expected, I would be called to testify before a U.S. congressional committee investigating "un-American activities." I resigned from the party in accordance with the party policy of rendering unqualified support to the U.S. war effort. After the war I was invited to rejoin. By that time the "line" had changed again. Earl Browder, who had coined the slogan "Communism is Twentieth Century Americanism" was replaced by an old timer, William Z. Foster. The hew "hard" line was transmitted to all the parties of the West by Maurice Thorez, the French Party boss. No trace remained of the United Front. Strict orthodoxy, primacy of the class struggle, etc. were the order of the day.

I had become especially sensitive to demagogy. I couldn't stomach it. I read Lenin's *Materialism and Empiriocriticism* and dismissed it as balderdash. I counted the number of "isms," with which Lenin labeled the views of people he castigated as tools of the bourgeoisie on the "philosophical front." There were fifty-two. The compulsion to condemn everything and every one by sticking labels on him, her, or it struck me as the most conspicuous manifestation of confounding verbal maps and reality. It was this degradation of language converted to a demagogue's weapon that finally led to my break with orthodox Communism. My "Kronstadt" was the Lysenko affair.[4]

I applied the same standards to anti-Communism. This too was a torrent of demagogy. In 1950 a colleague of mine, Alfonso Shimbel, Gwen, and I wrote an article entitled "Sanity and the Cold War." It embodied our common political outlook at that time. The article included a fantasy scenario embodying a renunciation of totalitarianism by the Soviet Union and its unilateral withdrawal from the arms race. In fact, it was an anticipation of Gorbachev's "conversion," which Gwen and I witnessed forty years later (Al died young). The way we saw it then, the sudden refusal on the part of the Soviet Union to cooperate with the U.S. in nurturing the global war machine would cut the political ground from under the U.S. military establishment.

At the time the prospect appeared to us to be entirely in the realm of fantasy. But it was not on that ground that Hayakawa refused to publish the article in *ETC.: A Review of General Semantics*. As co-editor I felt it was entirely proper for me to argue in favour of publication, for example by pointing out that Cold War rhetoric was a perfect example of language pathology—identifying verbally constructed images with reality; of completely polarized two-valued orientation, of demagogic manipulation, and so on, in short a textbook case study of language pollution on the global scale.

But there was no way to engage Hayakawa in a discussion where participants had to take sides. I was fond of debate, but Hayakawa hated every form of polemics. He often spoke contemptuously of people who were ever aching to "prove something." Human communication was to him a venture in sharing, not in "competing," as he conceived all forms of dispute. So I changed the subject. I recalled his saying one time something about the impossibility of "resigning from a culture." I asked him what he meant by it.

This put the conversation back on track. He said publishing our article would be tantamount to resigning from our culture. I asked him what "culture" he had in mind. If he meant the "mainstream" American culture, I said I didn't have to resign from it, because I never belonged. Then he told me about the "Nisei blues," the longing of American-born Japanese[5] to "make it" in the WASP world, which he certainly did. He escaped internment during the war. He was a celebrity, author of a best seller. I remember listening silently and gloomily. It cost great effort to refrain from leveling with him the same way, to tell him that he was mistaken in assuming that I experienced something akin to "Nisei blues" (a Jewish immigrant boy longing to make good in the WASP world—we both married WASPS). I had a deep affection for Hayakawa. So while in those days I felt little compunction in riding roughshod over some one's feelings, I held back. I was not to break with him until twenty years later when he supported the

Vietnam war and tried to prevent a paper of mine from being presented at a conference of the International Society of General Semantics.

Gwen, Al Shimbel, and I submitted "Sanity and the Cold War" to *Measure*, the University of Chicago magazine edited by Robert Hutchins, where it was published.

General System Theory

I mentioned the rise in prestige of science in the U.S. following the dramatic finish of World War II. Suddenly an abstruse mathematical theory was revealed as a source of knowledge conferring awesome power on its possessor. Generous support for developing a theoretical infrastructure for "high tech" spilled over into related "new fields" such as the theory of games, cybernetics, and information theory which all made their "public debut" within a year of each other.[6]

Among these was so called "general system theory," not nearly so widely publicized as the others but attracting considerable attention among academics in search of an intellectual base for counteracting the increasing isolation of specialized disciplines.

General system theory is usually associated with Ludwig von Bertalanffy, an Austrian biologist, and he, in turn, traced the underlying idea to the ongoing controversy between so called "vitalists" and "mechanists." The former maintained that life processes could never be completely explained in terms of laws (e.g., of physics and chemistry) governing the behaviour of non-living matter; the latter insisted that they could.

At one time the vitalists insisted that living tissue contains substances that do not occur in non-living matter. They called these substances "organic," whence organic chemistry got its name. This position had to be abandoned in 1828 when Friedrich Wöhler succeeded in synthesizing urea, an "organic" compound. This was, perhaps, the first of successive "defeats" suffered by the vitalists forcing them to retreat, one is tempted to say, to previously prepared positions.

In the first decade of our century, H. Driesch, a noted vitalist maintained he had shown experimentally the unique faculty of living tissue which he called "equifinality." He cut an embryo of a sea urchin in its early stage in two, put the two halves in separate containers with a nutrient medium and showed that both halves developed into normal sea urchins. Had the process of development been "mechanical," Driesch argued, the two halves would have developed into two halves of a sea urchin. That they didn't shows that the development was governed by a "goal," a "purpose," if you will, to become what the bit of living matter was destined to become—a sea urchin. He called this governing principle "equifinality," and asserted that it characterizes only the behaviour of living tissue.

Bertalanffy purported to refute this argument by pointing out that "equifinality" is characteristic of the behaviour of certain "open systems," that is, systems that exchange matter and/or energy with their environment, of which living organisms are certainly examples but not the only ones. Thus, the distinction between "open" and "isolated" systems becomes a fundamental one in theoretical biology. Indeed the apparent violation of the Second Law of Thermodynamics by living organisms,[7] sometimes cited by vitalists in support of their positions is not really a violation, since the law applies only to isolated systems.

The intellectual climate in the late forties was receptive to discussions about new "paradigms" in science, probably also a by-product of the dramatic consequences of applying "esoteric" theories (e.g., theory of relativity, quantum mechanics, mathematical theory of information) to new marvels of technology (harnessing of atomic energy, computerized thinking, automation).

Central to general system theory is the concept of a system as a portion of the world that somehow maintains its identity in spite of impacts of the environment that might destroy it. The most conspicuous manifestation of this faculty is the ability of living systems to resist encroachments on their integrity, continued functioning, and development. The designation "general" refers to the generalization of the notion of "system," particularly of "living system" to subsystems of an organism (cells, organs, tissues) and to supersystems containing individual organisms as subsystems, in the case of human aggregates, families, work teams, tribes, nations, the international system. The psychologist or the psychiatrist may single out the "psyche" as the focus of attention and seek to discover the way this "system" develops and maintains its integrity or, on the contrary, disintegrates, as in mental disease, and the way it influences other components of a human being.

It was probably this problem area that motivated Roy Grinker, a prominent specialist in psychosomatic medicine and psychiatrist at the Michael Reese Research Hospital in Chicago to organize an ongoing conference on general system theory in Chicago, in which I was invited to participate. We met twice a year. Some of us were permanent members of the conference; others were invited as specialists to participate in sessions devoted to some one or another aspect. It is in these sessions that I met Karl Deutsch, a "system-oriented" political scientist, whose book *The Nerves of Government* impressed me as an excellent example of combining suggestive metaphor (regarding governments as organisms) with rigorous analysis. I was later to engage in other analyses of this sort.

Grinker's conferences inspired a similar program at the University of Chicago, organized by James G. Miller, then chair of the psychology department, and Ralph Gerard, a physiologist, later a co-founder with Bertalanffy, Kenneth Boulding and myself of the International Society for General System Research. The idea spread to the Soviet Union, where a year book *Sistemnye Issledovania* (systemic investigations) soon made its appearance in a format similar to our *General Systems* the yearbook of the Society, edited by Bertalanffy and myself. Common interests led to my continuing contact and collaboration with the Institute of System Research in Moscow which have continued to the present day.

My sojourn in Chicago came to an abrupt end in 1954.

Witch Hunt

In 1950 the U.S. went to war against Communism in Korea, and the McCarthy "witch hunt" went into high gear. It was, of course, only a pale reflection of the paranoia that gripped the Soviet Union. It induced something like nausea rather than terror, but it nevertheless filled with despair people who hoped for a resumption of the promise of the New Deal interrupted by the war. Financial support for the University of Chicago (suspected of harbouring subversion) was drying up. To revive it, some assurance of loyalty to "American values" had to be shown. That meant that Hutchins had to go. A skilled money raiser unstained by either "intellectual elitism" or softness on Communism replaced him. The U.S. senatorial Jenner Committee (one of the committees investigating "un-American activities" on campuses) was welcomed at the University of Chicago.

A group formed including people who were likely to be called to the hearings. The big issue was whether to invoke the Fifth Amendment to the Constitution (the right to refuse to testify on grounds of self-incrimination). The Communists argued for invoking it. Most of the others argued against. They intended to answer bravely all questions except those that demanded incrimination of others. In doing so, they risked the charge of contempt of the Committee. But this was evidently an additional inducement, at least for some, to refrain from invoking the Fifth. It was a chance to publicly denounce the assault on American liberty and to suffer martyrdom on that account. I envisaged that fate for myself. Even though in answering the question "Are you or have you ever been…?" I intended to say, "I am not, but I have been," this is as far as I would go. I would steadfastly refuse to incriminate others.

It never came to this. I was not called. Three of my colleagues, members of the Committee on Mathematical Biology, were called. One of them was Al Shimbel, co-author of "Sanity and the Cold War." He did not invoke the Fifth Amendment, but hard as the committee tried, they could get nothing interesting out of him. Another colleague, who had done research in ballistics during the war was asked whether he was engaged in espionage at that time. He turned to an attorney and asked him whether if he answered that question in the negative, he would be obliged to answer other questions. The attorney said he would. Then my colleague invoked the Fifth Amendment and was excused from further testimony. He was fired. So was a third member of the Committee on Mathematical Biology. It was done delicately. Their contracts were simply not renewed. I never found out why I was not called.

With Hutchins' departure the atmosphere at the University of Chicago became oppressive. So when I was offered a year's fellowship at the newly established Ford Foundation Center for Advanced Study in the Behavioral Sciences in California, I accepted and resigned my assistant professorship.

In August 1954, we (Gwen, our two year old daughter, and I) put some belongings into our old Plymouth (Gwen's dowry) and set out for California. We did not intend to come back.

NOTES

1. *Othello*, Act III, Scene iii.

2. Later director of Energy Research and Development in the Federal Energy Office.

3. A logarithmic function of a variable increases with the variable at a decreasing rate; a linear function increases (or decreases) at a constant rate.

4. In 1921, sailors in Kronstadt, the principal Russian naval base, revolted against the Communist dictatorship. The suppression of the uprising by massive executionism led to resignation of many American Communists from the party. The notorious Moscow trials and the Hitler-Stalin pact on the eve of World War II led to further resignations. The successive disillusionments of American Communists, mostly intellectuals, led to the dictorum "Every American ex-Communist had his Kronstadt. Mine was the "purge" of geneticists from Universities and research institutes for "heretical" views inconsistent with the official philosophy of science. Trofim Lysenko became the ideological watch dog of biological science. For me that was the final straw.

5. Hayakawa was born in Canada but became an American citizen.

6. John von Neumann's and Oscar Morgenstern's *Theory of Games and Economic Behaviour (second edition)* and Norbert Wiener's *Cybernetics* were published in 1947; C.E. Shannon's and W. Weaver's *A Mathematical Theory of Communication* in 1948.

7. In the course of development, living systems become more organized. Some vitalists misinterpreted this process as a violation of the Second Law of thermodynamics, which supposedly requires a constant increase in entropy in physical systems. Such increase is characteristic of systems isolated from their environment, which living systems obviously are not.

CASBAH

8

The Center for Advanced Study in the Behavioral Sciences was located on the top of a hill overlooking the campus of Stanford University. The offices were entered directly from a patio; it looked like a motel. Perhaps its not quite accurate acronym was meant to suggest luxury—academic life without classes or committees. The idea was to produce an environment in which academics would have plenty of opportunity to "cross-fertilize" each other and plenty of time to do what they supposedly always wanted to do—engage in scholarship and research.

Some of the fellows said, perhaps half seriously, that the sudden imposition of leisure was threatening. I was reminded of an incident in my childhood. In early fall of 1918, before the Germans left Ukraine, it was still possible to travel between Feodosia and Lozovaya. We went to visit my grandparents. When the Germans left, the country was ravaged by civil war, and we were stuck in Lozovaya throughout the winter. Armies and guerrilla bands came and went. The Ukrainian nationalists were especially rough on the Jews. "Haidamaki" they called themselves, probably after Balkan Haiduks, who fought against the Turks. They wore bright red hoods attached to their caps. They "visited" grandfather's house five times during our stay on the pretext of searching for weapons. They found no weapons, but they settled for whatever they could find.

My grandfather was not a brave man. When these people came, he usually went to bed pretending to be sick. They were received by my uncle Misha (the one who had been prisoner of war) and my aunt Rose, who was able to talk calmly to them. One time they came early in the morning. Uncle Misha was shaving and came out with his face in lather and his suspenders hanging behind him. Their leader came right to the point. Sticking a nagan (a long-barreled pistol) in uncle's belly, he demanded, "Where is the money?"

Uncle Misha tried to say something, but only stuttering came out. Aunt Rose came to the rescue.

"Dobrodie," she said (the Ukrainian word for 'comrade'), "don't you see the man is too scared to talk. Put the gun away."

"You're right," said the Haidamak. He put the nagan behind his back and waved his fingers in front of uncle's face. "See? No gun. Now, then, where's the money?"

The CASBAH fellows were faced with a somewhat similar situation. See? No students. No classes. No committees. No papers to mark. Now, then, see what you can do. Joking aside, most of us felt great. Many did buckle down to write the book they had wanted to write for years. Some settled down to read. Some happily joined with others in seminars with unlimited discussion. Many went to each other's offices for intimate conversation. Some were loners. Their preference for solitude was respected.

There were roughly two categories of fellows. Among the solidly established academics was Ralph Gerard, a physiologist from the University of Chicago, Franz Alexander, who had worked with Freud, Clyde Kluckhohn, an anthropologist from Harvard, who spoke fluent Navaho, and Elsa Frenkel Brunswick, co-author of the much discussed book *The Authoritarian Personality*. The younger fellows were in their twenties and thirties. They were to become the cream of American behavioral science.

One of the "established" social scientists was Paul Lazarsfeld, an Austrian refugee, who had introduced empirical sociology in Austria. His classic study was a most detailed and meticulous description of Marienthal, an Austrian village in which every one was unemployed. (In Chapter 4 I mentioned another such village which I visited in 1933. I thought of it when I read Lazarfeld's work.)

One day Paul and I were having lunch in the CASBAH cafeteria. We agreed that we loved the place—a model of a genuine "community of scholars," which Robert Hutchins had always insisted a university should be.

"There's only one thing missing," I pointed out, "to make this place perfect. It should be in Europe."

Paul agreed.

Then an idea occurred to me. Or, perhaps, to him, or to both of us at once: why not? Austria was the obvious locale. To begin with, Paul was Austrian, and Austria was sincerely welcoming returning refugees. Second, Austria was between "East" and "West." (A year later a peace treaty would be signed guaranteeing Austria's neutrality.) Third, the Ford Foundation could, perhaps, be induced to fund an Institute of Advanced Studies somewhat similar to Casbah, which was also funded by the Foundation. Eight years later the Institute of Advanced Studies was founded in Vienna. Its founding fathers were Paul Lazarsfeld and Oscar Morgenstern, co-author with Von Neumann of *The Theory of Games and Economic Behaviour*. From 1980 to 1984 I was to be the director of that institute.

General System Theory

I mentioned my interest in General System Theory during the last years at the University of Chicago. Ludwig von Bertalanffy was also a fellow at CASBAH during that first year of its existence. The two of us together with Ralph Gerard, who had been a member of the General System Theory group at Chicago, and Kenneth Boulding, an economist at the University of Michigan continued the discussions.

The systemic approach emphasizes the interconnectedness of practically everything with everything else and makes much use of creative exploration of analogies. Poetry is, of course, very rich in analogies expressed in metaphors. However, these are indicative of similarities perceived subjectively and related to affect rather than to an understanding of underlying objective structural or functional identities. For example to say that an automobile "eats" gas can be taken to be literally, not merely figuratively, true in the sense that the burning fuel generates energy in the same way as digested food does.

I was particularly interested in analogies that could be deduced from mathematical models. They appeared to me to be the best illustrations of "unity in diversity," a principle which I thought formed a bridge between cognitive and ethical dimensions of the human condition. Exploration of mathematical analogies (isomorphisms), it seemed to me, should be a principal task of a "general system theory," that is, a theory based on postulating or discovering or studying properties common to "all systems." To make this programme meaningful, the term "system" should, of course, be sufficiently clearly defined, and this definition is then seen as one of the first tasks of general system theory.

One such definition is inherent in the mathematical physicist's conception of a system, namely as a portion of the observable world described by a set of variable quantities interacting with each other according to mathematically formulated laws. The solar system, a collection of interacting chemicals, an ecological system consisting of interacting populations of organisms are examples of analogies of this sort. The physical contents of two such systems may be different, but if the laws governing the interactions within them can be formulated by the same mathematical model, the same theory can apply to both. For example, an epidemic and the spread of a piece of information in a population of individuals interacting by random contacts could be described by the same mathematical model (cf. the discussion of this example in the previous chapter).

There is more. Analogies could be established between living and nonliving systems. The differential equations representing the interactions of substances in a tank could also represent the interactions of species in an ecological system, where the rate of change of each species population depends on the populations of other species. For example, the rate of growth (or decline) of a population of predators can well depend on the size of the available prey population and vice versa. In cybernetics reciprocal effects of this sort are called "feedback." Negative feedback is regulatory: increase of one of the reciprocally interacting variables induces a change in the other, which, in turn induces a decrease in the former. A system of this sort typically tends toward a steady state. Positive feedback, on the contrary, is destabilizing: increase in one variable induces a change in another, which induces a further increase in the former. Runaway arms races, inflations, outbursts of mass violence and so on can be represented by processes of this sort. Thus, a general system theory based on classes of isomorphic mathematical models could serve as a unifying theory bypassing disciplinary boundaries and contributing to deeper understanding of the world we live in.

Ralph Gerard, the physiologist in our group, had another idea of a general system theory based on a different classification scheme. To him the prototype of a system was the living organism, an entity far too complex to be represented in its entirety by a mathematical model. If we are going to look for fruitful analogies, Ralph argued, we should look at the analogues of living systems. Such analogues suggest themselves in both directions—"up" and "down."

Looking down, that is, at the constituent parts of the organism, we examine its "subsystems," for instance, organs, tissues, and cells of which the organism is composed. Looking "up," we examine collections of organisms, in the case of humans, small groups, e.g., families, work teams, clubs; larger organizations, e.g., firms, corporations, cities; still larger ones, whole societies, the international system.

Every one of these generalized "organisms," both "above" and "below" the classical organism has three aspects. Each has a structure, a way of behaving, and a history, or, as Ralph was fond of saying, being, acting, and becoming. Thus, the structure of a plant or an animal is its anatomy; of an institution its table of organization, showing lines of authority, channels of communication, etc. Each has a history, that is, goes through a process which is, in general, irreversible. A person, for example, starts as a zygote, turns into an embryo, then into a baby, then into a child, then into an adult, then into a corpse. The process has never been observed to go the other way.

The task of general system theory, according to Gerard, was to uncover analogies between the manifestations of the three aspects (structure, function, and evolution) across the levels of organization: cell, organ, individual, group, society. In the case of human systems above the individual, this task belonged to the social sciences; at the level of the individual and below to the biological sciences. In this way, general system theory would serve to integrate the biological and the behavioral or social sciences. In fact, if the levels are represented by the rows of a matrix and the aspects by columns, the cells of the matrix can be filled in by the disciplines concerned with particular aspects at particular levels. For example, cytology is concerned with the structure of cells; anatomy with the structures of organisms; sociology with the structure of societies, e.g., classes, castes, communities. Physiology is concerned with the functioning of organs, political science with the behaviour of states. Embryology is concerned with the evolution of a fetus, developmental psychology with that of a person, history with that of a society or a nation, or of humanity.

I liked Gerard's schematization. It emphasized unity in diversity, a concept that I believed provided a link between an optimistic epistemology and an optimistic ethos, that is, a rationale of a possibility of progress, which was being more and more persistently attacked by profound thinkers, explicitly by Spengler, implicitly by Toynbee.[1]

As our seminar progressed, we started to talk about founding a society of scholars interested in developing a general system theory. The annual meeting of the American Society for the Advancement of Science met in San Francisco that year. We arranged a session at which International Society for General Systems Research was founded.[2]

Among the younger fellows at CASBAH I had closest contact with Alex Bavelas, Stephen Richardson, and Duncan Luce.

Alex was a student of Kurt Lewin, the founder of group psychology. He succeeded in translating Lewin's tantalizingly suggestive ideas about group dynamics into rigorous mathematical language. The mathematics he used was based on a language of structure rather than the language of quantity and was more suited to a description of organized entities. Thereby the parameters of group structure, in particular its organization could be related to the parameters of group performance, which were quantities related to success or efficiency of problem solving or to group morale.

Stephen was a son of Lewis F. Richardson, a British meteorologist, generally regarded as the founder of peace research. He died in 1953 just a year before his son came to CASBAH. Stephen told me that his father left a large mass of papers. Some had been published, but most of this material had not. He asked me whether I knew of any one who would be interested in editing the collection and finding a publisher for a posthumous work. I asked what had been published, and he named "Generalized Foreign Policy." I looked it up and felt a warm glow of recognition as I read it. For here in another guise was Cournot's mathematical theory of duopoly as well as my own model of interaction between two individuals producing and sharing a substance. Richardson's version was a mathematical version of an arms race. There was the familiar pair of differential equations, whose solution revealed the trajectory of the system they represented. A point on the trajectory represented a steady state, which, depending on a relation among the parameters, was either stable or unstable. If it was stable, the arms race could persist in a sort of balance of power; if it was unstable, the slightest deviation from the steady stage set a positive feedback process in motion. The system would move irreversibly either toward piling up of armaments without limit (eventually presumably exploding in a war) or, toward disarmament depending from where it started. (In my model if the system was unstable, it would move toward parasitism. Which individual would become the parasite depended on the direction of the triggering disturbance.)

I told Stephen that I would try to get Rashevsky to undertake the editing job if he found the rest of the materials of sufficient interest, which he did. In 1960 two volumes of Richardson's life work appeared: *Arms and Insecurity* and *Statistics of Deadly Quarrels*.

Prisoner's Dilemma

Duncan Luce, who together with Howard Raiffa was to write the first textbook on game theory, led a seminar on the subject. It was he who introduced me to Prisoner's Dilemma. The game was discovered (not invented, as is sometimes said) by Merrill Flood and M. Dresher in 1950, who at the time were testing two types of solution of a non-zerosum game. The name was given to the game by

A.W. Tucker, a game theoretician, who invented the anecdote that illustrates the dilemma.

Two men are arrested on suspicion of burglary. The stolen items are found in their possession. This is sufficient evidence to convict them of possession of stolen goods but not of the graver offence, breaking and entering. The only way they can be convicted of B&E is on the strength of a confession by either of the men or both. The State's Attorney explains the situation separately to each of the prisoners, who are kept isolated from each other.

"We have enough evidence," the State's Attorney explains to them, "to convict you of possession of stolen goods. The penalty is a year in jail. We could convict you of breaking and entering if one or both of you confessed. If neither confesses, you will be convicted of possession of stolen goods and go to jail for a year. The penalty for burglary is five years in jail. However, if you both plead guilty to burglary, you will get only three years in jail. Now if one of you confesses, while the other does not, then the one who sings will not be prosecuted at all in return for having turned state's evidence. His buddy, who was stubborn and wouldn't confess, will be convicted on the strength of the other's evidence and will get the book thrown at him: five years in jail. Think it over."

Both prisoners think it over. Each reasons something along the following lines.

"Suppose my buddy confesses. Then if I also confess, I go to jail for three years; but if I don't confess, I get five years. So if he sings, I am better off confessing. But suppose he doesn't confess. Then, if I don't confess either, I get one year in jail for possession of stolen goods. On the other hand, if I confess, I go scot free. Even if he doesn't confess, I am still better off confessing. So it turns out that it is better to confess whether he confesses or not."

The other prisoner thinks along the same lines. In consequence, both confess, which is just what the State's Attorney wanted. Note, incidentally, that he didn't lie to them. He told them as it really is. So on the basis of valid information and "rational reasoning" each of them goes to jail for three years. If neither confessed, each of them would have gone to jail for just one year. So what is the rational thing to do: to confess or not to confess? This is the dilemma.

The connection between this situation and the situation produced by the arms race occurred to me at once. Suppose two states locked in an escalating arms race begin to feel the pinch and are willing to conclude some sort of arms control agreement. For simplicity suppose the agreement is to refrain from producing a new type of weapon. Inspection procedures have been agreed upon, but they are not cheat-proof. Each military establishment would like to cheat but is considering whether it would be worth while to do so. There is always the danger of being caught, but they have figured out procedures that can minimize the chance of detection. So each assumes that it is worthwhile to take the chance. By the same logic as in the case of the prisoner's dilemma, it appears that if the other refrains from cheating, it is advantageous to cheat; if the other cheats, it is imperative to cheat "in self defence." It follows that it is more advantageous to cheat than to abide by the agreement regardless of what the other does.

Consequently both, acting "rationally," cheat. But they had decided that both would gain from the arms control agreement; otherwise they would not have entered it. If both cheat, both are worse off than if both had refrained from cheating. So what is the "rational" thing to do: to cheat or not to cheat?

The dilemma arises in consequence of failing to see the distinction between individual and collective rationality. It is individually rational for each of the parties to cheat, just as it is rational for each of the prisoners to confess. But it is collectively rational for both parties not to cheat, just as it is collectively rational for both prisoners not to confess. There is an important difference between "each" and "both." "Each" refers to the parties separately; "both" refers to them collectively.

Now we see a counter-example to the conclusion drawn from the classical model of the free market. Adam Smith wrote about the so called "invisible hand," which guides the movements of prices (or exchange ratios) of traded goods according to laws of supply and demand. These ratios tend to an equilibrium, which benefits all the traders. Each trader pursues his individual advantage. He seeks to sell at the highest price he can get and to buy at the lowest price he can get. Yet the result of all these strivings benefits all. Is it possible that the two prisoners and the two states locked in an arms race demonstrate an opposite principle, which might be called the "invisible back of the hand"? Each acts "rationally," that is, does the best he can for himself. Yet both together do worse than they would have done if each had not been "rational" in this sense. The situation can be generalized to any number of participants.

Looking for an Anchorage

As the academic year was drawing to a close, it was time to be looking for a job. I had no intention of returning to Chicago. Neither did Ralph, whose wife had died. Jim Miller was also leaving Chicago. He held degrees in both psychology and psychiatry. Jim was most enthusiastic about general system theory. He thought that the problem of mental health was a typical systemic problem involving not only an individual but also his total environment, both physical and mental. Indeed, it made sense to be concerned with mental health not only of individuals but also of human groups on all levels of organization: families, work teams, institutions, whole societies. Gerard's scheme fascinated him. He modified it by expanding the second column of Gerard's matrix—function—so that it specified all the functions supposedly involved in keeping any living system alive, be it an individual, a group, a nation, or humankind. Thus, every living system contains "subsystems," corresponding to the organs or tissues of an organism, performing functions that keep the system alive. These functions include ingestion (of matter and energy) from the environment, excretions into the environment, coordination of activities performed in a living system by structures analogous to a central nervous system of an animal, receiving information from the environment (by sense organs), etc. Miller kept the rows of Gerard's matrix, representing living systems on different levels of organization and substituted his functions for Gerard's columns (being, acting, becoming).

During that year Jim was still at Chicago. He visited Ralph Gerard and me at CASBAH and told us about his plans for a mental health research institute along the lines suggested by the general system theory paradigm. In fact, he came to California to try to sell the idea to the University of California at Berkeley. While the negotiations were still going on, a concrete offer was made by the University of Michigan. So Jim Miller, Ralph Gerard, and I joined the faculty of the Department of Psychiatry at Michigan, Jim as Professor of Psychiatry, Ralph as Professor of Physiology, I as Associate Professor of Mathematical Biology.

I had misgivings about the scheme and about my role in it in particular. I agreed that the concept of mental health could be generalized to pertain not only to individuals but to groups, populations, societies, and the like. This sounded to me like an application of the basic ideas of Korzybski, who identified "sanity" with effective cognition of reality and "insanity" with the break of this contact effected by non-correspondence of the structure of language to the structure of reality. From this point of view degrees of "unsanity," of which "insanity" was conceived as an extreme form, were manifested in confusing abstraction levels, false-to-fact identifications, elementalism, two-valued orientation, etc. And it seemed to me that these symptoms were manifested in human groups on all levels of organization. I believed that group neurosis, mass psychosis, and, perhaps, other still to be identified forms of collective mental pathology were useful concepts with which to build a generalized theory of mental health. But I had misgivings about the way these ideas meshed with what the legislators of the State of Michigan had in mind when they approved the financing of the proposed institute. I was sure they expected a flow of results within a few years, results that would lead to a higher general level of "mental health" in the state (as they understood "mental health"), reduce the costs of hospitalization of the mentally ill (which was a substantial fraction of the entire cost of government sponsored medical care) and so justify the expenditures. I expected no such results.

So although I thought that the extension of the concept of "mental health" to families, institutions, organizations, and nations was a good idea and that the general systems outlook might contribute something to understanding the way these "living systems" behave and evolve, I didn't think that the approach had any direct relevance to the medical problems, or that it would suggest realizable preventive measures, effective care of patients, rehabilitations, and so on, which, I was sure, the legislators and the university administration had in mind. In short, I had misgivings about the way the idea was sold. But these misgivings did not suffice to prevent me from accepting the offer. So Gwen, our now three-year-old daughter, and I moved to Michigan.

Genesis of Superstitions

I am forever impressed by coincidences, not only because they amuse me but also because I believe they are the hard core of superstitions. There was a coincidence in our lives involving Ann Arbor. In the early years of our marriage, Gwen and I traveled by car a lot—in our old Plymouth, "whom" we called Eurasphitsia. (The name was suggested by the punch line of a shaggy dog story.)

As the mileage of aging Eurasphitsia approached the 100,000 mark, we wondered just where this would happen. It happened exactly (to the tenth of a mile) at the intersection of State and Huron Streets in Ann Arbor, Michigan. (We were on the way to Cleveland, Ohio.) At the time we wondered whether this had any significance in our lives. Perhaps it did! We spent fifteen years in Ann Arbor.

NOTES

1. Both Oswald Spengler in his *Decline of the West* and Arnold Toynbee in his *Study of History* essentially dismissed the concept of "progress" that dominated European thought in the eighteenth and nineteenth centuries.

2. It is now the International Society for the System Sciences. The focus shifted from scientific methodology and philosophy of science to problems of large scale engineering and management.

Ann Arbor

9

I was forty-four years old when we settled in Ann Arbor. For most people in academe, this is about the middle of adult life represented by a ten-to-twenty-year marriage, teenage children, probably the most productive years in their fields. For me it was like the beginning of adult life. Gwen and I had been married six years. We had one small child. Two sons were still to come, one a year and a half later, the other seven years later. We built a house. I had my first tenured position.

It was also a beginning in other ways. My interests had been brought into focus during the year at CASBAH. I still kept calling myself a mathematical biologist, a disciple of Rashevsky, and I still published occasionally in the *Bulletin of Mathematical Biology*. But my papers had only tangential relevance to my central interests—a general theory of systems and a general theory of conflict. I also intended to do experimental work, something that had no place in Rashevsky's group. In this indispensable adjunct to any science except mathematics I was a complete novice, as I soon learned.

Laboratories were established in the basement of a new building, where the just formed Mental Health Research Institute made its home. People in white coats worked there and published papers in physiology, biochemistry, and biophysics. There were also tiers of cages there, a death row, where animals waited their turn to contribute to human knowledge. There was none of this on the upper two floors. Nor were there any psychiatrists on the staff except director James G.Miller. Although the Institute was administratively within the Department of Psychiatry, it was scientifically completely autonomous. Experiments on human subjects were done upstairs. They were supposed to shed light on questions generated by the systemic approach to human behaviour. The world downstairs was expected to fit into the Miller-Gerard scheme on the "organ" level of a general theory of living systems. The upper stories were supposed to house research on the higher levels—individuals, groups, societies, etc.

The first task I considered undertaking was to put to experimental test the model developed in my very first papers on interactions between two individuals. There were ample provisions for building apparatus, and I consulted with a young engineer, one of the first to join the staff. I pictured two subjects, each having partial control of a "payoff" accruing to him as a consequence of setting the level of "effort." The relation between this "effort" (the input) and the "payoff" (the output) was to be defined by the pair of differential equations that constituted the mathematical model. The subjects would be told to try to maximize their payoffs by finding an appropriate setting of the knob controlling their "efforts." According to the model, if the efforts of the two are independent, their payoffs would tend toward a suboptimal equilibrium. If, however, the payoffs are interdependent (each being a function of the other), then an optimal equilibrium could be reached; that is, each would get the largest possible payoff under the given constraints. Moreover, for certain values of the parameters connecting efforts and payoffs, the equilibrium in the case of independent efforts could be either stable or unstable. In the unstable case one of the individuals would become "parasitic," that is the optimum level of his effort would be zero. He would continue to appropriate a certain share of their joint output "without working."

I asked Caxton Foster (the young engineer) whether he could build an apparatus for this experiment. He said he could, but expressed doubts about getting any sensible results. There would inevitably be "noise" in the system, he explained, some of it due to the imprecision of the subjects' hand movements controlling the inputs. To evaluate the results relevant to the theory of interaction, we would need a "base," that is, a pattern of hand tremors that contributed to the noise. Only after separating this noise out could we see anything meaningful in the way the outputs were related to the inputs.

This was too much for me. I conceded that problems of spectral analysis were interesting in their own right, but they were completely unrelated to what I wanted to know. Caxton, on the other hand, regarded the whole matter as a challenge to his own abilities and ingenuity and was quite willing to undertake the job. I let the matter drop and started thinking about other ways to pursue the questions that interested me.

I soon saw a way. I recalled the analogy between Cournot's economic model, describing the dynamics of duopoly, my quasi-biological model of parasitism and symbiosis, and Prisoner's Dilemma. All three were illustrations of the same phenomenon, namely, individual efforts in pursuit of individual interests resulting in an outcome that is not collectively rational. So why not experiment with subjects facing a decision problem isomorphic to Prisoner's Dilemma and see how they behave under various conditions? This required no elaborate apparatus. The "noise" could be confined to occasional errors in indicating decisions. But those decisions would be of utmost simplicity: the choice was between "cooperating" and "competing." In the context of the original Prisoner's Dilemma anecdote, "cooperating" meant not confessing (since cooperation referred to solidarity with the partner, not willingness to help the State's attorney). "Competing" meant confessing, that is, considering own interests instead of the common interest of the two accused. Unfortunately all three terms, "cooperating," "competing," and "confessing" begin with a C. To distinguish between cooperation and non-cooperation, I called non-cooperation "defection." Thus the two choices in Prisoner's Dilemma could be designated by C and D. I have had the satisfaction of seeing this notation widely adopted in the literature.

The First Prisoner's Dilemma Experiment

The first experiments at the Mental Health Research Institute (MHRI) involved triples of subjects instead of pairs. This was my first encounter with the way the donor of funds influences the direction of research. An invitation to submit a research project on effects of stress came from the U.S. Air Force. After considerable soul-searching I decided to refrain from self-righteous rejection of the invitation until I knew more about what this was all about. It would cost me nothing, I convinced myself, to find out, since Wright Field, from where the invitation came, was in Dayton, Ohio, only some forty miles from Greenville, home of Gwen's parents, whom we visited once or twice a year.

At Wright Field they told me the project was part of a large research programme related to the development of space exploration (See? No gun!). They showed me a mock-up of a space ship carrying a crew of five. Five dummies were seated in it, three facing one way, two the other. Confined in a small space for several days or weeks the men would surely be subjected to stress. It would be desirable to get an idea how stress would affect their performance.

"What aspect of the performance are you interested in?" I asked.

"Any aspect."

"Give me an example."

"We can't. Not now," they said. "No, it isn't for security reasons. We can't tell you, because we don't know ourselves. In fact, one of the aims of the research is to find out what aspects of the performance are particularly affected by stress. You choose the aspect that you want to investigate in any stress situation that interests you."

"And what sort of stress do you have in mind?"

"We don't know that either. This is something we want to know more about."

It was easy to rationalize the decision to submit a proposal. Applications would be in the context of a "peaceful" activity. I was also assured that the results would not be classified and could be published anywhere. I wondered what Norbert Wiener would have done. Would he regard this sort of investigation as "working on a military project," which he refused so demonstratively to do immediately after World War II? And if so, would I, who admired him for refusing to cooperate with the military, be obliged to do the same? There was no answer. I accepted the invitation and submitted a proposal, which was accepted.

One aspect of performance I undertook to study was the easiest to measure objectively, namely, reaction times. To provide some sort of theoretical framework for interpreting the results, I chose the amount of information in presented stimuli as the independent variable. As the dependent variable I chose the reaction time of a group making a coordinated response. Both of these choices were suggested by the general system paradigm. The relation of information to entropy had been investigated by Wiener and Szilard (incidentally, another prominent scientist, who had turned against the militarization of science). This identification of two seemingly unrelated concepts, one physical, the other cognitive, was a triumph of "systemic" thinking (cf. identification of space and time, of matter and energy, the complementarity of the particle and the wave properties of light).[1]

Reaction time was clearly a relevant index of performance in the sort of situation the sponsors of the project were interested in. The other aspect I chose, namely, the tendency to cooperate, could also be made to seem relevant; but the measure I intended to use would be at best a far-fetched one, namely, the propensity to cooperate in a Prisoner's Dilemma game. I was reminded of the story about the man who liked to putter around the house fixing things and who could use only two tools—a screw driver and a file. Wandering around looking for things to fix, he noticed some loose screws. So he tightened them with his screw driver. Soon there were no more screws to tighten. But he did come across some protruding nails. So he used his file to make grooves in the caps of the nails and used the screw driver to tighten them. Twisting the problem to fit the tool rather than finding a tool for solving the problem is a pervasive bad habit of specialized professionals. I was reminded of the bizarre fiasco of the rumour spread experiment, also a project sponsored by the Air Force.

Be it as it may, I went ahead with my plan to "apply" Prisoner's Dilemma as a tool of research on stress.

The stress I chose was sleeplessness. Subjects were to be deprived of sleep for thirty-six hours and the deterioration of their performance (if any) would be a measure of the effect of the "stress." The reaction time experiments showed expected results, which was reassuring as to the choice of measure but hardly interesting. In contrast, the Prisoner's Dilemma experiment was poorly conceived. The occurrence of cooperative responses in a three-person Prisoner's Dilemma played with communication excluded should be an extremely rare event without stress. So there was little "room" for this measure of cooperation to decrease under stress. However, a totally unexpected effect was observed, which had no bearing on the problem supposedly posed but was extremely interesting (at least to me) for quite another reason. It was unfortunate that the poor design of the experiment, in particular, the lack of proper controls precluded a convincing conclusion. (Later similar results were obtained by others in better designed experiments.)

The three-person groups of subjects played Prisoner's Dilemma in three different eight-hour periods of the thirty-six hour sleep deprivation period. (The other twenty-eight hours were used for different experiments.) They had a coffee break after four hours of play. The three of them and an experimenter sat at one table as they drank coffee. The experimenters were to see to it that the subjects did not make a deal, i.e., agree on choosing C every time, so as to maximize their joint payoff. They were not permitted to talk during the break.

When they resumed play, there was a dramatic increase in cooperation, and this in spite of the fact that they had gone longer without sleep, which, according to our questionable hypothesis ought to have reduced the tendency to cooperate. The only conjecture that suggested itself was that simply spending some time together, even without explicit interchange, somehow facilitated expressions and expectations of "trust," the state of mind underlying cooperation. Years later I read reports of experiments in which visual or auditory contact both increased the tendency to cooperate even if there was no opportunity of making explicit agreements to do so.

Those were the first Prisoner's Dilemma experiments I performed. About this time reports of other experiments started to appear mainly in journals devoted to social psychology. Their number rose sharply reaching a peak about 1970, then declined as in every such "wave." There was a revival stimulated by Robert Axelrod's excellent book, *The Evolution of Cooperation* (see below).

The First Visits to The Soviet Union

In May, 1961 I was a member of a U.S. delegation sent to the Soviet Union, hosted by the Soviet Academy of Pedagogical Sciences (because psychology was regarded there as an adjunct to pedagogical science). The delegates visited institutes in Moscow, Leningrad, Kiev, Tbilisi, and Tashkent. B.F. Skinner was with us. Regarded as a Pavlovian, he was somewhat of a hero in Russia.

In each city we were met by the head of the institution we visited, ushered into a conference room, and seated around a table on which there was always a bowl of apples and at each place a bottle of soft drink with a bottle opener.

Of these meetings the only memorable one was with Alexander Luria, who impressed me with his enthusiasm and erudition. Psycholinguistics was his forte. The persistent pressure to guide all research in psychology by the Pavlovian paradigm had no effect on him, while the pressure to produce "practical" results did not conflict with his own inclinations. He introduced us to a strikingly attractive and lively girl of about 17, who was blind and deaf. She learned to communicate by "writing" with her finger on the palm of the other's hand and received communications the same way. She "conversed" with us through Luria. We were shown samples of her sculptures. How she sculpted bodies was understandable: she could "see" them by touch. But one of her sculptures was a house, accurate in every detail. When we asked how she became acquainted with her "model," we were told she climbed all over the house including the roof, feeling every inch. Some of us couldn't believe that she was genuine, but we had no conclusive evidence one way or the other.

Another meeting that sticks out in my memory was with the entire staff of an institute, where we were to discuss "philosophy of science." Some of us and some of them were on a panel. The audience participated. I translated both ways. At one point one of our group asked to what extent dialectical materialism ("Diamat," as they called it familiarly), a compulsory subject in all university curricula) was regarded in the Soviet Union as an unassailable doctrine. Some one from the audience replied that it was indeed unassailable, because it was objectively true. It embodied, she said, the fundamental laws of existence and development and therefore served as a solid foundation of all genuine knowledge. All advances in science, she said, if they were indeed advances, stemmed from applications of dialectical materialism in the analysis of all phenomena and processes. At this point I could not help stepping outside my role as interpreter (who should under no circumstances interpose his own views in a discussion in which he serves in that capacity). I asked whether even the most productive models of the universe, for instance Newton's , were not ultimately outdated and replaced by more sophisticated ones, for example, Einstein's. The answer was that dialectical materialism was analogous to Einstein's view of the universe, not to Newton's, implying that this perfection of the mode of human cognition had already been accomplished.

Another instructive encounter took place at a pedagogical institute. A young teacher in an elementary school described an experiment that was of particular interest to me, because it was a neat way of assessing the relative weights of individual and collective interests of school children.

A class in an elementary school in Russia is organized in groups of 8—10 children. The group is called *zveno* (literally a link of a chain). The members of a *zveno* study together, undertake joint projects, etc. By and large the system encourages cooperation between the members of a group and, one would think, also competition between groups.

In the experiment described by the young teacher children were asked to estimate lengths of line segments, whereby underestimates would reduce the individual child's score, while overestimates would reduce her/his *zveno's* score. I liked this simple method of comparing children's orientations toward self and toward a collective. So I praised the experiment and pointed out its potential. For example, tests could be conducted on children in successive grades with the view of assessing trends: are the children becoming more individually or more collectively oriented, and so on.

Later the teacher asked me privately to be less lavish in my praise.

"This is just the way we see it," she said. "But we don't talk about it. The authorities may take a dim view of this business." I understood this to mean that the "authorities" frowned on any attempts to subject anything derived from the tenets of official ideology to empirical tests. The task of socialist education was assumed to be to inculcate certain values. Once certain educational policies have been prescribed, testing their effectiveness was regarded either as superfluous (if the tests showed them to be successful) or subversive (otherwise). At any rate testing them was interpreted as challenging them.

The following (possibly apocryphal) story illustrates this conception of education. A teacher of arithmetic, clearly of questionable competence, taught children to add fractions by adding the numerators and the denominators. An inspector visiting her class was shocked. But wishing to avoid scandal she told the teacher in private that she was doing it wrong and showed her the right way to add fractions. The next day the teacher addressed her charges as follows:

"Children, a new directive has come out. We will now add fractions as follows…"[2]

All in all, the impression I got of Soviet life on that first visit since I left as a child forty years before was a mixed one. In a sense, "destalinization" was in a full swing. We saw big portraits of Stalin standing in dark corners facing the wall where grime-free rectangles showed where they had been hanging. Contacts with Russians, Georgians, and Uzbeks outside official meetings were mostly relaxed. We were told that the "personality cult" was being dismantled, but the word "stalinism" (let alone "stalinshchina"[3]) was avoided. Nevertheless, everywhere we were reminded of ugly Soviet reality—by the hidebound thinking in cliches, by the mindless uniformity of the newspapers, by ubiquitous quarrels and dressings down of subordinates in public, by cringing before superiors, by the readiness to invent the flimsiest excuses to cover up signs not only of major foul-ups but also of petty mishaps.

I remember an incident in Sochi, a resort on the Black Sea, where we spent a couple of days of relaxation. The seaside hotel had a fine beach, divided by a fence in two halves. One, the crowded one, was for citizens; the other, almost empty, for foreigners. To go to the beach one needed a ticket. They were free, but one had to obtain one from the desk anyway. I guess this is the way segregation was enforced. At the desk we were told that we could not go to the beach at the time.

"Why not?" we asked.

"A storm is coming."

"But the sky is clear, and there is no wind."

"This means nothing. The weather report said a storm is coming."

"But there are so many people on the beach."

"They will soon be told to leave."

The conversation was in English. Evidently the ticket lady didn't know I understood Russian. When her subordinate, a young girl appeared, she started to scream at her.

"I told you a half hour ago I was out of beach tickets for the foreigners. I told you to get some. Instead you vanished leaving me to fight with them!"

Soon after I came home from this official visit, my family, that is, Gwen, Anya, now aged nine, and our son Sasha, aged four, and I started out for the Soviet Union, this time as tourists. After six years at the University of Michigan I was entitled to a Sabbatical, and we were to spend six months of it in Europe.

An Intourist guide was showing us the sights of Leningrad. She spoke English with an American accent. When we remarked on this, she explained that Intourist guides learned either British or American English and were assigned to British or American tourists accordingly. She was well read in American literature and praised Catcher in the Rye highly. She told us it had been translated into Russian.

Pointing across the broad Neva River, she called our attention to the Fortress of Peter and Paul, where Russian revolutionaries imprisoned in the tsarist days languished.

"When the Provisional Government was overthrown," she continued, "the ministers were imprisoned in the fortress. They were released in a few days. They were the last political prisoners in Russia."

I thought I had not heard. "You mean those were the last political prisoners in the Fortress of Peter and Paul?"

"No," she said, "they were the last political prisoners in Russia."

We met most of my relatives who had remained in the Soviet Union. During the war all of them had been evacuated to Central Asia. None were killed by the Germans. Of my mother's siblings five were still alive. They all came to Simferopol in the Crimea, where my cousins, with whom I had been very close in childhood lived. My male cousin, however, was in the Arctic, where he stayed after his release from the labour camp. I was to meet him ten years later, just fifty years after we parted as children. We corresponded for twenty-seven years, until he died.

Our daughter, Anya, may have been the last American child to see Stalin's face. Two months after we left the Soviet Union his embalmed body was removed from the Mausoleum (where he had lain beside Lenin for eight years) and interred in the Kremlin wall, the Second Class cemetery of the Soviet Union. The Mausoleum with only one corpse in it is the First Class hallowed ground, and the Novodevitchie Cemetery, where many celebrities are buried, is the Third Class. The latter contains a large white marble statue of Chaliapin but not his body (he died abroad). It reminds me of Mozart's statue in the Central Cemetery in Vienna. There is no body there either. The location of Mozart's body is unknown.

Warsaw

The last four months of my Sabbatical were spent in Warsaw, where I was invited as visiting professor in philosophy. I lectured on Korzybski and his general semantics.

Liberalization in Poland following the so called "Polish October" (1956)[4] went much farther than the so called "thaw" in the Soviet Union. The change of climate reflected the first attempt since the extension of the Soviet empire.

Gomulka, who had been repressed during the terror of the 1930's (which spread to the satellite states) became Premier. Khrushchev, accompanied by an awe-inspiring suite, came to Warsaw to read the riot act to the Poles. He was quietly rebuffed (told to watch his language) and backed down. Perhaps the brutality with which the Hungarian uprising was crushed a few days afterward was a panic reaction to the failure to intimidate Poland.

At any rate the smell of freedom in Poland in 1961 was much stronger than in the Soviet Union. Western newspapers were available in the reading rooms of at least one library. In the principal book stores of Warsaw I saw two tables, one with domestic and Soviet books, the other with books from the West. It seems that the division had to do with prices rather than with ideological content: the books from the West cost some ten to twenty times more, but they were there to buy and own. Freedom to read came to the Soviet Union only thirty years later. Translations of American comedies (e.g., *Harvey*) were produced. There was a Yiddish theatre providing simultaneous translation earphones. Most significantly, there was a satirical cabaret, where no one was immune from fun-poking. In a popularity poll the winners turned out to be Gomulka and Tadeusz Kotarbinski, a philosopher, whose wife still bore a concentration camp number in indelible ink on her forearm.

My host at the University of Warsaw was Adam Schaff, a member of the Central Committee of the Communist Party. We had met while he was visiting professor in the U.S. He was interested in Korzybski's ideas and ventured later to write a book entitled Introduction to Semantics, where the main ideas of general semantics were presented (a bold step at the time). I was to give a course on the subject.

"You will find," he told me, "that intellectual life in Poland gushes like a spring." (*Biot kluchom* is the Russian expression.)

I was not disappointed. Schaff and I became close friends. I imagine that his eventual loss of faith in Communism was much more traumatic than mine. He was dropped from the Central Committee in 1968, when the purge of Jews began in Poland. He remained on the faculty of the University of Warsaw but was prohibited from teaching. Since then his main activity has been at the European Centre for Documentation in the Social Sciences in Vienna. But he did not emigrate. He commuted between Warsaw and Vienna. Like me, he still clings to the vision of humane socialism.

Commitment

When I returned to Ann Arbor in February, 1962, I saw my commitments laid out for me. I would devote myself to the study of conflict and to what I started to call the three arms of the peace movement: peace research, peace education, and peace activism.

I had already written a book dealing with what I called three modes of conflict, entitled *Fights, Games, and Debates*. I conceived of a "fight" as a sequence of interacting stimuli and reactions. A dog fight, for example, appears as a sequence of this sort, proceeding from growls to grimacing (bared teeth), postures resembling coiled springs, finally exploding in overt violence. A quarrel escalating to a feud can also be described in this way. So can the unstable case of the Richardsonian model of an arms race. The common feature is the "systemic" nature of a fight-like conflict. It is neither planned nor conducted "rationally." It can be described without reference to available means and pursued goals. To the extent that one can speak of a "goal" at all in the context of a fight, one could say that it is confined to eliminating the opponent, perceived as simply a noxious stimulus, which one tries to remove by reacting to the irritation.

In contrast, a "game" is a "rationally" conducted conflict. It is characterized by clearly specified constraints governing the means employed in the pursuit of goals. The constraints may be agreed upon "rules of the game," as in parlour games (chess, bridge, etc.) or imposed by circumstances, taken into consideration in planning a course of action. "Rationality" in this context means ascribing "rationality" also to the opponent. The participant in a game may be motivated not so much by a desire to eliminate the opponent as by a desire to outwit him. This goal is particularly prominent in parlour games. Chess opponents may be the best of friends.

In a debate, as I depict it in *Fights, Games, and Debates*, the objective is neither to eliminate nor to defeat the opponent by a superior strategy but rather to convince the opponent, that is, to change his way of thinking, at least by inducing him to modify his views so as to bring them closer to one's own.

In Part II ("Games") of *Fights, Games and Debates* I introduced Prisoner's Dilemma as an example of a game in which the goals or interests of the players are not diametrically opposed as they are in almost all two-person parlour games.

In the latter what one player wins the other must lose. They are called *zerosum* games. Prisoner's Dilemma is a *non-zerosum* game in which a greater advantage of one player does not necessarily entail a greater disadvantage of the other. Thus the interests of the players are partially opposed and partially coincident.

Analysis of non-zerosum games shows that in that context the concept of "rationality" becomes ambiguous. It becomes necessary to distinguish between individual and collective rationality. Thus, a descriptive theory of conflicts of this sort must supplement a normative theory. A normative theory purports to prescribe how "rational" actors ought to make decisions. A descriptive theory purports to describe, at times to predict on the basis of observed regularities, how actors will actually behave in decision situations under specified conditions.

Experiments conducted by A.M. Chammah and myself at MHRI during 1962-1964 were reported in our book, Prisoner's Dilemma. In all experiments subjects played the game 300 times, whereby the outcome of each play was announced. Our principal independent variables were the four payoffs of the game: R (reward for "cooperation," i.e., for the choice of C by both players); T (the payoff accruing to the sole defecting player, hence a measure of "temptation" to defect); S, the payoff accruing to the sole cooperating player (the "sucker"); P, the payoff accruing to each player if both choose D, (i.e., the "punishment" for non-cooperation). Prisoner's Dilemma is characterized by the inequality $T>R>P>S$.

We also examined a difference in the way the game was played attributable to the gender of the players. We pitted men against men, women against women, and men against women in sequences of 300 plays.

The results showed clear shifts in frequencies of cooperative (C) choices in expected directions. That is, as reward for cooperation increased, or as punishment for defection became more severe, frequencies of C choices increased. As the defector's gains or the "sucker's" losses increased, frequencies of D choices increased. Being expected on a priori grounds, these results were not particularly interesting. They were, however, reassuring. They showed that we could increase or decrease the motivation of subjects to cooperate or to defect (statistically speaking) by manipulating the payoffs of the game.

Differences attributable to gender were not expected and therefore were interesting. Their interpretation presented a more challenging problem. In all long sequences of Prisoner's Dilemma the following trends are observed in the frequencies of C choices averaged over the players. On the first play about 50% of all players choose C. This is in itself interesting, because this choice violates the "sure-thing principle" of classical decision theory. The choice of D is more advantageous than the choice of C regardless of the co-player's choice. Next, the frequency of C choices tends to decline. This downward trend lasts about 30 plays in protocols of men playing against men. After that, the frequency of C choices starts to increase and flattens out at about 70%. Further, the frequencies of unilateral C or D choices decline throughout the sequence. Toward the end most pairs of players tend to "lock in" on either the CC (both cooperate) or the DD (both defect) outcome. Considerably more male pairs lock in on CC than on DD, which is reflected in the overall larger frequency of C choices. The results can be interpreted in terms of what the subjects seem to learn in the course of play. At first, they seem to learn that cooperation doesn't pay. An unreciprocated cooperative choice results in the worst payoff (the "sucker's" payoff). Eventually, however, the players seem to become aware of the advantage of cooperation: the reciprocated cooperative choice rewards both; reciprocated defecting choice punishes both. This accounts for the "lock-in" on CC. Those who locked in on DD failed to learn that cooperation pays in the long run.

The same trends were observed in women's protocols: initial decline of C frequencies, followed by a recovery and eventual "flattening out." But evidently the recovery started later and was weaker. Toward the end only about 35% of the choices in women's protocols were cooperative, less than the initial 50%. Still, the conclusion that "women are less cooperative than men" is not warranted at this point. A detailed analysis of the protocols points to a different source of women's "less cooperative" performance.

In addition to the frequency of C choices in iterated play, we examined the conditional frequencies, which reflect the probabilities of choosing C following the co-player's cooperative or defecting choice. As expected, the likelihood that a player chooses C after the co-player has chosen C is significantly greater than after the co-player has chosen D. In extreme cases, the former conditional probability is close to one, while the latter is close to zero. A style of play of this sort, that is, replying in kind, has been called TIT FOR TAT ("an eye for an eye"). We found that men tended to play TIT FOR TAT more frequently than women. It was later found by Chammah that TIT FOR TAT tends to elicit more cooperation from the co-player than other strategies. The "more cooperative" play of men compared to that of women could, therefore, be attributed to their greater propensity to play TIT FOR TAT. Years later the effectiveness of TIT FOR TAT in situations of this sort was dramatically demonstrated in two contests, and the relevance of this result to the theory of rationality was duly noted.

Prisoner's Dilemma A Study of Conflict and Cooperation was published in 1965. It was largely devoted to mathematical models purporting to describe the dynamics of iterated play, applying stochastic learning theory based on assumptions of how probabilities of choices in the simplest (either-or) decision situations are modified by feedback from the environment. This method was extended to game situations by P. Suppes and A.C. Atkinson.[5] We did the same with Prisoner's Dilemma and illustrated empirical testing of these models by comparing the deduced behaviour patterns with the protocols of the experiments.

All this was meant to be a contribution to descriptive decision theory. The point of departure was an exploration of the way people make decisions in a specific decision situation represented by the Prisoner's Dilemma game. Mathematics was used as a language in which the observed statistical regularities revealed in the protocols were described. However, the question arose how these findings were to be fitted in a normative theory where the central question is now ought a "rational" actor decide in a given situation.

The implications of Prisoner's Dilemma for a normative decision theory were discussed in *Strategy and Conscience* published a year before Prisoner's Dilemma.

Like *Fights, Games and Debates* it is in three parts. The first two are expansions of Part II of the former book. Part III is essentially another version of Part III of *Fights, Games and Debates*—a dialogue between a Western liberal and a Soviet Communist, this time paraphrased by some one who tries to trace the genesis of each ideology. The four chapters preceding the last are entitled, "What They Lack," "What We Lack," "What They Have" and "What We Have."

In attempting to summarize my beliefs and commitments (which is what I am trying to do in this book), I try to reconstruct their genesis. Partly this reconstruction is the content of the autobiographical narrative. I also try to put myself in the frame of mind reflected in the books I wrote thirty to forty years ago. In this respect, *Strategy and Conscience* is one of the most revealing. The two dominant themes in it are my abhorrence of the intellectualization of war and my conviction (at the time) that the ideological polarity, which dominated the four decades of the Cold War was another manifestation of a confrontation of a "thesis," and an "antithesis": and that the survival of humanity depended on the emergence of a "synthesis."

In spite of the fact that *Strategy and Conscience* developed the same thesis as *Fights, Games and Debates*, it got a very different reception in the United States. *Fights, Games and Debates* appeared in 1960. Herman Kahn's *On Thermonuclear War* and Thomas Schelling's *Strategy of Conflict* appeared in the same year. The title of Kahn's book was an obvious allusion to Clausewitz's *Vom Kriege* (*On War*), a sort of extension of the philosophy of war to fit into the nuclear world. *Fights, Games and Debates* could also be considered as a contribution to the philosophy of conflict in an age in which a monumental polarized conflict dominated all preoccupation, thoughts, and actions of important people, an attempt to understand the phenomena by examining its three aspects: the systemic, the strategic and the ideological.

Schelling was especially enthusiastic about this book, particularly about Part II, which, like his own Strategy of Conflict emphasized the importance of including non-zerosum games as models of rational conflict. In fact, two years before, Schelling published a long article on Prisoner's Dilemma in *The Journal of Conflict Resolution* (where I also published a lengthy review of Richardson's work). At the time he did not notice that our evaluations of non-zerosum games as conceptual tools in the theory of conflict were poles apart. I had not realized this either when I read Schelling's 1958 article. Only in the 1960 book was his position clearly revealed. The non-zerosum game, he pointed out, shows the way of extending Clausewitz's definition of war as an act of violence by mens of which we compel the opponent to submit to our will. This definition implies that in war there is always a winner and a loser. That is, war is properly modeled by a zerosum game, in which what one wins the other must lose. But in a nuclear war there is no way of escaping the prospect of a war without winners. And if one assumes that conflict among states, especially states aspiring to hegemony, is inevitable, it is imperative to develop an effective way of conducting a struggle for power without resort to overt violence. Possibly this goal would have been dismissed by Clausewitz as absurd, since violence was for him the sine qua non component of war, and war was the only form of struggle between states that he knew. On the other hand, he might have welcomed the extension of methods calculated to "compel the opponent to submit to our will," which is the central theme in Schelling's *Strategy of Conflict*. Wrote Schelling:

> We have learned that a threat has to be credible to be effective, and that its credibility may depend on the costs and risks associated with the fulfilment for the party making the threat. We have developed the idea of making the threat credible by getting ourselves committed to its fulfilment, through the stretching of a trip wire across the enemy's path of advance, or making fulfilment a matter of honour or prestige...We have considered the possibility that a retaliatory threat may be more credible if the means of carrying it out and the responsibility for retaliation are placed into the heads of those whose resolution is stronger.[5]

It appears that all these new lines of thought were opened up by the extensions of models of conflict to include non-zerosum games, since such situations create opportunities for communication and therefore for negotiation and bargaining. In a situation modeled by a non-zerosum game negotiation and bargaining serve no purpose. For negotiation to produce agreement there must be some area of common interest. The zerosum model provides no such area, since the interests of the players are always diametrically opposed: what is better for one must be worse for the other. Common interests exist only when some outcomes are preferred by both (or all) parties to other outcomes, and this can be the case only in situations modeled by non-zerosum games.

In this way, the theory of non-zerosum games points to a theory of strategic negotiation, and the problem that faces the negotiators is how to get one's way without war. There is room, therefore in the "defence community" (as the intellectuals serving the American war establishment started calling themselves) for a new type of strategist, one who thinks not in terms of weaponry and logistics but one who learns to utilize the common interests of antagonists to his own advantage so as to get his own way without risking outcomes disastrous for both.

I began to understand then why *Strategy and Conscience* was panned, in particular by Schelling, who had lavishly praised *Fights, Games, and Debates*, even though the later book was essentially an expansion of the earlier. Both books included a plea for "understanding the enemy," for taking into account the roots of two opposing ideologies in very different historical settings. Part of both books dealt with conflict resolution, which for a Western liberal intellectual is a "motherhood issue," something like the Christian imperative of loving the sinner while hating the sin. Likewise acceptable was the excursion into decision theory, where the inadequacy of the zerosum game model in describing real life conflicts (as distinguished from parlour games) was brought to light. In fact, this analysis was anticipated by Schelling. What was unacceptable to the defence community and to its academic fellow travelers was the critique of strategic thinking on moral grounds and the concomitant declaration of war against the defence community.

Here is what I wrote in the preface to *Strategy and Conscience*:

> One day a strategist came to our university to give a lecture on "defence and strategy in the nuclear age." The room was packed with standees. The tense

atmosphere revealed itself in ripples of nervous laughter which punctuated the speaker's ghoulish jokes. In the all-too-brief question period, waving hands were clamouring for the chairman's attention. Several of the questions were exactly of the sort that the lecturer might have anticipated. He was asked why instead of engaging in research applicable exclusively to war and to preparations for war (which the strategist maintained he abhorred "as much as any other farther of small children") the strategists did not direct their talents to research aimed at averting war. Why did the "unthinkable" which the strategist so bravely faced, include only scenarios of massive destruction? Why did the scheme not include other "unthinkable" situations, for example, the consequences of surrender?

The strategist's reply was exactly to the point. Much strategic research, he averred, was directed at preventing war. The possibilities of surrender were being considered. At any rate, there was nothing in the strategic approach that prevented such alternatives from being considered…Far from discouraging peace research, he maintained, the strategic mode of thinking actually encouraged effective peace research, in fact, guaranteed that recommendations for peaceful and accommodating moves in the game of diplomatic manoeuver were in effect conducive to the aims they were supposed to serve. Like many others (who later told me of their impressions), I felt engulfed in a wave of repugnance. I felt as if some one had taken Swift's "Modest Proposal" seriously and proceeded to defend it by ridiculing prejudice, by invoking the principle of "the greatest good for the greatest number" and by dismissing moral indignation as a symptom of "sentimentalism."

Succumbing to my feelings, I asked the speaker whether he would agree to a definition of "genocide" as a deliberate slaughter of helpless populations for political goals, adding that I was bringing up the subject only because he himself mentioned it in his talk. The speaker accepted my definition. I then asked him whether he realized that in view of the several precedents set at Nuremberg, Warsaw, Jerusalem, and elsewhere, genocide was a hanging offence, and, if so, how he would defend himself if at some future time he were a co-defendant in a genocide trial.

Again the reply was dignified and to the point. He said if mass destruction resulted, despite expectations, from policies based on his and others' analyses and if on these grounds he were held responsible, he would plead "partially guilty." The purpose of his research, he kept saying, was to avert war, not to kill people more efficiently. If war nevertheless broke out, he would be genuinely sorry. (Those were his words.)

After the meeting I learned that many of my colleagues thought my questions inappropriate. This feeling was shared, I was told, by the chairman, a convinced and active pacifist. The basis of the feelings was obvious. I had violated the standards of academic discourse. These standards include the constraint of keeping the discussion within the mode of reasoned argument and within the sphere circumscribed by the subject of discussion. It was expected, therefore, that questions would be confined to matters pertaining to the accuracy of the asserted facts, the consistency of stated assumptions, the validity of drawn inferences, and the like. Questions of morality, while possibly crucially important in themselves, were altogether taboo. I believe this departure from the accepted mode of academic discourse hit a raw nerve. Here is an excerpt from D.C. Brennan's review of *Strategy and Conscience* in the *Bulletin of Scientists*.[6]

> *Strategy and Conscience* is an anguished book, written by a man who points to some problems that more of us should spend more time thinking about. But its chief claim to distinction, unfortunately, rests more on the intensity of its anguish than on the accuracy of its reporting or on the perceptiveness of its analysis.
>
> The first serious complaint I have with this book is that the author has not specified and probably has not even clearly determined in his own mind just where he is shooting from, and this seems to interfere with his understanding of some important issues under examination. The great majority of us accept the idea that national military force may sometimes be used with justice in defense of important national goals or human values. Thoughtful people who adhere to this view are often confronted with line-drawing problems of degree. For example: Under what circumstances is it reasonable to threaten much military force? How many people can be risked as a consequence of some particular deterrent system?
>
> A few—pacifists—reject this kind of thinking altogether and hod that the best overall defense of human values resides in the complete rejection of military force, even when the rejection is by some countries only and not by all. For this view, the dominant problem is a missionary one, to convince the rest of us that we are working in the wrong general framework and that the gains of strict pacifism are worth the obvious risks.
>
> Now I do not find the author making overt missionary arguments that we should renounce all forms of military violence. The major part of his argument is couched in a mode that suggests that he accepts the standard framework, though I think he does not in fact. The book seems imbued with a kind of surreptitious pacifism.

This interpretation of my position as a kind of "surreptitious pacifism" illustrated most clearly what I meant by the intellectualization of war. Brennan assumed that there are two frameworks of thought, which can shape one's conceptions of war and peace—the rational framework, where thought is guided by examination of facts and by disciplined deduction, and the affective framework, where attitudes and convictions are determined by one's moral commitments, inclinations, and aversions. The strategist works in the former, the pacifist in the latter. He maintained that although I formulated my arguments in what he called the "standard" framework, I did this with the aim of concealing my true position—that of a pacifist.

What Brennan missed was my intent to expose the inadequacy of the strategic paradigm by demonstrating the ambiguity of the very concept of rationality. Once one starts to cast conflict situations in game-theoretic terms, one must examine the structure of non-zerosum games. Since most conflict situations (including those leading to war) can be realistically modeled only in terms of games in which the interests of the players are only partially opposed. And once one gets into this realm of analysis, one sees how the concept of rationality inevitably splits into at least two concepts—"individual rationality" and "collective rationality." Which of these concepts one chooses as a guide to "rational" analysis cannot be decided on "rational" grounds, since attempts to do so would inevitably lead to a vicious cycle. (In the same way, the postulates of a mathematical system cannot be proved by invoking these same postulates.) Thus, stepping outside the "standard" framework of thinking becomes a necessity when rational analysis is pushed far enough. The refusal to step out of this framework is what I call the "intellectualization of war." To be sure my repugnance of this process stemmed from moral outrage, but my critique was constructed on the strategist's own ground. I insisted that the analysis should be pushed sufficiently far. It should not stop when the preferred conclusion is reached.

A few examples will serve to illustrate the point. In his book *On Nuclear War*, Herman Kahn raised the question of how many civilian casualties would be acceptable to Americans in the sense of being worth the risk of a nuclear war in the process of resisting intimidation by the Russians. (I take this as an example of the kind of "line-drawing" that Brennan mentioned in his review.) Let us see how Kahn attempted to answer the question he posed.

> I have discussed the question with many Americans and after about fifteen minutes of discussion, their estimates of an acceptable price generally fell between 10 and 60 million, clustering toward the upper number.[7]

It is statements like this one that have moved people outside the defence community to condemn the callousness of the strategists and to dismiss "game theory" as a ghoulish perversion. In my opinion, this criticism misses the mark. It leaves intact the strategist's contention that theirs is the stance of tough-minded realism. Kahn's way of arriving at a figure representing "acceptable casualties" may be morally repugnant, but arguments of this sort only substantiate the contention of the defence community that its critics refuse to "face realities"; that they refuse to "think about the unthinkable," and therefore by-pass rational thought. There is a way of exposing the shabbiness of strategic thinking from the other end, as it were: it does not go far enough.

Consider the avenues of analysis opened up by the theory of games. At the very foundation of the theory is the recognition that in a conflict between "rational" actors, the outcomes are determined not only by the decisions of one of them, not even by the decisions of one of them together with external circumstances—the so called "state of the world at the time the decision is made"—but by the decisions of both or all players. For the chess player this is obvious. In contemplating a move, a chess player (if he is even minimally competent) must ask himself what the other's response to his move is likely to be; and this estimate must be made *from the other's point of view*. Therefore "rationality" from the point of view of a game-theoretic model of a conflict situation involves ascribing rationality to the opponent. So much the strategist understands. In fact, the appearance of the theory of games on the intellectual horizon was enthusiastically welcomed in the defence community, and research in the field was generously funded by the U.S. military establishment. For here was a highly sophisticated treatment of "rational" conflict. However, only two-person zerosum game models fit naturally into the "classical" framework of military thought: what one side gains, the other necessarily loses. So if Kahn's estimate that 60 million civilian casualties would be "acceptable" in a showdown with the Soviet Union were to be taken seriously, some implicit gains must have been projected to make up for the losses, which would necessarily be associated with corresponding losses by the other side. There was no evidence that such calculations were made. It seems that arguments of this sort are designed to give an impression of hard-headed "bottom line" projections, the usual practice in enterprise management cast in a framework of thought that is held in esteem.

An even more vivid example of the sort of mentality that simulates hard-nosed "rationality" can be seen in the following discussion of allocation of funds to various types of weaponry, designed to "deter" the enemy. The author appears to be doing a cost-benefit analysis of various allocations. He rejects the crude "bigger bang for a buck" standard of effectiveness. Not the size of the bang but the amount of destruction is the proper measure in his opinion; and even here one must carefully consider the different values the enemy places on things destroyed. For example if the enemy holds lives to be cheaper than industrial and military installations, then it is not rational to snuff out lives if for the same expenditures one can put more installations or missile silos out of commission.

> The number and value of enemy targets that can be destroyed (for a given budget)…takes into account not only the numbers of our offense bombers and missiles but also their operational effectiveness…It still is, of course, an ambiguous criterion and requires more precise definition. For example, what target systems—population, industry, or military bases—should be used to keep score.[8]

It has been said that at the meetings of his security advisors during the Cuban missile crisis in 1962, President Kennedy asked each in turn to estimate the probability of a nuclear war with the Soviet Union if U.S. attacked Cuba. Presumably such estimates were made—30%, 60%, etc. Again the procedure reflects a stance—a sort of sober rationality, in a situation in which submitting to sentiment or emotionally induced stress would lead to panic.

Finally consider the following account by Herman Kahn of how Americans learned to think "rationally" about the unthinkable. Kahn did a great deal of lecturing on matters pertaining to nuclear strategy to audiences consisting, as he writes, of "college students, businessmen, members of the League of Women's Voters, etc. To illustrate the point about exercising control, he would ask them what they thought would (or should) happen, if a single hydrogen bomb were dropped on New York. At first the answer would be that the President should order a crushing retaliatory blow on the Soviet Union. A few years later, however, presumably after exposure to lectures on flexible response, the audiences became much more sophisticated, as Kahn notes with satisfaction. A lively discussion would follow. Searching questions would be asked. Someone would suggest that the President get in touch with his opposite number in the Kremlin and inquire why there was only one bomb.

Kahn would stimulate further discussion by explaining that the one bomb on New York was indeed a deliberate act by the Soviet Union and that the Soviets made it clear that they would destroy the U.S. totally unless the U.S. did this or that. Then,

> ...almost all would agree that there should be retaliation but that it should be limited. Most suggest that Moscow should be destroyed, but many objected to this on the grounds that this city is much more important to the Soviet Union than New York is to the United States. Those usually agree that the destruction of some smaller city, such as Leningrad or Kiev, would be an appropriate counter-escalation.[9]

People who are appalled by discourse of this sort usually call it immoral or obscene. At times I have also reacted to it in the same way. However, the main thrust of my criticism of strategic thinking in *Strategy and Conscience* was along other lines. I challenged the claim that the arguments of the strategists were based on rational analysis. To show this, I spelled out the details of constructing a game-theoretic model of a conflict situation, since these models represent an application of the most sophisticated mode of strategic analysis. I felt justified in setting up the game-theoretic paradigm as a model, since in the excerpts cited explicit or implicit allusions are made to the fundamental concepts of game-theoretic analysis, for example, to utilities of outcomes of decisions both to self and to the opponent, probabilities of outcomes of actions, which are involved in so called "calculated risk," another widely used expression related to rational deliberations, and so on.

First, let us examine the notion of utility. Roughly, a utility of some thing or state of affairs indicates how much it is "worth" to a specified actor, whereby utilities are assumed to be represented by observable quantities, for example, in business by amounts of money. The answer to the question how well a firm is doing is often assumed to be the "bottom line" of a quarterly statement, representing gains or losses. Also in evaluating the efficacy of a drug, doctors look at the percentage of patients cured, perhaps corrected by incidence of undesirable side effects, which may include fatalities.

Similar calculations can enter evaluations of military strategies or tactics. Casualties are clearly observable and are simply quantifiable by being counted.

But to exhibit countable or measurable products of an activity is not to establish measures of utility. Even the utility of money is not necessarily proportional to the amount of money. A dollar is worth more to a poor man than to a rich man. Even more problematic is the establishment of the utility of, say, a drug, based on the numbers of lives saved weighted against the number of lives lost through side effects. Are the latter simply to be subtracted from the former? That is, are the saved and lost lives to be weighted equally? To fix ideas, suppose a 100% effective vaccine against leukemia is discovered in the sense that every one inoculated with it is immune to the disease. However, a tiny fraction of the vaccinated are killed by the vaccine. Suppose the number of lives saved exceeds the number of lives lost by a factor of ten.

Does this mean that a parent's refusal to let a child be vaccinated is "irrational"? Or does it simply mean that in the parent's estimation the "disutility" of the child's death from vaccine weighs more heavily (in the sense of post-decision regret) than the "utility" of being safe from the disease, given the a priori of whether that particular child will be stricken by it? The point I am making is that utility is necessarily subjectively estimated. It is not given by "nature" like, say, the mass of an object, or the capacitance of a condenser. This subjectivity of utility need not preclude rational analysis in arriving at decisions, but it must be explicitly recognized. In the strategists' discourse, however, this inherently subjective nature of utility (or disutility) is completely disregarded. Kahn believed that he established the disutility of 60 million civilian deaths (to be balanced against the utility of "standing up to the Russians") by recording the estimates of "several Americans." But he did not specify who his respondents were (perhaps his colleagues at the Rand Corporation, where he worked at the time) nor whether they would name the same figure at some other time or if he had posed the question differently or had described in some detail the reasonably foreseen consequences of various decisions. In other words, the method used in this case at arriving at a "rational" decision violates the most elementary standards of objective analysis, supposedly a mark of enlightened strategic thinking. Pointing this out completely bypasses the formidable moral issue involved in decisions of this sort.

No more "rational" are arguments based on considerations of risk involving estimates of probabilities. In certain businesses, notably insurance or commercial gambling, estimations of probabilities enter the process of arriving at "rational" decisions. These estimates are based on observed frequencies of events, for example, accidents of a given type or the results of spinning a roulette wheel, or of drawing a number of cards from a deck. These estimates are realistic as long as the observed events can be regarded as repetitions of the same event. Specifically, although every turn of the roulette wheel is different in detail, and the circumstances of every accident differ, the events have enough features in common to be regarded as repetitions. It follows that this justification does not apply to events which by their nature cannot be repeated many times. An obvious example is a nuclear war. The occurrence of several nuclear wars all basically alike and all in apparently identical circumstances is highly unlikely. Thus, an estimate of the "probability" of a nuclear war, which sometimes enters considerations leading to formulation of diplo-military policies of nuclear powers has no basis in reality. On what, then are such estimates based? In the case of the Cuban missile crisis, they may well have been based on hopes and fears or similar mental or emotional states of Kennedy's advisors. Those who wanted an attack on Cuba may have tended to make smaller estimates of the "probability" of a nuclear war; those who did not relish the prospect of such an attack tended to make larger estimates. Calculations of "reasonable risk" had nothing to do with these estimates.

Teach-ins

Hard as I tried during my first years at Michigan to confine criticisms of strategic thinking to the strategists' own ground, the moral and emotional issues could not be avoided when the U.S. launched air strikes against North Vietnam, initiating ten years of horrendous destruction of a Third World country.

Shortly after the bombing began, Alice Herz, an elderly lady, immolated herself in Detroit as a gesture of protest. A group of faculty members and graduate students met to discuss possible ways of publicizing our repugnance. A strike was suggested, but the idea was soon dismissed. Some 40 to 50 faculty members expressed support for the action, and this presaged failure, which would do far more harm than good to the emergent protest movement. Next, some one suggested devoting a class hour to acquainting the students with the background of the war in Vietnam (which had already been going on for twenty years). This idea was also dismissed. Very few of the faculty felt competent to present this information, and those who did could be easily singled out for punitive sanctions. The action might be interpreted as breach of contract, which specified the number of hours per week a faculty member undertook to teach a specified subject. Finally, the idea of the "teach-in" took shape.

The teach-in was conceived as an analogue of a sit-in strike. In the 1930's, the turbulent years of energetic union organizing, striking American workers, instead of picketing the premises, occupied them. It was much more difficult to dislodge them than to break-up picket lines. The novelty of the tactic also attracted much more attention. The teach-in was like the sit-ins in that it involved occupying the premises. But breach of contract could not be easily established since those events were to take place outside the normal teaching hours.

The first teach-in took place at the University of Michigan on the night of March 24-25, 1965 from 8 P.M. to 8 A.M. The format was a combination of mass meetings and seminars. Lecturers and seminar leaders from several universities participated. Administration cooperated by making several lecture halls and seminar rooms available. The affair was meticulously planned along the lines of a meeting of a professional society, that is, as a tight programme of lectures, workshops, etc., interspersed with plenary sessions. Kenneth Boulding, one of the eleven organizers, made an excellent suggestion that undoubtedly contributed to the success of the affair, namely, to provide free sandwiches and coffee to be consumed in the ten minute breaks between the sessions. "Nothing like food to keep spirits up," Ken pointed out.

We expected a few hundred students. About three thousand showed up. There was a counter-demonstration. A dozen or two supporters of the war picketed the meetings. They carried signs urging some one to "drop the bomb" and expressing support for the President ("LBJ all the way!"). There was a bomb scare. The halls had to be cleared while they were searched. This rather raised the morale of the protesters, making them feel that they were pitted against the forces of evil. The next day a group of people from the State Department staged a counter-teach-in. There was just one session attended by about 300. Possibly the participants of the teach-in slept all day.

The teach-in quickly spread to American and Canadian campuses. They culminated in the national teach-in Washington, D.C. on May 15, 1965. A nation-wide telephone hook-up broadcast the proceedings to some fifty campuses.

The opening session of the national teach-in was to be a confrontation between the opponents of U.S. intervention in Southeast Asia and the government. The government was to be represented by McGeorge Bundy, President Johnson's advisor, generally regarded as the architect of the Vietnam war. After protracted negotiations, Bundy accepted the invitation on the condition that the pro-war side be represented not by him alone but also by a panel of academics. There were, of course, many of those, and they were duly invited to participate.

Bundy, however, did not show up. On that day he was sent by Johnson to the Dominican Republic to explain to the Dominicans the occupation of their country by the marines, which coincided with the affair in Washington. Whether this coincidence was accidental or arranged we have no way of knowing. In effect it prevented the confrontation, which we had hoped would make the anti-war protest something to be politically reckoned with. Instead, it was presented to the public as a debate between academics.

Five thousand people attended the national teach-in. The government asked and got three hundred reserved seats. Possibly this was another ploy. The intention may have been to create the impression of poor attendance since the seats remained empty. If so, the move back-fired. Attention was called to the empty rows and it was explained why they were empty. (The rest of the ballroom was packed.) Attention was also called to the empty chair on the rostrum, where McGeorge Bundy was supposed to sit.

We got excellent coverage—four pages in the *New York Times* with some of the speeches reported in full. In one story McGeorge Bundy was featured as "the nation's Number One Drop-out."

The affair was well organized. The "headquarters" hummed with activity. I had the satisfaction of telling Barry Commoner (who had been skeptical about our being able to stage a "national event"), when he came to headquarters to ask what he was to do, "Your marching orders are just being typed, Barry. They'll be ready in a few minutes."

Every resource person was assigned to one or more workshop sessions. At the plenary session we featured Henry Morgenthau, author of *Politics Among Nations*, a widely used textbook on international relations, representing the so called "realist" school of political science. Like Barry Commoner, Morgenthau was one of our "stars." We worked him hard to the extent that he complained about his "teaching load," the heaviest he had ever had.

Morgenthau was a staunch opponent of the Vietnam war, and he explained his position as being consistent with the "realist" conception of international relations. In this view, the principal virtue in the conduct of foreign policy is "prudence," that is, a realistic appraisal of the relative power of states, which determines the rational course of foreign policy. The exercise of such prudence discourages adventurism and (which is especially important) tends to preserve a "balance of power"—the essence of stability of a world order. Among the considerations entering the assessment of one's power is a realistic determination of one's proper sphere of influence. It was on this ground that Morgenthau energetically opposed U.S. involvement in Vietnam. Southeast Asia was definitely outside the proper sphere of influence of the United States, and consequently United States had no business there. In an article entitled "Speak Truth to Power," Morgenthau harshly criticized American foreign policy of those years.

The teach-ins provided an anchorage for my conception of the peace movement as consisting of three "arms"—peace research, peace education, and peace activism. I now perceived the peace movement as the twentieth century continuation of eighteenth century Enlightenment. I considered the essence of enlightenment to be the acquisition of a way of thinking appropriate to a current state of development of the human race. In the eighteenth century the enlightened portions of humanity no longer supported an authoritarian political system. The stranglehold of absolute monarchy and of the established church were broken. The task of the enlightened portion of humanity in the twentieth century now seemed to me to be the abolition of the institution of war. The cutting edge should be political action. But political action directed toward the goal of ultimate dismantling of the global war machine had to be based on solid knowledge. Moral condemnation of war and abhorrence of war were obviously not enough. The dissemination of relevant knowledge was essential: of history, politics, even physics and biology for properly understanding the implications of nuclear warfare. The task of peace research I saw as that of acquiring this knowledge, the task of peace education of disseminating it, and the task of peace activism of applying it.

Peace Research

In looking over the list of papers I published in 1966, that is, papers written soon after the start of the teach-ins, I note that of the thirty papers sixteen were on some theme relevant to war or peace, conflict or conflict resolution. Most were on my uses of experimental games in research on the psychology of mixed-motive conflict; but some were more general. The underlying theme in all was the complementarity of the strategic and non-strategic approaches to the theory of conflict and to the practice of conflict resolution.

In the 1960's and 1970's the Mental Health Research Institute sponsored an extensive programme of peace research, "Correlates of War," led by J. David Singer, who had a joint appointment with the Department of Political Science. As the title suggests, the programme could be interpreted as a search for the "causes of wars." However, the establishments of correlations does not necessarily mean identification of causes. A correlation (that is, a tendency to occur together) between events or conditions A and B may be observed if A is the cause of B, if B is the cause of A, if each is a cause of the other or neither is. Nevertheless the establishment of a significant correlation between the incidence or the duration or the severity of wars and certain objectively identifiable conditions may be taken as some evidence that these conditions are contributory causes of war.

The method of uncovering correlates of war was used by Lewis F. Richardson. His research is summarized in one of the two posthumously published volumes of his life work, *Statistics of Deadly Quarrels*. Richardson defined a "deadly quarrel" as any conflict between human beings ending in one or more fatalities. He classified all such "quarrels" by magnitude represented by the logarithm to the base ten of the number of victims. Thus, a murder of one individual is classified as a deadly quarrel of magnitude 0 (since the logarithm of 1 is 0). A riot resulting in ten deaths is assigned magnitude 1; a bloody suppression of a demonstration resulting in 100-1000 deaths would be of magnitude between 2 and 3; the two world wars were of magnitudes between 7 and 8. A war of magnitude between 9 and 10 would wipe out the human race.

This classification of war by magnitude without regard for any other features reflects Lewis's pacifism. He deliberately ignores distinctions between economically, politically, or ideologically instigated wars. These distinctions do not interest him any more than they interest any pacifist, say of Tolstoyan persuasion, for whom all war is simply the ultimate manifestation of evil. Ignoring the usually advanced causes of wars, Richardson believed he was assuming a stance of complete "objectivity," the point of view of the proverbial extraterrestrial being, who records only overtly observed events classified by some easily identifiable criteria.

"Correlates of War" was conducted in the same spirit, except that the "objective criteria" were more widely conceived. Any criterion on which good data were available and which could have some conceivable relevance to the incidence of war were "thrown into the pot." Examples:

"Formal Alliances 1815-1965"
"Measuring the Concentration of Power in the International System."
"Variables, Indicators, and Data: The Measurement Problem in Macro-Political Structures."
"Status, Formal Organization, and Arms Levels as Factors Leading to the Onset of War."
"Bipolarity, Multipolarity, and the Threat of War."
"The Road to War Strewn with Peaceful Intentions."

In pondering the role of research on war and peace as a component of the peace movement, I tried to assess the contributions of the Correlates of War project. In many ways it was conceived as an analogue of medical research. It was surely medical research, disciplined by scientific rules of evidence that contributed to the eradication of several diseases and to the dramatic prolongation of life expectancy. Further, the bulk of medical research was concentrated on a search for the causes of diseases. It is also worth noting that in this context discovery of necessary conditions of diseases leads more directly to practical results than the discovery of sufficient conditions. The latter are often complex and difficult to identify. Necessary conditions are often simple and easy to identify. For example, the tubercle bacillus is a necessary but not a sufficient cause of tuberculosis. Without it tuberculosis cannot occur; but a carrier of the bacillus need not have the disease. Thus, the discovery of a necessary cause of a disease, be it a specific organism, a diet deficiency, or a genetic defect, often portends a break through that leads to eventual prevention, control, or cure of the disease.

The same reasoning could be applied to peace research. Sufficient causes of wars are complex and often obscure. Moreover, they may be very different in different historical periods. In the eighteenth century European states went to war to determine whose nephew would be the next occupant of a vacant throne. Wars of succession are not likely to be resumed. On the other hand, after the Treaty of Westphalia, religious wars, such as the Thirty Years' War was conceived to be, were no longer fashionable. World War II could, perhaps be classified as an analogue of a religious war ("ideological war"). But this conception could be challenged, as, in fact, it has been challenged by political scientists of the "realist" persuasion. Thus, besides changing from one historical period to another, sufficient causes of war may be highly controversial.

In contrast, a necessary condition of war, besides being conspicuous and easily identifiable by objective indices, is weapons. Without weapons wars of the sort that most people are most concerned about would be impossible. Adherents of the "You can't change human nature" school of thought may point out that even complete and general disarmament will not eradicate "wars" fought by sticks and stones. But this argument should not concern us any more than the inevitability of the common cold concerns the medical scientist searching for a cure for cancer.

The parallel between medical research and peace research breaks down when we turn our attention to how the knowledge gained by research can be applied. The results of medical research are applied to solving problems as a matter of course. If an effective vaccine against AIDS were discovered, the disease could be eradicated as thoroughly as small pox was eradicated. This could be done because an infrastructure in the form of a network of institutions exists designed to utilize new knowledge, namely, hospitals, clinics, the medical profession, pharmaceutical industries, departments of public health, and so on. No such infrastructure exists in the form of institutions designed and empowered to convert results of peace research, no matter how promising, into action. By contrast, a vast infrastructure exists in the form of institutions ready to apply knowledge produced by war research: arms industries, military schools, institutes of strategic studies, and so on. Knowledge of the obvious necessary conditions of war, namely, the existence of weapons, and the advances in ever more destructive weaponry, contributes next to nothing to the solution of the "problem" that modern war poses to humanity. However, the recognition of the institutional obstacles to the solution of the "problem" does suggest a fruitful direction of peace research and also a way of converting the knowledge generated by it into action.

It has been said that one of the most valuable contributions to peace research has been the study known as *The Pentagon Papers*, an investigation of the administrative background of the United States involvement in Southeast Asia. As a sort of self-study, it is vivid evidence of the intellectualization of the defence community. Availability of this material to the general public was not intended, and energetic attempts were made to suppress its publication; but the Supreme Court ruled that suppression would be a violation of the First Amendment to the Constitution. So in effect, the gathering of the materials for the Pentagon Papers could be regarded as an example of "investigative journalism," long established in American tradition and known in its early days as "muckraking."

Muckraking dealt primarily with political corruption. Investigative journalism need not be confined to exposing actions and conspiracies subject to criminal prosecution. It could well lead to public exposure of activities and institutions, which, while legal, can in certain kinds of political weather be extremely embarrassing to the perpetrators. In this way, investigative journalism can be regarded as one direction of peace research that is relevant to the attack on the central problem—a search for ways and means of removing institutional obstacles to the obvious "cure" of the war "disease," namely, the elimination of weapons.

Farewell to U.S.

I am frequently asked why we left the United States, and I often answer, "Because we had growing sons." This was not the main reason, but it is related to what I believe was the real reason, which is not easy to explain.

Our sons were aged eleven and five and so would not be threatened by the draft for several years. Nor did I undergo what could be seriously called harassment. Soon after we came to Ann Arbor, I was accosted by a man in a car parked near our house. I came up expecting to be asked directions. The man turned out to be a government agent. He invited me to come into his office for a talk, which I did the next morning.

Two or three others were present at the conversation. In answer to the carefully worded probing about whether I knew any one who was at the time or had ever been connected with the Communist Party. I told them I had been a member myself. I felt good about it. I thought I would be going through what I should have been going through in Chicago. But the interview was devoid of all drama. The men were annoyingly polite and friendly. They asked how much time I had. I told them I was free all morning, that my only worry was that the parking meter on the street below would run out. One of them went down to put a nickel in the meter.

They did ask me whether I remembered any of the other members of the party. This was the moment I looked forward to in Chicago, when I intended to say calmly (not defiantly) that I was ready to tell them anything they wanted to know about myself but that I would not speak about any one else. But the situation was so devoid of drama that this sort of self-righteousness seemed out of place. I recall saying that I didn't really remember any one and that anyway they all used pseudonyms.

They encouraged me to talk about my political views, and I did. They kept the conversation going by asking intelligent questions and offering mild counter-arguments. I enjoyed myself. At one point, they asked whether I could from time to time come in for a talk about what was happening on our campus. They explained they were neither interested nor empowered to intimidate any one, that to do their job properly (guarding the internal security of the country) they had to be informed about everything that was going on. They told me that I could see for myself that being compared to the secret police of totalitarian states does them a grave injustice. I said I agreed, but nevertheless felt that doing what they asked me to do would not be "collegial," and they said that they did not agree but that they respected my opinion.

On another occasion a member of the university administration asked me to come in and told me that he received information about my being associated with "subversive" groups in the 1930's. Specifically two events in Chicago were mentioned. I played piano at a fund-raising affair sponsored by the Communist Party at the home of the Goldbergs (whose friendship with the Rapoports is now on the level of the fourth generation). The other affair was my joint recital with Misha Mishakoff, sponsored by the Friends of the Soviet Union. This time I did ask "defiantly" what he was going to do about it. He said "Nothing." So once again I was disarmed.

From these episodes one might surmise that what I found lacking in the United States was an opportunity to suffer for my convictions. This is not so. Some of my colleagues were cruelly harassed during the McCarthy witch hunt; some went to jail. Probably, if I had gone about it in the right way, I could have been among them. But I didn't really want to be a martyr. And in the brief period when I was engaged in "safe" political activity in the 1966 election campaign, I did it half-heartedly wishing I didn't have to.

Many faculty members were involved in that campaign and worked through the Ann Arbor Democratic party. A split occurred between those who saw the Vietnam war as the primary issue and those who believed that the primary goal was to get the Democratic candidate for Congress elected. Although the chairman of the Ann Arbor organization (a young beginner in politics) was on "our" side, we could not induce the candidate to denounce the war. We then switched our support to Elise Boulding (Kenneth Boulding's wife), who ran as a "peace candidate." She took enough votes away from the machine candidate to get the Republican elected, which made me *persona non grata* not only in the Democratic party organization (recaptured by the state machine) but also with some of our friends.

This experience made me wonder whether I could feel at ease in any situation in which the main task is influencing people to move in a pre-determined direction. What repelled me most in American political life was the salesmanship aspect. It reminded me of two similar highly distasteful experiences: trying to get people to install a radio "on a trial basis" (Chicago, 1926) and trying to get them to sign a petition to put the Communist candidate on the presidential ballot (Peoria, 1940).

It would seem the two situations were widely different. In one case I was trying to get people to do something that would bring a profit to a business without the slightest regard for the people I tried to influence. This was real exploitation, a far cry, to be sure, from the exploitation of an underclass by a ruling class that Marx wrote about, but exploitation nevertheless—using people for one's own benefit. In contrast, gathering signatures was supposed to be relegated to spreading political enlightenment. I really believed at that time that a Communist victory at the polls would benefit the majority of the American people. The fact that such a victory was a virtual impossibility was irrelevant. The campaign was a trickle that I thought would one day become a mighty stream.

Still, what was involved was arm twisting of sorts. The people I approached had no inkling about what I was talking about. For the most part they suspected some sort of scam or gimmick of the sort to which they were repeatedly exposed. Those who signed were probably used to making a positive response to any encroachment, having learned that a positive response gets rid of the intruder, and as long as no money outlay was required, they didn't give the matter further thought. So this, too, was exploitation—making use of people's ignorance or their apathy or their inability to defend themselves.

In retrospect I think those two experiences in salesmanship gave me a new slant on exploitation. A proper criterion of exploitation is not whether the exploiter benefits at the expense of the exploited but whether the effect of his gain on the exploited is of any consequence to the exploiter. Being manipulated into buying something may at times benefit the buyer. The buyer is, nevertheless, exploited if the salesman gives no thought to whether the transaction will benefit or harm the buyer. On the other hand, even if compliance harms the target but if the persuader is genuinely convinced that the target would benefit, the act of persuasion should not be regarded as exploitation.

What about teaching? I had been a teacher of something or other since I was fourteen years old. I taught children to play the piano; I taught physics to aviation cadets, English to Russian pilots, Russian to American pilots. In universities I taught mathematics, semantics, psychology, control theory, and decision theory. I have always loved teaching, was told that I was a very good teacher, believed it, and was proud of it. But is not teaching essentially influencing people to move (mentally or spiritually) in a predetermined direction? So why should teaching not be regarded as manipulating people, even though the teacher may be sincerely convinced that he is doing it in the student's interest? And was it not the manipulative aspects of a political campaign that I couldn't take, even though the sort of persuasion I used could not be subsumed under "exploitation"? I think the crux of the matter lies elsewhere. In a teaching situation (at least in those in which I took part) it was the student who came to me. I did not initiate the contact. Therefore I imagined my role to be a reactive one: responding to a question equivalent to "How?" or "Why?" or to a challenge like "Show me!" or "Say it!" That's all I needed. I could take it from there without feeling that I was encroaching on some one's autonomy or arousing suspicions that I wanted something and was trying to get it by getting some one to do something or want something.

In short I found I had a deep aversion to everything connected with salesmanship or advertising or propaganda. I found that I rejected competition in any except strictly circumscribed situations, where the outcomes implied no more than recognition of excellence or of virtuosity. I accepted competition in sports, where victory did not depend on influencing some one's inclinations or perceptions, where, in fact, any such attempts are equivalent to cheating. By the same token I rejected activities that reflect striving for dominance. In fact, I rejected the three most prestigious fields of American professional life—the two traditional ones—competitive business and competitive politics—and the new one established in the middle of our century—war.

One might surmise that this was the main factor in my decision to leave the United States—a reaction to its major cultural values, the values inherent in the success cult so admirably spelled out in Dale Carnegie's little masterpiece, *How to Make Friends and Influence People*. But this was not so. I did find a niche in academic life. This is not to say that competition does not exist in this life as it does in everything else in a success-worshiping culture. But it is possible to opt out of it, and I thought I had. What I found impossible was to continue business as usual, while the country to which I owed at least formal allegiance made the slaughter of civilians (which is what counter-insurgency and nuclear warfare entail) a component of its role in the international arena. It was not enough for me to insist that in my active opposition to this policy I was not resigning my loyalty to the country I lived in, that, on the contrary, acts of opposition were acts of loyalty on a level higher than that of conventional patriotism. The real difficulty was that the only acts of opposition that I regarded as effective in those days revolved around political organization and intense continual public protest. A way out was to go to live in a country that was not committed to a messianic role—a small peaceful country with no aspirations to major power status.

I talked things over with Gwen, and she agreed. She had worked in different branches of the cooperative movement, with people trying to establish a people-oriented health care system, with consumers cooperatives, with community organizers. She was a more consistent opponent of violence than I was. She had opposed U.S. participation in World War II while I had volunteered and had justified it for many years afterward.

And there were the children. The youngest was only three in 1965, but the elder boy, the eight-year-old was already deeply involved in what was going on.

When I came back from Washington (from the national teach-in), the first thing he asked me when I walked through the door was "Did you win?" I thought that if I were to be a role model for my sons, I would have to make active dissidence my principal activity, if we continued to live in the United States. I doubted my competence as a full time dissident. I believe in retrospect that the opportunity to escape from this responsibility was an important factor in my decision to emigrate.

I let it be known through the academic grapevine that I was "available," and in the course of 1967 I got three offers: one from the National University of Mexico, one from the Technical University of Denmark, and one from the University of Toronto. The prospect of living in Denmark seemed most attractive. Denmark was a small country, in no way a threat to any one.

To me the idea of returning to Europe was especially appealing. Ever since my student years in Vienna I hoped to live in a culturally rich city in a European country that had long opted out of power politics. I looked forward to living in a city with crooked streets, a city with a rail road station in the heart of it with a central core preserved, not rotting, possibly with a royal palace occupied by a monarch stripped of all power but respected as a father or a mother figure. I liked to travel in trains with cosy compartments, where people could engage in a conversation, and occasionally walk up and down the corridor, where each car carried a plaque with names of a half dozen famous cities on it in a half dozen countries. I loved to hike or cycle through villages a few kilometres apart, each with a central square, a commemorative fountain or monument, and a seventeenth century inn, but no used car lot with strings of little flags advertising it.

In contemplating leaving the U.S., where I had spent 37 of my 56 years, I thought of what I was sorry to lose and of what I was glad to get rid of. The biggest loss would be the loss of frequent, easy contacts with intimate friends. All my closest friends, some from adolescent years, were in the U.S. My relations with European colleagues never went beyond cordiality. What I looked forward to leaving behind me, forever, if I could help it, was seeing the gutted centres of great cities—the core of Detroit that looked like the bombed out cores of European cities in 1949, the slums of Chicago, the deserted "down towns" of practically all midwest cities.

So we decided on Denmark. In the meantime I received an invitation to spend three months at the Institute for Advanced Studies in Vienna (the one that Paul Lazarsfeld and I plotted to establish, when we were at CASBAH). I left Ann Arbor in March, 1968. I took our life savings with me and deposited them in a Zurich bank on my way to Vienna. I got an apartment in Grinzing (one of the wine suburbs of Vienna), bought a Volvo and lived to greet my family at the modest little Vienna airport. I watched them come—my beloved Gwen and my beautiful sixteen-year-old Anya and solemn eleven-year-old Sasha carrying his French horn and the not quite six-year-old Tony. A month later we set out in the Volvo for Copenhagen with the intention of settling there.

It didn't work out. Before returning to Ann Arbor for the "terminal year" (as was required after a Sabbatical), we bought a house in Copenhagen. We gave power of attorney to a lawyer, who was to handle our affairs until we returned. Some alterations were to be done on the house, for which we engaged an architect recommended by the lawyer. During our absence the architect did things to our house, which we never authorized. In fact, we found the interior gutted when we returned in the spring. The upshot of the whole business was that we had to sell what was left of the house for half of what we paid for it (we had paid cash). There was no way of getting recourse without spending possibly years in litigation. The affair made us bitter, and I resigned heavy-hearted the professorship at the Technical University. We went back to Ann Arbor. I phoned the University of Toronto to ask whether they still wanted me to come. They said yes. In September 1970 we moved to Toronto, where I got a cross appointment in the departments of psychology and mathematics.

NOTES

1. Korzybski's insights into how language molds conceptions of reality was expressed in his notion of "elementarism"—separating what is in reality not separable. It took operational analysis of these conceptions to establish then as alternative aspects of underlying unified reality—"space-time," in relativity theory, "wave propagation-particle stream" in quantum mechanics. Other examples of conceptual separation of inseparable categories: "mind-body," "heredity-environment," etc.

2. Later it occurred to me that the teacher's method of adding fractions might be proper in certain contexts. Suppose in one department of some enterprise 20 of 50 employees, that is 2/5 are women and in another 50 out of 70, that is 5/7. What fraction of employees are women in the two departments combined? Answer: 7/12, that is 70 out of 120. In this case it is, apparently legitimate to write "2/5 + 5/7 = (2+5)/(5+7) = 7/12." If this was the context in which the teacher taught the children to "add fractions," the reference to the "directive" is even more disturbing.

3. The suffix "shchina" has a pejorative connotation in Russian. It usually means "a badism."

4. Ironic reference to the October Revolution in Russia.

5. T.C. Schelling, *The Strategy of Conflict*. Cambridge, MA: Harvard University Press, 1960, p.6

6. Volume 21 (1965), pp. 25-30. My reply was published in the same issue.

7. *On Thermonuclear War*. Princeton: Princeton, University Press, 1960, p.25.

8. Hitch, C.J. and McKean, R.N *The Criterion Problem. In American National Security.* M. Berkowitz and P.G. Bock, eds. New York: The Free Press (1965).

9. Kahn, H. *On Escalation. Metaphors and Scenarios*, New York: Frederick A. Praeger (1965).

Toronto

10

I often interpret my leaving the United States as escape from responsibility. But I don't really have guilt feelings on that account. The responsibility I left was that of participating in concrete party political action. My incompetence in that area as well as pronounced lack of inclination provided a basis for rationalization.

There was no dearth of serious problems in Canada in 1970: virulent violence-prone separatism, political murder, martial law. I confess being comforted by my status of foreigner.

I applied for landed immigrant status and waited for three years to get it. On one occasion Gwen inquired about the delay and was told that information was awaited from the Soviet Union about my early life. This was absurd, and Gwen told them so. Aside from the fact that I left when the Soviet Union did not exist (it was founded a year later) survival of records during the years of civil war and during the total destruction of World War II was out of the question. We continued to wait.

The reason for the delay became apparent when an RCMP man visited me at the office in 1973. He asked me whether I visited the Soviet Union in 1971. I said I did.

"And I understand you had some sort of contact with the KGB on that occasion?"

"I did."

"And did they give you an assignment?"

"You mean involving espionage? They did not. And if they had, I would have declined it."

"Then what was the nature of the contact?"

I told him. I visited my cousin whom I had last seen fifty years before when he was nine and I was ten. In 1934 he made a remark to the effect that the cause of socialism was delayed for a century by the forcible collectivization of the peasants. For that he was exiled to Central Asia for three years.

He was not imprisoned and could find work; so life was bearable. When the three years were up, he was called in by the "security organs." He expected to be discharged. Instead he was sent to a labour camp in the Arctic for a ten year term. He did not return to Crimea, where his mother and sister lived, until 1970.

When my cousin met me at the Simferopol airport, he told me I was to stay with him. This surprised me, since I knew that close contacts with foreigners were strongly discouraged and sometimes severely punished.

"That's quite all right," my cousin assured me. "The 'organs' know all about it. I have permission to have 'intense contact' with you."

We talked all night, telling each other the stories of our lives. When he accompanied me to the airport, he gave me a slip of paper with a telephone number on it and told me to call that number when I was in Moscow and ask for Vassily Ivanovich.

I was astonished. What was my cousin involved in? In what was he trying to involve me?

"That's quite all right," he assured me again. "Just do as I tell you."

However I was worried. Suppose, I thought, I called the number and called Vassily Ivanovich (name and patronymic only, no last name), and they said "Vassily Ivanovich who?"

Nevertheless I did call and asked for Vassily Ivanovich.

"Speaking," said the man.

"I was told to call you. What is this about?"

"Ah, yes, Professor Rapoport. I wonder if you could spare me some time. I would like to talk to you about game theory."

I invited him to the hotel. Gwen and the children went sight seeing, and I took him to breakfast. Back in the room I asked him what he wanted to ask me about game theory.

"Actually I wanted to talk about something else," said Vassily Ivanovich. "I wanted to ask you why they insist in America that Jews are persecuted in the Soviet Union. You must know that this isn't true. Your cousin, Vladimir Yakovlevich is Jewish. Does he feel that he is persecuted?"

I thought of my cousin and the twenty-two years he spent in the Arctic.

"No, he wasn't persecuted because he was Jewish," I said. I wanted to add that he was persecuted for speaking his mind but checked myself in time. I imagined he might be invited by the "organs" to explain why he used the permission to have "intense contact" with a foreigner to slander the Soviet Union.

"Antisemitism appears in various forms," I said. "For instance in Poland Jews are persuaded or, in some cases, forced to leave the country, simply because they are Jews. You don't have this form of antisemitism. On the contrary, you make it very difficult for Jews to emigrate. And they feel that it is a form of discrimination. Or take another comparison. In Poland, admittedly a country where antisemitism is endemic, a monument was erected on the site of the razed ghetto to the victims of the Holocaust with an inscription in Polish and Yiddish. Your poet Yevtushenko, much esteemed abroad, wrote a poem about Babiy Yar, which begins with, "There's no monument in Babiy Yar..."

"There will be," said Vassily Ivanovich quickly.

"And what will the inscription on the monument say?"

"To the victims of fascism."

"That's what I heard," I said, "when I was in Kiev. I was shown the site of the massacre and was told that was where they shot the prisoner of war soccer team, when they refused to throw the game to the guards, who challenged them."

The conversation went on along these lines. I tried to steer it away from the question whether there was antisemitism in the Soviet Union (thinking of my cousin and his possible vulnerability in spite of his "rehabilitation"). I concentrated instead on explaining why people got the impression that there was.

I reported the extent of my "contact with the KGB" to the RCMP man, and he seemed satisfied. Shortly after that we were given landed immigrant status.

Rationalist and Systemic Views of Behaviour

Until my official (mandatory) retirement in 1976, I lived the quiet life of a university professor. I had a cross appointment in the departments of psychology and mathematics. I taught courses in control theory, decision theory, inferential statistics, mathematical psychology, and social psychology. I gave papers at conferences. I looked forward to the three week Christmas break and the Reading Week in February and to the long free summer. I no longer felt the compulsion to participate in "practical" politics. The rationalization provided by the status of foreigner worked. However, preoccupation with what I regarded as the central global problem, namely, the confrontation of the superpowers, remained.

I wrote four books during those six years: one on the confrontation (*The Big Two*), one on a systemic approach to large scale conflict (*Conflict in Man-Made Environment*), one with two colleagues from Michigan on the 78 species of the simplest conceivable game (*The 2 x 2 Game*), and *Semantics*.

The Big Two: Soviet-American Perceptions of Foreign Policy was written at the invitation of Pegasus Press. It was to be the first volume of a series entitled American Involvement in the World. I don't know whether the series was ever continued. I think not, because I believe Pegasus went out of business shortly afterward. In this book three conceptions of international relations are compared: the "realist," the "ideological," and the "systemic." In the realist view states are viewed as more or less rational beings acting to advance their "interests" along which the preservation of own power and limitation of the power of other states dominate. From this point of view it is natural to ascribe to states motivations ordinarily considered to underlie actions of individuals. For instance it is commonplace to read in textbooks on political science, "Germany felt threatened by..." or "France could not allow..." or "Russia's aim was to..." It is natural to interpret these statements as descriptions of fears, desires, or intents of individuals, who determined the foreign policies of states. But underlying this interpretation is an assumption that individuals can determine policies of states and that they can translate these policies into goal-directed actions of states—an assumption that is not regarded as a reasonable one in other conceptions of international relations.

The ideological conception does not ascribe rationality either to states or their leaders. An ideology is a framework of thought within which events are interpreted. Some ideologies severely limit the range of concepts in terms of which events can be interpreted. For this reason ideological interpretations of foreign policies are less voluntaristic than "realist" interpretations. Acts of states are assumed to be driven by compulsions rather than by rational calculations of "national interest."

The systemic approach is the least voluntaristic. In it states do not appear as "actors." Instead, large scale political events appear as consequences of the behaviour of a system, determined by its own inner dynamics. Considerations of national interest or ideological justifications of politics appear as rationalizations of what is happening actually independently of intents, goals, or aspirations of political leaders.

In *The Big Two* I strongly emphasized the systemic interpretation, which was further developed in the next book *Conflict in Man-made Environment*.

In *Semantics*, originally intended as a textbook in what I hoped would be an introductory course on the psychology of human cognition, I stated what I thought was the most valuable in Korzybski's general semantics, and in Hayakawa's subsequent exposition of these ideas in a language the average college student could understand. The four parts are entitled, "Man and His Language," "From Symbol to Meaning" (semantics proper), "From Meaning to Knowledge" (the role of language in cognition), and "From Knowledge to Responsibility," (the relation between science and values, the theme of my first book, *Science and the Goals of Man*).

The 2 x 2 Game explores the structures of the simplest possible situations in which two actors make decisions, whose outcomes depend on the way these decisions interact. From the point of view of "classical" game theory (based on prescriptions dictated by individual rationality) a single concept—that of equilibrium—serves as a basis for a unified theory. This approach amounts to the exclusion of psychology from decision analysis. In *The 2 x 2 Game* the principal concern is with the psychological pressures generated by the decision situation involving interests which may be coincident, diametrically opposed, or only partially opposed, against a background of images the actors have of themselves and of each other. The bulk of my research in Toronto was in this field and comprises what I regard as my principal contribution to it.

Spin-offs of Prisoner's Dilemma

The central idea underlying all my work in the field of decision theory is embodied in the concept of the "social trap"—a situation in which each of two or more participants acts "rationally" in pursuit of own interest but nevertheless the outcome is bad for every one concerned. Arms races, runs on banks and other varieties of panics are well known examples. The Prisoner's Dilemma game is the best known formal model of a social trap. It has inspired hundreds of experiments purporting to determine conditions that facilitate or inhibit escape from this social trap, i.e., make it easier or harder for players to recognize that they can best serve their individual interests by cooperatively pursuing their collective interest.

The experimental format best suited for this purpose is the iterated game. A pair of subjects play many times in succession, and are informed of the outcome of each play. They thus have an opportunity to learn that even though it is always advantageous to "defect" (not cooperate) on any particular play, in the long run cooperation pays, since defection is most likely to be retaliated, resulting in a loss for both. Indeed in long iterations of the game "lock-ins" on the cooperative choice are frequently observed. Each player refrains from defecting to avoid retaliatory defection by the other. Once the subjects have "learned" to cooperate a sort of deterrence effect keeps them cooperating.

Nevertheless "rational analysis" of the situation prescribes unconditional defection to both players if the number of times they are to play is known to both. Deterrence is not effective on the last play, since no retaliation can follow D (the uncooperative choice). We can therefore conclude that a pair of "rational" players will choose D on the last play, since D is better than C (the cooperative choice) regardless of the other's choice. Thus, the outcome of the last play is a foregone conclusion, and the next-to-last play becomes effectively the last play to be examined. The same reasoning now applies to it; so that the next-to-last outcome is also bound to be DD (mutual defection). And so on. This "backward induction" leads to the conclusion that ALL D (unconditional choice of D) is the only "rational" strategy in Prisoner's Dilemma played a known number of times. In other words, two individually "rational" players who can think the problem through rigorously to the inescapable conclusion must refrain from cooperation throughout the sequence be it 200, 2,000, or 2,000,000 plays long, each time getting less than they might have got by cooperating.

One consolation left to some one not impressed with this analysis is that real people are not fully competent, fully dedicated strategists. As repeatedly demonstrated in experiments with iterated Prisoner's Dilemma, quite a number of them do learn to cooperate. The question arises what strategies do they use, and which ones are more successful than others, in the sense of bringing in bigger total payoffs in iterated play.

To answer this question, Robert Axelrod of the University of Michigan announced a contest. Participants were invited to submit strategies for playing Prisoner's Dilemma 200 times. The strategies were to be submitted as computer programmes. A pair of programmes would be matched against each other to produce a protocol of 200 plays. The programme that accumulated the largest total payoff (having played against every submitted programme including itself) would be the winner of this round robin contest.

Fifteen programmes were submitted. I submitted TIT FOR TAT. It won the contest. A few years later another similar contest was arranged under the same conditions except that the number of plays was now a random variable, that is, an encounter could be terminated after any play with a certain probability. The average duration of each encounter was 151 plays. This time 63 programmes participated. I again submitted TIT FOR TAT, and it was again the winner.

The results of the contests attracted considerable attention. I was frequently asked how I came to discover the "unbeatable" strategy for playing iterated

Prisoner's Dilemma. I pointed out that far from being "unbeatable," TIT FOR TAT cannot possibly beat any strategy in a paired encounter. In order to get more points in iterated play with another strategy TIT FOR TAT would have to play more D's than the other, for only unilateral defection brings a payoff larger than the opponent's. But TIT FOR TAT cannot play D more frequently than the opponent, since the only time it can play D is after the other has just played D. The question naturally arises why, if TIT FOR TAT cannot beat any strategy in a paired encounter, did it win both round robin contests. The answer is that all the "stronger" strategies, each of which beat TIT FOR TAT, lost points when matched with other "strong" strategies.

So the first lesson to be drawn from these contests is that while in individual encounters the "stronger" programme usually wins, in a field this may not be so, since the strong in fighting the strong may "harm" each other (i.e., reduce each other's score). In fact, an elementary example shows how this can happen. Consider a truel, that is, a duel fought by three persons, whereby each shoots at the other two until there is either a single survivor or no survivors. Suppose one of the three is the best shot, one the second best, and one the worst. In many situations of this sort the worst shot can be expected to have the best chance of survival, since each of the others would rather eliminate the stronger opponent, who presents the greater threat. Moral: at times in weakness there is strength.

The other lesson reveals the connection between some results deduced in the theory of games and mechanisms driving evolutionary processes. Axelrod used the computer programmes submitted in his contests to simulate evolution by natural selection. Programmes were pitted against each other and the accumulated points of a programme were translated into reproductive advantage or disadvantage. Replicas of programmes accumulating more points were added to the population of programmes. Less successful programmes were withdrawn. In this way the population of programmes "evolved." Eventually in five out of six simulations, the population consisted almost exclusively of TIT FOR TAT programmes, showing that in some situations "nice guys finish first."[1]

Axelrod's experiments showed how games based on social traps could be used to simulate evolutionary processes, in particular how to demonstrate the evolution of cooperation in a population of "egotists" as a result of a selection process. In a population of aggressors, bullies, hard competitors on the one hand and non-aggressive, trusting, cooperators on the other, the former will have the advantage. But if this advantage is translated into larger reproductive rates, while the non-aggressors are decimated by exploitation, eventually the aggressors will find few non-aggressors to exploit and will turn on each other. Then they will be the ones who will be reproductively disadvantaged. Perhaps this is what was meant by the prophesy, "The meek shall inherit the earth."

Games representing social traps became a standard tool in computer simulations contributing to theoretical biology. In particular, the concept of "evolutionarily stable strategy," introduced by J. Maynard Smith proved to be especially theoretically fruitful.[2]

Vienna Again

In 1976, having reached the age of 65, I was officially retired from the University of Toronto. However, I was asked to stay on to teach a course in statistics and one in decision theory. I saw the latter as a nexus between hard formal analysis and the sort of enlightenment that makes commitment to certain values imperative.

Through the years 1977, 1978, and 1979 I bestowed on myself the honourary title of migrant worker. I taught or participated in research in Berlin, in Hiroshima, in Louisville, Kentucky and in Vienna. The latter visits were at the Institute for Advanced Studies, founded by Paul Lazarsfeld and Oscar Morgenstern. I mentioned my meeting with Paul Lazarsfeld at CASBAH, where the idea of the Institute was born. Morgenstern was Von Neumann's collaborator in laying the foundations of the theory of games. So the two also represented a nexus between hard analysis and moral commitment. Lazarsfeld's classical study of Marienthal, the Austrian village with 100% of the population unemployed, was a meticulously objective study of those people, undertaken with the obvious objective of arousing social conscience.

The seed money for the Vienna Institute was provided by the Ford Foundation, the same foundation that provided the seed money for the Center of Advanced Study in the Behavioral Sciences in California. The original goal of the Vienna institute was to re-establish graduate studies in the social sciences in Austria, which had been devastated during the war. Morgenstern was primarily interested in advanced studies in economics, for which Vienna had once been famous. Lazarsfeld was interested in introducing empirical sociology, which, aside from his seminal work, was practically unknown in Austria. Following my visit as guest professor there, I was asked to join the Scientific Advisory Board, and invited to become the Director in 1979.

Anya, aged 27 was in Knoxville, Tennessee, studying veterinary medicine. Sasha, aged 22, had been in Vienna since 1975, studying music at the same *Hochschule für Musik* where I had studied fifty years before. Tony (aged 17) was in New York studying at the Julliard School of Music. I had a three year contract at the Institute, automatically renewable (unless three months notice was given by either side) for another three years.

Between Christmas and New Year's, 1979 we were met at the Vienna airport by Herr Johann Auner, the care-taker of the Institute, with whose family we had became friends on my previous visits. We rented the spacious apartment of my predecessor, who had gone to Germany. It was within walking distance of the Institute. After the holidays I made my appearance, was installed in the director's office and was briefed by the outgoing director. I already knew the formal structure of the Institute. There were five departments: economics, sociology, political science, management science, and mathematics. Two year fellowships, including modest stipends were given to graduates of universities or other post-secondary schools. These were called "scholars." Courses in fundamentals were given by "assistants." Most of them aspired to the higher degree of "dozent," which entitled them to teach in a university, the usual step to a professorship. In addition, courses of two weeks to three months duration were given by guest professors invited from all over. The most unusual, one could say utopian feature of the institute was the student-teacher ratio. There were at any time about 50 scholars and about 25 assistants. Not quite as favourable was the ratio of independent to contracted research done by the assistants. Most of the funded research was contracted. The clients included the government and also enterprises of various sort. It was obvious that this work was undertaken not with the view of advancing or deepening knowledge but rather with the view of keeping the Institute going at a level considerably higher than could be subsidized by unencumbered funds.

I did not mind this bread and butter activity. I rather liked the idea of young social scientists doing "practical" work. It was something like having engineers work on an assembly line or doing repair jobs, a sort of an internship. It should not prevent those who loved to work and think from doing "creative" research in addition to the required chores. (I had, however, overestimated the proportion of scholars who were sufficiently dedicated to their chosen professions to work beyond the required hours.)

More disturbing was the information my predecessor gave me about the political situation in Austrian institutions. Every important institution, he told me, had two directors. To be sure, one of them was called "director," and the other "associate director," but actually each was expected to keep a check on the other. I wanted to know in what way. I was told that one of the directors was informally known as the "red" director, the other as the "black" director. The "red" director was an appointee of the Austrian Socialist Party; the "black" director was an appointee of the Austrian People's Party (the conservative one). Which was the "director" and which the "associate" director was determined by which party was in power. Since currently the Socialists were in power, the "red" director was the director, and the "black" director was the associate director. So I was the "red" director, he explained, as he had been. The associate ("black") director was staying on. His contract had just been renewed.

I wanted to know how this arrangement worked in practice. He told me it was reflected in the governance of the Institute. The governing body was a "Kuratorium" of fourteen members—seven red, seven black. The red faction was led by Bruno Kreisky, the Chancellor of Austria. The black faction was led by the president of the Austrian National Bank. He was also the president of the Kuratorium. The body met twice a year in one of our seminar rooms. The president sat at the head of the table. The reds sat on one side, the blacks on the other. Since party discipline was absolute, that is, each faction voted as a block, no matter could be decided except by consensus. Therefore all decisions had to be made prior to the meeting, hammered out by wheeling and dealing. The voting at the meeting was entirely pro forma. (Although members of the Kuratorium were frequently absent, their party colleagues had their proxies.) This was the Austrian way, my predecessor said.

Each party worked out its strategy, presumably for the interim periods, in a caucus meeting. That is, before the meeting, each faction met separately in two seminar rooms. Ordinarily each director would attend the caucus meeting of "his" party. In my case this practice would probably be suspended. The reason, my informant explained, was in the way I got to be invited. His term had expired, and they could not agree on the next red director. Every proposal of the reds was blocked by the blacks. I was a compromise candidate. Every one agreed that my politics was "red" yet I was not beholden to the Austrian Socialist Party, that is, did not owe my career to its patronage and could not be expected to stay in Austria after the expiration of my term. Thus I could afford to be politically independent and did not have to attend caucus meetings. In fact, I probably would not be invited to attend them. (The Austrians, it seems, are fairly consistent in keeping political bargains except when it is distinctly advantageous to break them.)

Part of the compromise, my predecessor went on, was a formal division of authority between the two directors. By and large, I was to be in charge of the academic side of the business and the associate of the administrative side. This suited me fine. In fact, the arrangement seemed ideal.

This was in the first week of January, 1980. The Kuratorium was to meet in a few days. I was shown the agenda. There were the usual items of business: confirmation of invitations to visiting professors, reports on projects ongoing and completed, financial statement (we were in excellent shape), and, what turned out to be the first harbinger of things to come, confirmation of assistants' contract renewals. Assistants had two-year contracts, renewable virtually automatically twice. Five or six contracts had expired. I was to propose renewals of all of them except one. The assistant whose contract was not to be renewed was the daughter of a late prominent Communist politician. The Socialists thought highly of her, because she worked on projects which in our day would be called "politically correct." One was entitled "Sources of Social Inequality in Austria." It was funded by a ministry, and its findings could be used by the Socialists as political ammunition. The People's Party establishment was intent on getting rid of her. Somehow they succeeded in getting the Socialists to sacrifice her, possibly in return for some quid pro quo. And possibly (I can only guess) the Socialists saw an opportunity of using the inauguration of a new director to reverse the decision. At any rate, I received a telephone call on the day of the Kuratorium meeting from a Socialist member, who asked me whether a proposal to renew the assistant's contract would be made at the meeting. I replied that all the proposals to be made at the meeting had been decided upon before I came, and being new I did not feel qualified to make last minute changes. A lengthy conversation followed in the course of which the Kuratorium member filled me in on the background of the affair and put me under considerable pressure. The upshot of the matter was that I promised to recommend the sociologist's re-appointment.

I told the associate director of my intention, and he took it pretty hard. He warned me against yielding to political pressures. I explained that I had other reasons for recommending extension of all contracts that came up for renewal. The action would be something like a general amnesty announced by a new ruler, a morale raising action that would in the long run "pay for itself." He remained disappointed. And so were the Kuratorium members who sat on the left side of the table from where I sat, that is (properly) on the right side from where the president sat at the opposite end. The members on his left looked pleased.

During my four years at the Institute I alternately alienated the one or the other faction of the Kuratorium, which accounts for the curtailment of my intended stay by two years. Friction arose mostly on matters of recommended appointments. I was to recommend assistants and senior assistants who were to be heads of departments. The Kuratorium was to approve the appointments. I was guided by my opinions about the qualifications of the candidates and, in the case of senior assistants by their leadership potential (as I assessed it). When the senior assistant of the economics department left to work for the Organization for Economic Cooperation and Development (OECD), a successor could not be found immediately. The associate director suggested that a "red" be appointed for six months, then a "black" for six months. By then a successor from the outside would be found. This was done. But when the associate director suggested that the "black" be kept on as the senior assistant, I demurred. Instead we got a "red" from the Technical University. This got me in bad with the "blacks." Later I recommended the appointment of a "black" as senior assistant of the mathematics department, whom I regarded as qualified. This got me in bad with the "reds."

I could have left a year earlier if I had responded properly to the admonition administered to me by the president of the Kuratorium. The associate director and I were summoned to the president's office presumably to hammer out the differences between us. Instead the president read the riot act to me.

"Professor Rapoport," he said, "The Institute for Advanced Studies was established by the two leading political parties of Austria. Your job is to see to the interests of the Socialist Party. The present associate director's job is to see to the interests of the Austrian People's Party. We shall get along better if you keep this in mind."

"Mr. President," I should have replied. "Had I been told of this when I was invited to be the director of the Institute, I would surely have declined the invitation. Consider this a formal notice that I am resigning my position as of December 31. You will get a written confirmation by mail. My compliments." ("*Habe die Ehre*," I would have said, as a Viennese does.)

This is what the French call *pensés d'escalier*—staircase thoughts, what one wishes to have said as one goes downstairs after a dramatic encounter.

The final break came a year later exactly four years after I came. On December 22, 1983 we had a farewell dinner, to which we invited the care taker of the Institute (now retired) and his family. I was deeply touched by the surprise he had prepared for me. He had found in the archives of the Musikverein Society programmes of two performance of mine in Vienna. One was my debut recital on March 9, 1933. The other was a performance with orchestra of three piano concerti, Rachmaninoff's Third, Stravinsky's Concerto for Piano and Winds, and

Tchaikovsky's B Flat Minor, on December 22, 1933, exactly fifty years before the farewell dinner. He had the programmes photographed and framed and presented them to us.

This gesture may have been a stimulus for resuming musical activity, which had been barely glimmering during my forty odd years in academe. I had occasional minor engagements mostly at universities. I had given a "farewell recital" when I was leaving the University of Michigan, at which my elder son, then thirteen made his debut as a composer with a D minor piano sonata. I had given another in Toronto when I was leaving for Europe, uncertain whether I would return. After returning I played a recital arranged jointly by the Department of Psychology and University College and thereafter every spring jointly with my younger son, a violist, usually including a composition by my elder son.

The Peace and Conflict Studies Programme

During our four-year stay in Vienna we spent summers in Toronto. (I was still teaching a summer course in social psychology.) In 1982 I met with some colleagues of mine in the mathematics and physics departments, who told me of a newly formed organization, Science for Peace, devoted to encouraging applications of science to the promotion of peace and discouraging applications to the service of the military establishment and their industrial, scientific, and educational adjuncts. The organization was working toward establishing a chair of peace science at the University of Toronto. I expressed interest in joining the organization but was not free to do so until the end of my appointment in Vienna. The end came sooner than I expected. We returned to Toronto at the end of 1983. I joined Science for Peace and was elected president.

An endowed Chair at the University of Toronto required a fund of about 1.5 million dollars. Immediate prospects for raising so much money were poor. If, however, the objective was to establish a permanent centre of peace education, there was another way. In addition to conventional studies focused on particular disciplines represented by university departments, a number of interdisciplinary studies offered in the colleges focused on some problem areas, for example, environmental studies, women's studies, studies of aging, etc. Programmes of this sort required comparatively modest funding. Most of the courses comprising them were already given at the university. Whatever funding was needed was for whatever additional courses were to be added. I proposed to Science for Peace to work for the establishment of a Peace and Conflict Studies Programme to be offered by University College. I would teach two courses in the programme, an introductory course on the origins of conflict and violence (psychological, ideological, strategic, and systemic), and a course on decision theory which would include the findings obtained in experiments simulating conflict situations, particularly social traps.

The establishment of the programme required the approval of the departments in which courses were given that students in the programme were required to take. With some exceptions the approval was freely given and after traversing the administrative channels, the programme was in place after two years. It is a four-year undergraduate programme leading to a Bachelor of Arts degree. It attracts young people who hope to make conflict resolution or peace-making their profession. They get a background in areas of psychology, sociology, economics, political science, and philosophy that are directly relevant to the study of peace and war, conflict and conflict resolution. Perhaps my children or theirs will live to see the day when peace professions attain a status comparable to that of the war professions in our time.

Funding was finally obtained for a professorship in the area. My successor took office in 1996. I could therefore look forward seriously to my next retirement.

NOTES

1. Axelrod showed that all the programmes that did best in his contests were (1) "nice," that is, never the first to defect; (2) retaliatory, that is, always responded with defection to the co-player's defection; (3) forgiving, that is, "forgave" previous defections by resuming cooperation as soon as the co-player did; and (4) simple.
2. Cf. J. Maynard Smith, *Evolution of Cooperation and the Theory of Games*. Cambridge, Mass: Cambridge University Press, 1982.

I Believe That...I Believe In

11

Some forty years ago, if I remember correctly, a large circulation magazine ran a series entitled "What I believe." Persons prominent in public life were invited to contribute. I have often thought what I would have written if I had been invited.

Rereading what I actually wrote since then, I find that my beliefs have remained fairly constant. Experience, however, has accumulated, and I think I understand better why I believe what I believe. Explaining these beliefs to whoever reads this and to myself is a way of taking stock, my reason for writing this book.

As I said at the outset, "believing" is used in at least two senses. We may believe that something is or is not the case; or we may believe that something ought or ought not to be the case. To "believe in" is often used in both senses. Thus, we may believe or not believe in ghosts (namely, that they exist or do not exist); or we may believe or not believe in capital punishment in the sense of approving or disapproving of it.

The ambiguity was pointed out by Mark Twain when some one asked him whether he believed in baptism by immersion.

"Why of course I believe in it," he is said to have replied. "I've seen it!"

The quip ridicules the confusion between "believing that…" and "believing in…," but it misses an important aspect of belief: the two meanings cannot always be separated.

To see this, consider another famous quip of Mark Twain's.

"If you called a dog's tail a leg, how many legs would a dog have?"

Mark Twain's retort to the answer "Five" was "Wrong. He would still have four legs no matter what you called the tail."

But would he? I recall my first piano lesson. Anna Andreyevna told me not to let my thumb hang below the keyboard; that it belongs on the keyboard together with the other fingers. How many fingers does a person have? The pianist says five. The violinist says four. The pianist refers to his thumb as the first finger; the violinist to his index finger. Further, it is not wrong for an English speaker to say that a person has four fingers and a thumb. There is no special name for the thumb in Russian.

Beliefs that the name of a thing somehow reflects its "essence" have been sources of delusions throughout the history of human thought.

> Lord God formed every beast of the field and every fowl of the air and brought them unto Adam...and whatever Adam called every living creature, that was the name thereof. (Genesis, 2:19.)

One way of interpreting this story is that from then on animals were called by the names that Adam gave them. Another is that Adam *guessed the true names* of the animals, evidence of man's inherent perspicacity. The first interpretation is based on the recognition that words reflect existing *agreements* about how to refer to things, that is, a realization of what is; the second reflects a conviction that there are right ways and wrong ways of referring to things, that is a feeling about what ought to be.

A Hindu scholar, Swami Harihanarand Saravasti wrote:

> The things *named* and their *names* are both parallel manifestations resulting from the unison of Brahman (the undifferentiated principle) and the Maya (appearances)...But between the two aspects of manifestation the relation remains close, there is a fundamental identity between...words and objects.

We need not go to India or search among the archives to encounter such views. The following was written in the U.S. in 1948.

> I should urge examining in all seriousness that ancient belief that a divine element is present in language. The feeling that to have power of language is to have control over things is deeply imbedded in the human mind. We see this in the way men gifted in speech are feared or admired; we see it in the potency ascribed to incantations, interdictions and curses...knowledge of the prime reality comes to man through the word; the word is a sort of deliverance from the shifting world of appearances. The central teaching of the New Testament is that those who accept the word acquire wisdom and at the same time some identification with the eternal.[1]

Korzybski's constantly repeated slogan, "The word is not the thing" was directed squarely against this conception of reality.

Hayakawa, applying the same principle to the teaching of English, emphasized distinctions between reports, inferences, and judgments. Reports are accounts of direct observation. Inferences are interpretations of observations. Judgments are expressions of attitudes. "The boss threw the telephone directory at his secretary" is a report. "The boss was angry" is an inference. "The boss is a brute" is a judgment.

The power of language to shape our cognition, Hayakawa pointed out, stems from the fact that syntax often fails to distinguish between reports, inferences, and judgments. "All men are created equal," being in the indicative (declarative) mode, sounds like a statement of fact. As such it can be easily shown to be false in many respects. But the point of departure of the American Declaration of Independence should not be understood as a statement of fact. Rather it should be interpreted as an expression of an attitude. Its "true" meaning is "All men should be treated as if they were created equal." Similarly when Anna Andreyevna told me that the thumb was a finger like the others, she was telling me to treat the thumb like the other fingers. Whether it "really" is or is not a finger is a nonsense question. So is the question of whether the dog's tail "really" is or is not a leg. To say that it is not is to call attention to differences between the tail and the other appendages; to say that it is to ignore them.

Awareness of these different functions of language, namely, the descriptive (calling attention to what is) and the normative (calling attention to what we ought to be aware of) seems at first thought to point to a fundamental distinction between "scientific" and "value-oriented" modes of cognition and to support the contention that the language of science ought to be descriptive, i.e., "value free." One of the principal tenets of my belief system is that the separation of scientific cognition and value orientation is neither possible nor desirable.

Degrees of Belief and Disbelief
In important matters my beliefs in what is true are based on what has been established in the course of scientific investigations or their analogues (to the extent that I am informed). The "strength" of these beliefs is determined by the strength of the evidence supporting the findings. Here there is plenty room for doubt. In the face of strong evidence to the contrary a belief may be discarded. A subjective element enters per force in the formation or discarding of beliefs. This is readily seen when statistical evidence evaluated against a background of prior beliefs.

In the behavioral sciences a standard method of evaluating the weight to be attached to experimental evidence is by way of assigning a *level of significance* to the findings. Suppose, for example, we wish to find out whether a larger proportion of men (or of women) put sugar in their coffee. To get some idea we may station ourselves somewhere in a cafeteria where we can observe men and women taking coffee and record proportions of each population taking sugar. We may observe a difference between the proportions. But the difference does not yet establish a finding in which we can have confidence. It may reflect merely a chance fluctuation in the observed samples of male and female populations. We can, however, establish a degree of confidence in the result by estimating the probability that the observed difference was only a reflection of chance fluctuations. This probability determines a level of significance of the result. The smaller this probability, the higher the level of significance.

How low this probability should be to justify our belief that the observed difference reflects a "real" difference, rather than a statistical fluctuation in our samples, is a matter of choice. The stronger is our prior belief that there is no difference to speak of, the lower the probability should be that the difference was due to chance to make us change our mind. How strongly we hold to our *prior belief* may depend on how strongly we want to hold on to it. In the case of men's and women's preferences in this case I couldn't care less. So I probably would cheerfully accept 0.05, the conventional "level of significance" of the difference in either direction (a chance of one in twenty that the difference in the observations was due to chance). In certain beliefs, however, I have a vested interest. This means that I will demand very strong evidence to abandon my belief or (as in the example I am about to give) my disbelief.

I do not believe in extrasensory perception (ESP). I think I would change my mind if enough evidence were offered for its existence. How much is enough? Suppose I were invited to observe results of experiments, purporting to demonstrate telepathy. In a standard experiment of this sort a deck of cards is used consisting of five different patterns. The experimenter looks at each card and "tries" to transmit the pattern he sees to the subject. The subject tries to guess the pattern. In a large number of trials the subject is expected to guess correctly merely by chance about 20% of the time. A significant excess of cards guessed can be attributed to something other than chance, perhaps to some sort of transmission (the nature of which need not be specified) from the sensory apparatus of the experimenter to that of the subject.

This format is a standard one in experimental psychology. Here a well formulated hypothesis is being tested, namely that the subject will make more correct guesses than can be "reasonably" attributed to chance. Note, however, that a low probability of the observed result (that the subject guessed more than the number of cards expected by chance) will not amount to a "proof" that telepathy exists, only to a more or less strong corroboration of the hypothesis that it does. But how low should this probability be? I set my own level of significance for the result of the experiment to change my mind about telepathy. In the case of deciding whether men take sugar more frequently than women (or vice versa) I was willing to settle for a 0.05 level of significance. In the case of the telepathy experiment I will demand a much greater significance of better than chance guessing to make me give up my disbelief.

The choice of prior beliefs can be based on prior experience or prior generalizations of experience or on preconceived notions or, not infrequently, on prejudice. I have heard or read about many instances where charlatans exploit people's gullibility for profit. Belief in so called extrasensory perception or other "psychic" or supernatural phenomena offers a fertile field for fraudulent activities of this sort. So setting a very high significance level for experiments in telepathy and other alleged extrasensory phenomena I am really comparing probabilities that I assign (subjectively) to different "causes" of what has been observed, namely (1) a real effect, (2) a trick designed to deceive me, (3) chance. I choose the explanation that I deem most probable:—either (2), or if evidence of fraud is lacking, (3)—a personal choice.

The same principle guides my interpretation of events. The amazing list of coincidences related to the assassination of President Kennedy is a case in point. Consider the following "parallels."

- Lincoln was elected in 1860; Kennedy in 1960 one hundred years later.
- Lincoln was succeeded by Johnson, a southern Democrat. Kennedy was succeeded by Johnson, a southern Democrat.
- The first Johnson was born in 1808; the second in 1908, one hundred years later.

- Lincoln's presumed assassin, John Wilkes Booth was born in 1839; Lee Harvey Oswald was born in 1939, one hundred years later.
- Neither presumed assassin ever came to trial; both were shot.
- Both Lincoln and Kennedy were shot in the back of the head in the presence of their wives.
- Lincoln was shot in a theatre and Booth was found hiding in a warehouse. Kennedy was killed by a shot from a warehouse and Oswald was found hiding in a theatre.
- Lincoln was shot was in the Ford Theatre. Kennedy was shot while riding in a Lincoln, a car made by the Ford Motor Company.
- The first name of Lincoln's private secretary was John, which was Kennedy's first name.
- The last name of Kennedy's private secretary was Lincoln.
- Lincoln's and Kennedy's last names both have seven letters. The two Johnsons' first names both have six letters. Booth's and Oswald's full names both have fifteen letters.

I dismiss all of these "parallels" as coincidences. But I do not dismiss the "mysterious deaths" of several witnesses involved in that assassination as an artifice or coincidence. *Executive Action*, a movie about the assassination used the following as a promotional hype:

In the three year period which followed the murder of President Kennedy and Lee Harvey Oswald, eighteen material witnesses died—six by gunfire, three in motor accidents, two by suicide, one from a cut throat, one from a karate chop, three from heart attacks, and two from natural causes.

An actuary engaged by the *London Sunday Times* concluded that on November 22, 1963, the odds against these witnesses being dead by February, 1967 were one hundred thousand trillion to one.[2]

These coincidences I regard as strong evidence of a conspiracy. Clearly I have a vested interest in dismissing the first set of coincidences and taking seriously the second set. I cling to my belief in the ruthlessness of participants in power struggles and their frequent resort to murder, and I cling to my disbelief in mystical determinants of prominent events. I realized the strength of the latter disbelief when I came across another Lincoln-Kennedy "parallel." It seems that the first public suggestion to nominate Abraham Lincoln for president in the election of 1860 was made in 1858 by one Israel Green of Findlay Ohio. The suggestion was published in the *Cincinnati Gazette* on November 6 of that year. Suggested for vice-presidential candidacy was former secretary of the navy under President Millard Fillmore. His name was John Kennedy![3] My dismissal of the whole business as a string of coincidences became mildly disturbing. Was it a symptom of a closed mind impervious to evidence contradicting a priori beliefs? In this case, perhaps.

Superstitions

I regard some superstitions not merely as instances of cognitive immaturity but as symptoms of extreme egocentrism. What disturbs me most is not the egocentrism itself but the exploitation of it. My friends sometimes chide me for ranting against the daily astrology column in newspapers. What harm, they ask, is there is taking this nonsense seriously? That depends on what is meant by harm. Note the limits of the setting in which matters discussed in the astrology column are confined. They comprise: money management, career advancement, romance, family tensions and nothing else. It may well be that these matters exhaust all the concerns of the "average reader" (although this, of course, is open to question). What I find particularly repugnant is the reinforcement of the notion that these matters are of central concern to whoever is running the universe (a form of blasphemy).

I subsume many forms of so called "conventional wisdom" under superstitions, in the sense that evidence in support of certain widespread beliefs is either non-existent or misleading. As an example, consider the widespread view that a country's security is positively related to its war potential. Evidence for this view is usually suggested by citing instances of wars in which one country was defeated by another, supposedly because it was militarily weaker. But if victory in war is assumed to be evidence of military superiority, we surely have an instance of circular reasoning: a country was defeated; consequently it must have been militarily weaker. On the other hand, if one uses a priori measures of military potential, as military professionals are wont to do, it is a moot question whether military potential established in this way will be found to be correlated in a statistical sense with victory in war. Examples can be cited, of course, but a "for instance" is not a proof. Selected corroborating cases can be used to prove anything.

Next consider the conventional wisdom embodied in the belief in so called "deterrence." Consider World War III, a war that may well have been averted but was surely expected until a few years ago. It was widely believed (and is still believed by many) that colossal expenditures of material and human resources were necessary to prevent that war or, failing that, to win it. Ambiguity of victory, which has steadily grown through the twentieth century, is evident. For efficacy of deterrence there is no evidence. The non-occurrence of World War III can be attributed to anything at all with equal justification or with no justification at all. The efficacy of the sun dance in making the sun rise can be tested by omitting it sufficiently many times. I submit that such a test would refute the hypothesis. However, this method of testing the efficacy of the rain dance cannot be applied to testing the efficacy of deterrence of a nuclear war, because by the nature of such a war, it cannot occur with a frequency that would provide opportunity for repeated tests.

In spite of the total lack of evidence, at least in our time, for testing the belief that the security of a country depends on its military potential, or in the efficacy of deterrence, the beliefs persist. They can, therefore, be regarded as superstitions.

Another pervasive instance of conventional wisdom, especially in America, is the belief that a war economy nurtures economic robustness and hence prosperity. This superstition is certainly at variance with common sense. If prosperity means anything at all, it must surely be related to the availability of consumer goods and services. When resources are diverted to production of things that are said to perform their function best if they are not used, such as weapons of total destruction, and to services needed to keep producing these things, the resulting economy cannot possibly contribute to prosperity. If it is argued that part of general well being (and therefore prosperity) is a feeling of "security" supposedly induced by military technology, this reduces the belief in one superstition to the belief in another.

To be sure, the belief that a war economy generates prosperity can be related to observations. As a matter of fact, however, most superstitions can be related to observations. What puts them in question is the fact that *generalizations* based on such observations are not justified. In the United States a connection between war economy and prosperity was established in the minds of most people by what happened some forty odd years ago. The preceding decade was characterized by an economic disaster. In the richest country in the world in which even the poor were rich by world standards, quite suddenly most people became really poor. On the face of it, this sudden impoverishment was bewildering. It seemed that all the means for producing the necessities of life and many luxuries were in place. So was the work force. Why were machines and people idle? It seemed that something was lacking that in "normal" times brought the work force and the technology together. What was that something? The machines were owned by corporations. To be motivated to keep the machines running, the managers had to expect a profit. They could expect a profit only if sufficient quantities of what was produced were sold. But to buy these products people had to have money. People out of work did not have money. They could not be expected to buy the goods. The managers of corporations could not expect to make profits. So factories closed. People remained out of work and without money. The goods produced could not be sold. And so on. And so on.

It was believed that if something could be found to "kick-start" the economy, perhaps it would function again. Say the factories were activated regardless of expectation of profit. People would have to be hired to work in the factories. They would be paid. Then they could buy what was produced, and the production would go on. Throughout the 1930's attempts were made to get the process going without much success. But when war broke out in Europe and the prospect that the U.S. might be drawn in became real, large scale production could be started of things that did not have to be bought by consumers, namely, war equipment. Moreover, existing plants had to be expanded and modified to produce those things. So people were hired in droves. Unemployment vanished. People had money to spend, and they were eager to spend it. As a matter of fact, demand began to exceed supply. When the country went to war, even rationing was introduced. Paradoxically scarcities produced prosperity, just as previously abundance produced poverty.

Enlightenment

I identify the so called "Enlightenment," as the spirit of eighteenth century Europe was called, with dispelling of superstitions, and with the consequent re-definition of human values. This brings me to discussing my own beliefs in the sense of what I approve of and what I hope for.

I believe in enlightenment both in the sense of approving of it and in the sense of hoping that it will come about. Frankly speaking, I cherish the old fashioned and widely discredited belief in "progress." However, the concept of "progress," just as that of "belief" needs to be carefully examined.

I distinguish between belief in the sense of faith and belief in the sense of hope. I don't have much *faith* in a "better future" for humanity in the sense of betting on it if I were an outside observer. However, I don't see myself as an outside observer, trying to guess the future of humanity. I am an interested party; so I shrink from making a sober assessment of chances. What interests me is what can be done to improve the chances that our children will live in a better world and who can be expected to do it. That is, I cling to *hope* that conditions for it can be brought about.

To begin with, I must define "progress" in the sense in which I will be using the term. The common conception of progress has been that which characterized the spirit of Western Europe throughout the nineteenth century. It was closely linked with the growth and spread of technology. In my childhood and youth I, too, thought of progress in this way. As a child I was fascinated by the romances of Jules Verne; as a youth by those of H.G. Wells. To be sure, more of H.G. Wells' science fiction was devoted to anti-utopias than to utopias, but a faith in the ultimate victory of human progress over degradation was still dominant.

Today people who care about the future of humanity are bitterly disappointed in megatechnology for obvious reasons. First and foremost, the fantastically accelerated technological progress was diverted and continues to be diverted to serve the global war machine. And even the so called "peaceful" uses of megatechnology are seen as ultimately destructive—in the first instance through degradation of the environment and also by facilitating the concentration of power in the hands of those who control its further development and applications.

Distrust of technology spills over into distrust of science. I believe that the proliferation of cults that celebrate mysticism, assorted "psychic phenomena," and the like are symptomatic of hostility to science.

However, technology was only a by-product of progress in science, a sort of side effect that has shown both a positive and a negative side. The positive by-product of scientific progress was an improvement in the mode of cognition (aside from the mode of production), which induced distinctions between reliable knowledge and misleading beliefs. It is true that technology spawned its own superstitions, but like all superstitions these can be dispelled by further enlightenment. It was enlightenment in the first place that opened the road to technology by dismantling the hand-me-down images of what the physical world was like. And it was enlightenment that revealed the potential dangers in unbridled development of technology. And if anything can alleviate these dangers, it is further technology coupled with further enlightenment.

The one area of human activity in which progress in the sense of enlightenment, growing complexity, and unidirectional development cannot be denied is science. Ambivalence arises in evaluating this progress. Is it good or bad? At the foundation of my beliefs is the conviction that the enlightening effects of progress in science are good and that all other effects must be judged in relation to this aspect. While I am convinced that progressive enlightenment is a necessary condition for a better future (in fact, it enters my definition of a better future), I am not sure whether it is a sufficient condition. To cope with this question I must spell out more concretely what I mean by a "better future."

Good and Evil

Just as it is easier to define disease than good health (except as absence of disease, which is side-stepping the problem), so it is easier to define evil than good.

The cardinal evil, as I conceive it, is treating human beings as if they were objects, as one treats, say, tools, that is, means to an end. This conception of human beings is reflected in military terminology. In the czarist army, the strength of an infantry unit was expressed not in terms of the number of men, but in terms of the number of bayonets. The strength of a cavalry unit was expressed in terms of the number of sabres. This way of counting people spilled over into the language of industry. People working in factories were traditionally counted as "hands," just as cattle are counted as "heads."

Clearly, using people as means to an end amounts to having power over them. Thus, aspiration to power over people appears to me as the ultimate source of evil.

Aspirations are fueled by needs, innate or acquired. Needs can be non-addictive or addictive. Non-addictive needs occur in cycles. Normally, the need for food, sleep, or sex disappears on being satisfied, then grows until it is again satisfied. The peak intensity remains about the same. In contrast, the intensity of an addictive need keeps increasing with each satisfaction, as is the case with addictive drugs.

Not all addictive needs are destructive. For example, curiosity and refinement of aesthetic sense can be addictive, but in general they enrich life rather than impair it, as other addictions do.

Aspiration to power over people is an addictive need. We see it manifested in potentates who achieve power by violence, i.e., by destroying their enemies, real or imagined. Each purge or blood bath is likely to make more enemies, so that the repressions go on and on. We have seen dramatic demonstrations of this phenomenon in the twentieth century.

Arms races are manifestations of addiction. Arsenals are accumulated as a way of increasing potential power over an adversary. Since, however, the adversary is driven by the same motivation, the need spirals into addiction.

It appears to me, therefore, that "progress" depends on preventing concentration of power. In fact, the essence of any conception of democracy is prevention of concentration of political power. However, formal decentralization of political power, as in constitutionally defined democracies does not preclude using people as objects. Conflicts in the form of struggles for power can continue to pervade competitive business and competitive politics, whereby people can still be used as means to ends. In the absence of mechanisms of direct coercion, masses of people can be persuaded to buy things—one is tempted to say things they don't need, except that they do need them, since needs, often addictive ones, can be induced by mass persuasion. People can also be persuaded to vote for candidates beholden to the power elites with private agendas rather than to the people who elect them. In fact, people can be persuaded to identify their interests with those of the power elites.

Another way of distinguishing between social good and social evil is by comparing the extent or intensity of conflict and cooperation in a given society. From this point of view enlargement of political units appears as a progressive tendency. As clans merge into tribes, tribes into chiefdoms, chiefdoms into states or empires, internal conflicts are attenuated. However internal pacification is often accompanied by intensified external conflicts. Unification is often facilitated by perception of a common enemy. Conflicts erupting in institutionalized interstate warfare more than make up for pacification within states.

Besides, enlargement of political units has been often the result of conquest and subjugation rather than of mutually advantageous unification. Internal stability based on apparent absence of conflict was characterized by Johann Galtung as "structural violence," that is constant threat of violence by which ruling elites maintain their position of exploitative dominance over a population.[4]

If we subsume structural violence under (potential) conflict, we can rank societies according to three modes of social control in the order of decreasing amount of conflict and increasing amount of cooperation. Kenneth Boulding called these three modes Threat, Trade, and Love respectively.[5] Threat induces *compliance* by the use of "unless" and "to you": unless you do (or do not) do this, I will do that to you. Trade induces *reciprocity* by the use of "if" and "for you": if you do this for me, I will do that for you. Love induces cooperation by inducing identification and by the reference to "all" and "are": we all do this because we all are...In this sense, "love" does not necessary imply sentiment or passion. In fact the choice of this term was unfortunate. "Hard-nosed" social scientists look askance at it. Eventually Boulding used "integration" instead. I assume that "love," in the sense in which he used it, referred to the inducement to do something for others not because of what they do but because of who they are. We nurture and protect children not because of what they can do to us if we don't and not because we expect payment but because they are children. Here affection is usually involved. But it needn't be. Universal social services are apportioned independently of sentiment or affection simply because the recipients are entitled to them by being members of a society, by being integrated into it.

Threat is the mode of control dominant in totalitarian societies; trade in a commercial societies. Integration is the mode envisaged in a cooperative commonwealth. I agree with Boulding that the three modes are in ascending order of morality and interpret this to mean that capitalist democracy is morally superior to dictatorship and social democracy to capitalism.[6] This ranking is consistent with the ranking along the conflict-cooperation scale if threat is associated with dominance, dominance with structural violence, and structural violence with (potential) conflict.

The We-They Dichotomy

Since the end of World War II, countries now subsumed under "The West" (victors and vanquished alike) have developed close ties. Foundations for a United Europe (by which Western and Central Europe was understood) were apparently laid. It seemed that with the end of the Cold War the union would include the Soviet satellite states, perhaps even the Soviet Union itself. Instead, forces of disintegration set in. In 1992 and 1993 twenty two new countries were admitted to the United Nations with many more expected to seek admission. "Nationalities" that hardly any one had heard of before are clamouring for recognition. What has come to be called "ethnic nationalism" threatens to spawn the sort of chronic violence that dominated Europe since the disintegration of the Roman Empire. The ethnic war in former Yugoslavia may be a harbinger of things to come—a materialization of ghosts of the past. The Moldavans see the Russians and Ukrainians living in their newly hatched country as enemy aliens. The Abkhasians see the Georgians as oppressors; the Ingushetians, the Ossetians, the Armenians living in Azerbaidjan have their own axes to grind. Slovakia seceded peacefully from Czechoslovakia but now faces its own resident aliens clamouring for the same rights—the Hungarians who along with the Kurds and the Palestinians have their own diasporas. Policies based on preservation of ethnic purity of states are from the point of view of democracy, tolerance, and enlightenment as vicious as those based on preservation of "racial" purity and for the same reasons: pure ethnicity, like pure "race" is an evil myth and loyalty to either instigates violence culminating in genocide.

What are the sources of we-they dichotomies?

Here is the way a high official of Lilliput tells Gulliver about the origins of the war between Lilliput and Blefuscu, the neighbouring empire.

It began in the following way. It is allowed on all hands, that the primitive way of breaking eggs before we eat them, was upon the larger end, but the present Majesty's grandfather, while he was a boy, going to eat an egg and breaking it according to the ancient practice, happened to cut one of his fingers. Whereupon the Emperor, his father, published an edict, commanding all the subjects, upon great penalties to break the smaller end of their eggs. The people so highly resented this law, that our histories tell us there have been six rebellions on that account...These civil commotions were constantly fomented by the monarchs of Blefuscu...Now the Big-endians [exiles] found so much credit in the Emperor of Blefuscu's court, and so much private assistance and encouragement from their party here at home, that a bloody war has been carried on between the two empires for six and thirty moons.

There are many ways of identifying a person as "one of us" or "one of them": by the way they look, talk, dress or make the sign of the cross. The Lilliputians identified their friends and enemies by the way they broke an egg. Some of these symptoms may seem trivial to us, but actually all of them are indicators or are believed to be indicators of important distinctions, namely, between ways in which people perceive themselves, others, and the world, in short between what they believe and what they believe in.

Beliefs are essentially preferences, and preferences can be represented by scales with a positive and a negative pole, a true-false scale, a good-bad scale, and a pleasant-unpleasant scale. Give the last a more lofty name, say beautiful-ugly, and we have the three values recognized in all cultures: Truth, Virtue, Beauty. I believe that underlying all hostilities associated with the "we-they" dichotomy are incompatible conceptions of what is good, what is true, and what is beautiful. A butler in one of P.G. Wodehouse's novels says he disapproves of the Swedes because their heads are too round and of the Irish because they are Irish. But this is simply an instance of how all the features that determine an attitude are collapsed into a single identifying label, which serves as a triggering mechanism for unleashing hostility.

If conflicts arise and are aggravated by incompatible notions about what is good, true, or beautiful, it seems that they can be resolved if people can develop tolerance for other people's value systems. It seems to me that tolerance is easiest to achieve in the realm of aesthetic or sensual gratification. I can attest to having no difficulty accepting the fact that some people are homosexual or that some people regard fried scorpions as a delicacy, even though I can't imagine myself deriving vicarious pleasure either from others' homosexual erotic experience or from watching others eating fried scorpions. In the realm of aesthetics it is not so simple. People worry about standards of taste in music, painting, literature, etc. That is, attempts at conversion or missionary work in these areas continues. However, differences of commitment to criteria of aesthetic excellence seldom lead to bloodshed.

With regard to conceptions of good and evil the situation is very different. In this realm people with different criteria are often regarded as evil, at times condemned to extermination, for example, heretics and other ideological enemies. People regarded as evil present a constant threat. Putting it in another way, the essence of a community is commitment to shared values, that is, agreement on what is good and what is evil. Those who do not share such commitments are most easily seen as enemies.

Conceiving the enemy as an embodiment of evil provides a way of overcoming what may be an instinctive aversion against killing one's own kind. The aversion may well have been incorporated in the human psyche (as in the psyche of most mammals) in the process of natural selection. One distinctly human activity is adapting the environment to own (immediately perceived) needs rather than adapting self to the environment, as other animals do. Clearing land, whether of stones or of trees is a conspicuous example. Possibly the primitive wars of extermination, vividly described in the Old Testament, were undertaken with the same aim as land clearance. Here people rather than stones or trees were a conspicuous obstacle to settlement. However, inhibition against killing one's own kind may have been a hindrance. Identifying the local population as the embodiment of evil may have been effective in overcoming the inhibition. Witness the tribal god Yahweh's commands to the Hebrew invaders:

> Of the cities of these people, that the Lord thy God giveth thee for an inheritance, thou shalt save alive nothing that breatheth, but thou shalt utterly destroy them: the Hittite, and the Amorite, the Canaanite, and the Perizzite, the Hivite, and the Jebusite; as the Lord, thy God commanded thee; that they teach you not to do after all their abominations, which they have done unto their gods, and so ye sin against the Lord your God. (Deuteronomy 20: 16-18.)

It is not only allowed but also commanded to kill evil people. In discussions of problematic human traits (criminality, intolerance, racial prejudice, predilection to violence) the "nature vs. nurture" issue often crops up. Long before the study of inheritance became a science (genetics), conventional wisdom often attributed patterns of behaviour or dispositions to inheritance. People were judged by the sort of families they came from; privileges were justified by descent.[7]

For the most part emphasis on hereditary determinants was associated with reactionary politics, Naziism being the most vivid example. Leanings toward liberalism are generally associated with scepticism or outright denial of genetic determinants of attitudes or behaviour and with emphasis on environmental factors. In particular, contemporary peace activists are for the most part convinced that attributing wars to a natural human propensity to aggression and violence is a dangerous delusion.

In my book, *The Origins of Violence* I discussed the pros and cons of an "aggressive instinct" in humans. I admit that the findings of ethology (study of animal behaviour) and of socio-biology (the study of the evolution of social behaviour) cannot be dismissed out of hand. The principal argument for the existence of an aggressive instinct or drive in many animals, particularly in vertebrates, is based on the demonstration that such an instinct could well have conferred a reproductive advantage. The stronger, more aggressive male would have had a better chance to inseminate more females (or in monogamous species to find a mate) than a weaker, more timid one. Consequently the corresponding genotype would have been selected for in the process of evolution.

Recently I came across a genetic explanation of the assumed innate propensity to internalize we-they dichotomies, which unfortunately, from my point of view, reinforces the assumption that aggression, violence, xenophobia, etc. may be incorporated in human nature.

The argument, presented by Carl Sagan (whose credentials as a humanitarian are unimpeachable), is based not on reproductive advantage but on the evolutionary advantage of the so called "genetic drift," which accelerates the evolutionary process. The effect of this drift is strongest in small interbreeding groups. On the other hand a small completely interbreeding group is more prone to extinction if the genetic drift pushes that population over the brink, so to say. Both incest taboos (which we share with several other primates) and random breeding in a large population counteract the effects of genetic drift and contribute to prevention of extinction. How can the advantages of genetic drift (accelerated rate of evolution in a changing environment) and those of incest taboos coupled with opportunities for random matings in a large population (insurance against extinction) be combined? Sagan writes:

> What would it feel like from the inside if you were a member of a species that had, through natural selection, made arrangements for a genetic drift? You would enjoy living in small groups. You would hate crowds...You would conceive a passionate loyalty to the group, something like intense family feeling, superpartriotism, chauvinism, ethnocentrism...You would also need to avoid any merger of your group with another, because much bigger groups would avoid accidents in sampling [i.e., genetic drift—A.R.]. So it would be helpful if you conceived a passionate hostility to other groups, a real sense of their deficiencies, something like xenophobia or jingoism.

> These other groups are, of course, composed of individuals of the same species as you. They look almost exactly like you. To fan the flames of xenophobia, you must examine them with minute attention and exaggerate whatever differences can be discerned, always to their disadvantage. They have slightly different heredities and slightly different diets, so they don't smell quite the same as you and yours. If your olfactory powers are sufficiently finely tuned, may be their scents will render them grotesque, hateful, odious.

> It would be even better if you could *establish* some differences. If differences in dress and language are unavailable—having not yet been invented—differences in behavior, posture, or vocalizations would be helpful. Anything that could distinguish your group from the others would work to keep hatreds high and resist merger.

> At the same time, avoiding too much inbreeding and guaranteeing at least occasional outbreeding are essential. So you would feel revulsion against incest, or at least among the most consanguineous matings. Outbreeding might be officially proscribed—perhaps among humans. by young men attacking males from other groups who, even accidentally, wander into the neighbourhood, or by fathers mourning, as if dead, daughters who run off with foreigners. But despite the pervasive ethnocentrism and xenophobia, now and then you would find members of other hostile groups unaccountably attractive. Surreptitious matings would occur. This is, more or less the theme of *Romeo and Juliet*, Rudolph Valentino's *The Sheik*, and a vast industry of books on romance targeted at women.

A promising survival strategy, in short, is this. Break up into small groups, encourage ethnocentrism and xenophobia, and succumb to occasional sexual temptation provided by the sons and daughters of enemy clans. Devise your own culture. The more your species is capable of learned behavior, the greater the differences that can be established between one group and another...

A solution has been found to the problem of how to arrange for gene frequencies to respond quickly to a volatile, changing environment. And the solution seems eerily familiar. After a journey into an abstract world of population genetics, we turn a corner and suddenly find ourselves gazing at something that looks very much like...ourselves.[8]

It is in problem areas related to perceptions of the human condition or expectations about human destiny that beliefs in what is and beliefs in what ought to be are sometimes difficult to distinguish. The appearance of Darwin's *Origin of Species* in 1859 was enthusiastically greeted

in Europe by the political "Left" (republicans, free thinkers) and condemned by the clerics, who saw it (correctly) as incompatible with biblical accounts. In our own day the political Left looks askance at sociobiology—a sophisticated elaboration of Darwinian theory—suspecting sociobiological investigations of fostering racism, an offspring of genetic determinism.

Awareness of one's own ideological bias may be a salutary antidote to it. I confess being shocked when I read the following passage:

Throughout recorded history war has been common in tribes and nearly universal among chiefdoms and states. The spread of genes has always been of paramount importance. Moses gave instructions identical in result to the aggression and genetic occupation by male langur monkeys. Combinations of genes able to confer superior fitness in contention with genocidal aggression would be those that produce either a more effective technique of aggression or else the capacity to prevent genocide by some form of pacific maneuvering.[9]

The passage expresses a firm belief that war is a genetically determined trait of human nature. I feel a compulsion to refute the argument. But I must do so by means compatible with certain rules in marshaling and evaluating evidence. Moreover, I must prepare a "safety net," that is, a position I can retreat to if I fail to refute the argument decisively. The influence of my ideological commitments must be minimized in the first part of the task but not in the second, because the "position to retreat to" rests not on beliefs about how things are but on beliefs about how they ought to be.

The discovery of a "gene for war" or something of this sort would be a definitive corroboration of E.O. Wilson's position. At this time, the chances of such a discovery are minimal. But failure to discover such a determinant would not "disprove" the "genetic theory of war." Nevertheless I can point out that whatever may have been the reproductive advantage conferred by successful wars and concomitant "genetic occupation" (killing the males and carrying off the females as langur monkeys do), it is unlikely that such reproductive advantage has been operating for the last several centuries. The question remains to what extent the genetic predisposition for war (if it was ever established by reproductive advantage) still remains in the human make-up.

The same question remains with respect to aggressiveness as a genetically determined predisposition of human males. It is the source of my most persistent and most disturbing doubts. On the one hand, it is reasonable to assume that aggressiveness conferred reproduction advantage on pre-historic man (i.e., on man before the effects of cultural evolution eclipsed those of biological evolution). On the other hand, it is not at all certain to what extent aggressiveness has declined since then as a basic drive in human males.

One of the most remarkable characteristics of the human psyche, probably related to the capacity to think and communicate by symbolic language, is the tendency to "link" preferences, appetites, phobias, etc. Specifically the sexual drive can be linked to a great variety of attractions or repulsions. Most noteworthy is the fact that in some men it is linked to dominance and brutality, in others to empathy and tenderness. Is this difference a manifestation of genetic variation or of conditioning? Belief in the one or the other alternative seems to be a belief in what "is." But preference for the one or the other (in my case the latter) is not based on weighing evidence. It is based on what actions seem appropriate if the one or the other belief is chosen. In general, commitment to action is the nexus between cognition and value orientation.

Relativity of Values

To be human, to my way of thinking, means to seek autonomy. At the same time survival of humankind depends on integration. Can the two imperatives be made compatible? I think they can. As far as we know, we are the only beings capable of acquiring "higher order knowledge," i.e., not only knowledge of how things are, but also of how they might be. Further, humans can acquire knowledge about *how* we see things and *why* we see them the way we do and how we could see them otherwise. It is this faculty of self-examination that suggests the possibility of achieving integration without jeopardizing autonomy, that is, of achieving unity in diversity. This brings me again to the central question related to the realization of this possibility. Are there values that can be justifiably called universal human values?

If there are universal human values, then living in peace with others must surely be one of them. Because of pervasive differences among people, tolerance must be a concomitant of shared values. But the concept of tolerance is beset with problems. If one values tolerance and aspires to practising it, should one tolerate intolerance?

Relativity of values was at one time, perhaps still is the ethical foundation of cultural anthropology. The modern cultural anthropologist regards the so called "primitive" (now called "indigenous") cultures as so many endangered species and has the same emotional stake in them as the most ardent conservationist has in endangered biological species. This feeling stems partly from feelings of repugnance against the brutality of conquerors, the greed of colonizers, and the arrogance of missionaries, religious and secular. Another source is admiration for the objects of one's study, which stems from expertise. Just as the archaeologist admires everything that is old enough so the cultural anthropologist, because of his expertise, appreciates the refinement, sophistication, and spirituality of a culture which the uninitiated may see as "primitive," ridden with superstition and ignorance, or simply evil.

Problems arise when this attitude—call it tolerance, call it recognition of the relativity of values, call it empathy—is juxtaposed to the ideal of global integration of humanity, that is also a commitment to humane values. Are the two ideas compatible?

I never could accept the idea that the scientific view of the world is just another view, no more valid than the view of the mystic or of assorted "believers." I also disagree with the view that the scientific outlook is a special product of Western civilization and therefore culture-bound. It knows no cultural boundaries. However, justification of "proselytizing" the scientific outlook presents a problem. The justification that most readily suggests itself is that universal or at least widespread acceptance of the scientific view of the world is a prerequisite for the solution of global problems, and the solution of global problems is a prerequisite for the survival of the human race, and the survival of the human race...well, it's an end in itself. (Or is it?)

But how is the onus of "missionarism" to be removed from sincere proselytizing of enlightenment? How is best intentioned dissemination of knowledge about efficient agricultural methods, about disease-preventing practices, about contraception to be convincingly distinguished from spreading the Good News about the salvation of humankind through Jesus's self-sacrifice, from teaching "modesty" to women accustomed to going bare-breasted, or from Robinson Crusoe's teaching Friday that it is all right to eat goats but not people?

We are witnessing a rebirth of cultures not quite but almost totally destroyed by conquerors (who called themselves "discoverers") of the Americas—the Maya, the Inca, the Cherokee, the Iroquois. Those who have come to recognize the evil done to those people welcome these attempts of reconstruction, support the struggles of indigenous peoples for autonomy and dignity. Frequently these same people cherish also the ideal of a world community—a warless world. But are the two commitments compatible? How about the aspects of some cultures that starkly contradict ideals of tolerance and peace? If Aztec culture is to be revived and protected, does this mean that human sacrifice, once an integral feature of Aztec culture, is to be revived and will be protected from outside interference as a "cultural right" analogous to a human right? If the cultures of North American plains Indians are to be resurrected, does this mean that tribal warfare, scalping, etc. are to be tolerated? To what extent will intervention, say in defence of human rights (recognized by global consensus) be justified or even imperative?

To take an example, the punishment prescribed by the Koran for adultery is stoning people buried up to their neck with "stones that are not too large, so that they are not killed by one or two." Intervention would involve violation of sovereignty of Saudi Arabia. In the opinion of many, raising the question of intervention is already prejudicial, since it is symptomatic of paternalism or arrogant cultural bias. However, these questions cannot be evaded without evading responsibilities imposed by the global outlook. Answers in each concrete case are clear in my mind. I strongly condemned U.S. intervention in Vietnam, in Iran, in several Latin American countries. I strongly condemned U.S.-led intervention in the Persian Gulf. But forty years ago I was convinced that the war against the Axis was justified (a view which I cannot unambivalently hold in the light of what happened since then). As I write this, I am ready to support military intervention in Haiti, as the only way of disarming gangs of thugs terrorizing a helpless population with the aim of preying on it. Nevertheless, apparently the same intention led to murder of civilians by UN sponsored "peace-keeping" forces. On the one hand, it seems, violence inevitably breeds more violence, so that the use of violence for suppression of violence appears perpetually self-defeating. On the other hand, there seems to be no way of protecting the helpless against murderous violence and ruthless exploitation except by at least disarming the predators, which almost certainly requires resort to violence.

The question that I find most bothersome is how to resolve the apparent incompatibility between freedom of the individual, autonomy of a culture, sovereignty of a nation on the one hand and the imperative of establishing a basis for universally shared values on the other. It is easy to agree that individual freedom ought not imply the freedom to kill, rob, or rape. But does the justification of restrictions of individual freedom imply justifications of analogous restrictions of cultural autonomy? Does it imply justification of intervention with the view of eradicating certain practices permitted or even prescribed by some religions (e.g., stoning adulterers) or by traditions (e.g., virtual enslavement of women) or by conceptions of self-esteem (e.g. the conviction that a man without a weapon is a man without honour)? I firmly believe in total prohibition of international arms trade. But enforcing this prohibition would probably involve encroachment on sovereignty of states. In fact, it could most easily be implemented by military force, as the prohibition of slave trade was once enforced by the British navy. Would such enforcement be incompatible with a "just world order" based on equality of states? These questions define the battle between my certainties and doubts.

Myth

I envisage global integration in terms of concentric circles of "loyalty layers." At the core is the Self with its sacrosanct sense of identity, which I am willing to assume to be biologically determined. Then comes the nuclear family, parents and children, also probably biologically determined (a mammalian heritage). Although alternative arrangements for child care are possible, I believe that the nuclear family provides the most favourable environment for emotional growth and a link to the higher loyalty levels—community, culture, humanity, and beyond.

Each loyalty level is firmed by some psychic mechanism. At the level of the nuclear family the cohesive agents are sexual and parental love. At the higher levels we observe a wide range of we-they dichotomies, all of them (I firmly believe) culturally established independently of biological determinants. (In fact, it is on this question that I reject the sociobiologists' basic assumptions, about the genetic basis of cultural evolution.)

Throughout human history religion has been a most important and conspicuous binder of loyalty. Indeed the word "religion" in languages derived from Latin is etymologically related to the verb "to bind."

In pointing out the complementarity of conflict and cooperation, I often call attention to the double role of we-they dichotomies. They unite and they separate. Nationalism induces loyalty to fellow citizens and often hostility to foreigners. Its positive facet is patriotism; its negative one is chauvinism.

Most religions do the same and so cannot be bases of global loyalties. Universalist religions represent attempts to transcend the we-they dichotomy but so far without success. These religions (e.g., primitive Christianity, Buddhism, etc) developed within circumscribed cultural frameworks and so inevitably absorbed dominant characteristics of their social environment including imperatives of culturally dominant we-they dichotomies.

Loyalties are nurtured by myths. Myths play an especially prominent part in religions. From the point of view of positivist science, a myth is a blown-up superstition—a belief in something that is demonstrably not true. At the same time, the cohesive function of myths cannot be denied. So if myths contribute to the cementing of loyalties and if the harmful effects of myths (as elaborate superstitions) can somehow be counteracted, could they not be utilized in working for global integration?

In pondering this question, I find that my reservations stem from a profound disagreement with a school of thought once prominent among social scientists (especially cultural anthropologists) called functionalism. Functionalists compare a society or a culture to an organism which, to be understood, must be perceived in its entirety. Customs, laws, taboos, networks of kinship or of other social relations—all serve some functions and in their totality keep the society or culture "alive" as it were. Removal of any component could impair the viability of this "organism," just as impairment of a vital organ can kill a living being. In this sense myths are clearly seen as vital components of human societies.

I agree to that some components of a culture are indeed vital in this sense. But I don't accept the implication that every society or culture is worth preserving. Here is where I inevitably draw fire. When functionalists think of "culture," they usually have in mind the violated ones in danger of extinction. They usually accept the paradigm based on relativity of values and therefore reject any distinction between a "good" and a "bad" culture or between "good" and "bad" aspects of any culture. Being a believer in universal human values (although I cannot claim to know with any confidence what they are), I am willing to judge aspects of cultures (or even entire cultures) as "good" or "bad" in accordance with whether they enhance or detract from values that I assume to be universal. These distinctions give me leverage for judging myths as "good" or "bad" or to rate cultures on a "good-bad" scale. In particular I regard cultures that spawned totalitarian dictatorships as "bad" as well as the myths that supported their internal cohesion. For example, the "theory" of the master race, with its blood mystique is as clearly a myth as are the stories of creation, of the origin of peoples, etc. These are, in my estimation, a prime examples of bad myths.

I can name two other myths that I regard as bad. One is the doctrine of the Original Sin and of its redemption by a blood sacrifice. The other is the account of a covenant between the Jews and God, which gave the Jews title to lands in the Middle East and a license to slaughter the residents of the region. I feel no compunction in attacking these myths regardless of their importance to believers. How am I to square this readiness with a sincere desire to respect beliefs that may be essential in preserving a culture that is worth preserving? Or, if the concept of culture does not apply to racism or Christianity or Judaism, how then can a "culture" be distinguished from an ideology or a religion? Is the concept, perhaps, applicable only to the way of life of the Arapesh or the Tibetans? Only, perhaps, to the oppressed and the exploited, whose way of life is in danger of extinction? If so, shall we exclude from the category "culture" the Hellenic or the Arabic, or the Chinese systems of thought and everything generated by them?

This brings me to the "good" myths, say the nature myths of native North Americans, which, it is said, kept them in balanced harmony with their environment. Consider the address of Onitositah, an adviser to Cherokee chief Oconostota on the occasion of the defeat of the Cherokee nation by the settlers.

> The Great God of Nature has placed us in different situations. It is true that he has endowed you with many superior advantages; but he has not created us to be your slaves. We are separate people! He has given each of us lands, under distinct considerations and circumstances; he has stocked yours with cows, ours with buffaloes; yours with hog, ours with bear; yours with sheep, ours with deer. He has indeed given you an advantage in this; that your cattle are tame and domestic, while our are wild and demand not only a larger space for range, but art to hunt and kill them. They are nevertheless, as much our property as other animals are yours.[10]

In all these arguments, advanced by people encroached upon by invaders, there are indirect references to a creation myth in the form of explanations of what was "meant" to be, which is another way of stating what "ought" to be, i.e., a statement of value, in this case the right to live as one has been accustomed. If so, then arguments about the "truth" of a creation myth are irrelevant. But when everything is said and done, having made a case for taking the creation myths seriously as expressions of moral imperatives, I still feel no pangs of conscience in pointing out the absurdities in the arguments of Jehovah's Witnesses about "scientific corroborations" of the Genesis accounts of Creation, the Flood, etc. Can this mean that I regard those arguments as analogues of blasphemy, i.e., insults to my own "religion," positivist science?

Unity in Diversity

This brings me back to what I perceive to be the role of the scientific outlook as a foundation of a better future for humanity: its potential for discovering unity in diversity. I already discussed this potential in the context of the lesson that can be drawn from the theory of relativity. The theory rests on the discovery of a new invariant. Thus, observers may disagree about the length of a long rod, or about the time interval between two events, each measuring these in his own system of space and time coordinates. But they will agree on the space-time interval between two events, which is the same for all observers.

As a matter of fact, the most important insights in the history of science have been discoveries of ever more general invariants. Geometry progressed from studies of congruence (invariance of configurations subjected to rigid motion) to studies of similarity (invariance under isotropic expansion or contraction) to studies of invariance under projections, to invariance under continuous transformations as in topology, each invariance being more general than last. An in-joke among mathematicians is, "A topologist is some one who doesn't know the difference between a coffee cup and a doughnut." (They both belong to the same topological genus.) The foundations of physics rest on the fundamental unity of what resides in a lifted weight, in a coiled spring, in boiler of a steam engine, in electric potential, and in a nuclear reactor—stored energy, subjected to the same conservation laws. The foundations of biology rest on classification of living things, that is, on the recognition of what a rabbit, a shrew, and a rhinoceros on the one hand or an octopus, a clam, and a snail on the other have in common, indeed what all living things have in common and how they are all interdependent.

I cling to the hope that the unity in diversity principle, which underlies the insights of the scientific outlook can be eventually internalized by human beings in matters pertaining not only to beliefs in what is but also to beliefs in what ought to be.

NOTES

1. Richard M. Weaver, *Ideas Have Consequences*. Chicago: University of Chicago Press, 1948.
2. Quoted in Henry Hunt, *Reasonable Doubt*. New York: Holt, Rinehart and Winston, 1985, pp. 412-13.
3. See *The Magazine of American History*, Vol. 29 (1893), pp. 282-83.
4. Cf. J. Galtung, "A Structural Theory of Aggression," *Journal of Peace Research*, 1964, No.2: 95-119.
5. Cf. K.E. Boulding, "The Relation of Economic, Political, and Social Systems." In *Collected Papers*, L.D. Singall, ed., vol. 4. Boulder, Colorado: Associated University Press, 1974.
6. Similarly, I feel that prostitution is morally superior to rape and conjugal love to prostitution.
7. Cf. Edmund Burke's justification of hereditary aristocracy in M. Morton Auerbach, "Edmund Burke," *International Encyclopedia of the Social Sciences*.
8. Carl Sagan, *Shadows of Forgotten Ancestors*. New York: Random House, 1992, pp. 254-56.
9. E.O. Wilson, *Sociobiology. The New Synthesis*. Cambridge, MA: The Belknap Press of Harvard University Press, 1975, pp. 572-73.
10. R. Wright, *Stolen Continents*. London: John Murray, 1992.

Looking Back and Ahead

12

I could describe the first half of my life as a succession of disappointments. As a child in war-torn Russia I looked forward to America as a land of peace and plenty. My father did not tell me about his life as a worker in a cigar factory during his earlier sojourn in Chicago. He spoke of five cent ice cream cones and roller skates and fireworks on the Fourth of July. They were all there, but I missed my father, who worked long exhausting hours on the milk wagon or in a neighbourhood grocery, and I missed my Russian cousins with whom I acted out episodes from English and American adventure literature.

I was thrilled to live in Vienna in the 1930's, a city governed by a socialist administration, where I watched forests of red flags floating over the marchers on the Ringstrasse on the First of May and on the Twelfth of November. But I witnessed a brutal putsch blessed by the established church.

I had hoped that the New Deal would initiate a process culminating in a peaceful "proletarian revolution." Instead, the depression was forgotten and with it the rising "class consciousness," as the U.S. drifted into war. At first I opposed the drift to war, because that was the Communist Party line before the Soviet Union was attacked. Then I supported it (when the Nazis invaded the Soviet Union). I was convinced that *this time* victory would usher in a lasting peace. Instead I witnessed the lowering of the Iron Curtain and preparations for World War III. I had hoped that victory over Germany would mean the end of dictatorship in the Soviet Union. Instead, I witnessed its paranoid xenophobic phase.

Then I settled in academic life and married Gwen. Since then my private life was marked by contentment. I loved my work and my family. I was in good health. Like almost every one I knew, I was adjusted to the constant threat of annihilation, partly because it was irremovable like the threat of being killed in an earthquake or in a plane crash and partly because there was practically complete unanimity among the people who mattered to me that the threat emanated from our common enemy—the war establishment.

Freeman Dyson made this we-they dichotomy especially vivid. In his book, *Weapons and Hope* he pictures the gulf between the Warriors and the Victims. His

Warriors are the people in the service of the global war machine. The Victims include every one else.

I modified this image to bring it in accord with my own. I pictured the Warriors not as people but as roles, and I broadened these roles to include vast infrastructures of the war machine, that is, the war industries, the research institutes, the think tanks, the lobbies vying for defence contracts, and, of course, the world wide arms market. In this way the dichotomy appeared not as a people vs. people confrontation—like all other we-they dichotomies—but as one that pitted people against a system, which it was salubrious to hate. Indeed, Dyson himself implicitly pictured the Warrior-Victim dichotomy in this way by pointing out that he belonged to both camps. He was an active member of the "strategic community" and regarded himself also a member in good standing of the human race.

Still in presenting his case, Dyson emphasized the people-vs.-people confrontation. His stated aim was to bridge the gulf between the Warriors and the Victims, to present both as concerned human beings and to induce each to understand the legitimate concerns of the other.

I made a similar attempt twenty-five years earlier in presenting an imaginary "ethical debate" between a sincere Communist and a sincere Liberal. In reading *Weapons and Hope* however, I could not draw a parallel. I could not imagine either a synthesis of the two positions or a compromise between them, essentially because I refused to see the Warrior-Victim dichotomy as a people-vs.-people dichotomy. I saw only people (both in the roles of Warriors and of Victims) threatened by a system—a global institution, the institution of war.

So instead of placing my hope (as Dyson did) on an understanding between people who see war from different points of view, I placed it on the mortality of institutions. History is cluttered with dead or moribund institutions: chattel slavery, human sacrifice, hereditary absolute monarchy, dueling, infanticide, to name a few. There is no reason to exempt war from the same fate.

Thus, the perception of a common enemy seemed to be a foundation on which to build a global community. In fact, this had been the basis of all important political integrations and also the reason why conflicts, instead of being alleviated by the process, were often aggravated. That is, internal pacification was usually accompanied by externally directed belligerency. The Cold War and the polarization of the world induced by it was the latest and most threatening manifestation of this "law." By casting a faceless institution in the role of a common enemy, the dilemma of conflict-cooperation duality could be resolved, it seemed to me.

Throughout the Cold War I was reinforced in my conviction that aspiration to power, addiction to power and worship of power were the principal sources of violence and that violence was the overt manifestation of evil. Further I became firmly convinced that the abolition of war as an institution was an indispensable prerequisite in making headway with the other central global problems, environmental protection and the establishment of a just world order based on equitable distribution of resources and guaranteed human rights. This conviction protected me from further disappointments. I no longer expected anything "positive," as long as the global power struggle continued. In particular, the repeated aggressions, interventions, and subversions by the United States appeared to me not as betrayals of humanitarian or democratic ideals but as consistent implementations of policies guided by addiction to power. The failure of Khrushchev's attempt at de-Stalinization appeared not as a temporary setback in the progress toward democracy but as retrenchment of totalitarianism. I was not shocked by the brutal intervention in Czechoslovakia (as I had been shocked by the attack on Finland in 1939), because I now expected it.

Thus, while during the second half of my life, that is, since my becoming rooted in academe and establishing a family, the world did not appear any brighter, I think in retrospect that I have spent a personally happy life.

My contentment was partly rooted in a sense of belonging. I suppose it corresponds to a "sense of identity," that psychologists, sociologists, and anthropologists of the "humanist" persuasion talk about. I agree that people seek a "sense of identity" and suffer if they lack it or have lost it. It also seems to me that this "sense of identity" generates we-they dichotomies and with them a love-hate mentality and the horrendous social problems associated with it.

The complementarity of love and hate (attachment and aggression to use behaviourist terms) was eloquently described by Konrad Lorenz in his book *On Aggression*. He notes that intraspecific aggression is most characteristic among vertebrates. It is also among vertebrates, particularly among mammals and birds that attachment between individuals most commonly occurs. Moreover, among vertebrates absence of bonding (e.g., among herding animals) intraspecific aggression is less common.

Although I have often questioned the assumption of some socio-biologists that cultural as well as biological traits are established predominantly by Darwinian selection, I have recently become receptive to the idea that aggressiveness in particular may be among these traits, so that the explanation of pervasive we-they dichotomies as a manifestation of "human nature" ought not be dismissed out of hand. I still insist, however, that *where* the line between Self and Other is drawn is a product of socialization, not a consequence of genetic determinism. In the case of humans there is nothing natural about making inclusions and exclusions on the basis of "race," sex, politics, or species. So I ascribe my own definition of identity to the way I have been socialized. As I said in the last chapter, I picture it in terms of concentric spheres of empathy, affection, or loyalty. The inner sphere includes the immediate family and intimates. On the next level are like-minded persons—those who share my convictions of what is true, or, more precisely, how one arrives at truth; and those who share my convictions of what is good or evil. Beyond that is humanity; beyond that the biosphere, not as a collection of identifiable species but as a system on which the existence of humanity depends. So when I have to fill out blanks on visa applications or customs declarations, identifying myself as "male" or "American" or so many years old evokes in me no sense of "belonging." The answers are forced on me by bureaucratic procedures.

In contrast, identifying myself as a "professor," I feel different: somewhat embarrassed by the pompousness of the designation, yet somewhat gratified that to a certain (very slight) degree a basis of my self-identification is touched upon. It is also somewhat touched upon on the rare occasions when I am asked to state a religious affiliation and answer "none." For, as I said, my sense of identity is based on what I do and on what I believe and extends to people who think and feel more or less as I do.

In sum I believe that the satisfaction I have derived from the second half of my life stems in large measure from clarity of identification.

The innermost sphere of empathy, changed only in consequence of births and deaths, has been my family. We are currently nine. Our daughter Anya, a veterinarian occupies a basement apartment in our home with her several dogs. Our elder son Alexander (Sasha), a composer, lives with his wife Katharine (Kathy), a violinist, and our grandson Leo within five minutes' walk. Our younger son Anthony (Tony), a violist, his partner Helen and their baby daughter Erin live within a twenty minute subway ride. Seven of our birthdays fall in seven different months and are all celebrated with festive dinners. I prepare a "numeroscope," essentially an elaborate twisting of the number representing the age of the subject so as to exhibit recurrences of the first three perfect numbers, 6, 28, and 496. In this way I demonstrate the old saw that if you torture data long enough, they will confess to anything. Both my sons chide me for "abandoning" music, a not quite just accusation, since Tony and I still play a joint recital every spring, which sometimes includes a composition by Sasha.

To my family this book is dedicated.

Acknowledgments

The next sphere of identification is with people personally closest to me, those with whom I am most comfortable discussing my innermost thoughts, convictions, enthusiasms, and aversions. Life in the "developed" world being what it is, most of them live far away, and I see them only on rare occasions. But they remain nevertheless a part of my life, the firmest ties to the past.

Stretching my memory to almost the very beginning of my consciousness, I invoke the image of a three-year old, my cousin Vladimir, whom I mentioned several times in the course of this narrative. He was named Isaac, but insisted on being called Volodya and so remained.

A few years ago he left Crimea, which both of us always regarded as our home, that is, the place we name when people ask us "where we are from." Together with his sister Sonya, whom I revered in childhood, his daughter and her two sons he emigrated to Israel. Sonya died in 1995, Volodya in 1999. Volodya was the only person with whom I have been exchanging long letters at least once a month since 1971.

A friend from adolescence is Alex Tulsky. We both graduated high school aged sixteen. (In fact, Al had not yet reached his sixteenth birthday.) Music brought us together. Al played the clarinet. We organized a chamber ensemble, originally with a violinist and a cellist. Others sometimes joined, sometimes left. Al and I were the core. We played "classical selections," which I arranged for whatever instruments we had, mostly excerpts from operas, such as the intermezzi from Carmen or the triumphal march from Aida (which sounded fine when a trumpeter joined us).

Al came from an impoverished proletarian family. To help ends meet he sold papers from a corner stand. The papers cost two or three cents in those days. Profit was one cent. Al must have had some business sense. The stand was on a busy thoroughfare (Madison Street). Not many people crossed the street to his stand. He dispatched his kid brother to the other side with a few papers, thus increasing the volume of business. I sometimes visited him at the stand. He told me he was following the serialized translation of Remarque's *All Quiet on the Western Front*, with which he was much impressed. When I was in Vienna, he was in medical school. Already in high school he was fascinated with gynecology. When I returned in 1934, he was an intern. In his parents' flat on Chicago's West Side, he showed me the beat-up chair and desk at which he crammed medical knowledge for five years. Eventually, he became head of gynecology and obstetrics in Chicago's prestigious Michael Reese Hospital. Like me, he still teaches and, I suspect, for the same reason: a passion for passing on what he knows, the same sort of passion that many have for passing on their accumulated wealth to those they care for.

On almost the family level of intimacy are the Goldbergs, who live in Chicago, and the Greenbergs, who live on the West Coast. The two families never met. The Goldbergs have two sons, Carl and David in that order. The Greenbergs have two sons, David and Carl in that order. All four are pushing or past fifty now. When Gwen and I and their parents went out together, the two Goldberg boys stood on adjoining window sills, motionless with their hands behind their backs, looking down on us as we got into the car—a silent gesture of reproach.

I met Milton Greenberg (Moy) in Bengal in the last year of World War II. He was a navigator in the Air Force, just torn away from Alice, whom he had married less than a year before. I believe Alice was able to send him some goodies now and then (since I can't imagine where he else got them from). Among them were anchovies, of which I was fond. Moy would promise me an anchovy or two for playing the piano. Later he insisted that he would actually dangle an anchovy to induce me to play, but I don't recall any of that.

In Bengal I also met Lee Lorch, a mathematician and a "leftist" like me. Unlike me, he was persecuted in the U.S. for his views during the McCarthy witch hunts. We met again twenty-five years later in Toronto and resumed our close friendship.

Chandler Davis was another mathematician, whose emigration to Canada was motivated by the same considerations as Lee's and mine. It was largely due to his initiative that I was invited to the University of Toronto, where I continue spending a happy old age.

There were two other colleagues, who, like Chandler, Lee, and myself emigrated from U.S. to Canada for (I assume) similar reasons: psychologists Alex Bavelas and Bill Livant. My debt to these is not easy to specify. I think what attracted me to them was sparkling imagination manifested in at times striking metaphors and an undisguised contempt for pretensions pompousness.

It was common interest in general semantics that brought Günther Schwarz and me together shortly before the close relationship between Hayakawa and myself was ruptured.

Before World War II Günther had studied political economy and upon graduation became director of a motor factory in Darmstadt. In 1944 the factory together with most of the city was destroyed by an Allied air raid. Günther and his family moved to the countryside. Once coming by bicycle to what had been Darmstadt, he saw lying about what seemed like charred pieces of lumber. Looking more closely he saw that they were human bodies. It was this sight that made Günther a life-long anti-war activist.

After the war there was first an attempt to destroy completely Germany's industrial capacity (the Morgenthau Plan). Günther had to find other ways of making a living to feed his family. He became a free lance salesman of packing materials, tin cans and the like.

Concurrently he resumed his education, attending lectures on political science, philosophy and psychology at the Darmstadt Technical University. He was shocked to learn that the students knew next to nothing about Naziism—there was no literature on the subject.

In the fall of 1956 the Russians crushed the Hungarian uprising. The threat of World War III became imminent. Again Günther discovered to his dismay that the students had no idea about what was going on.

Günther became editor and publisher of *Darmstädter Blätter*, digests of articles, excerpts from books, etc. published all over the world dealing with global issues. It could be appropriately designated as a *samizdat* publication, an allusion to the Soviet *samizdat*, the outlet for dissident thought and discussion in pre-Gorbachev Soviet Union. The name is a sardonic analogue of *gosizdat*, the acronym of "state publishing house," where *sam* (self) replaces *gos* (*gosudarstvennyi*=state), hence "do-it-yourself publishing house." *Samizdat* literature was typed on thinnest paper, ten carbon copies per page and surreptitiously distributed. The issues were anything but attractive. The same could be said for the early issues of *Darmstädter Blätter*. Of course there were no comparable obstacles to free expression and communication in post-war Germany, but it took money to publish something on one's own.

Once Günther translated and published an article from *Etc.: A Review of General Semantics*. This led to an invitation from Hayakawa to the 1965 conference on general semantics in San Francisco. There Günther saw Hayakawa's *Language in Thought and Action*. He translated it into German, rented a booth at the Frankfurt Book Fair and exhibited his translation as the only book. Soon afterwards *Darmstädter Blätter* became a book publishing house. Hayakawa's book was followed by several of mine, one of which it appeared in German three years before it appeared in English.

Besides general semantics two other themes became central in Schwarz's publications: the plight of the Jews throughout European history and peace. The peace theme became the foundation of extensive collaboration between us. Translations of *Conflict in Man-made Environment, The Origins of Violence and Peace: An Idea Whose Time Has Come* followed. Schwarz also published my Russian translation of the latter book and his own German translation of this autobiography. For the Russian translation, the latest computer technology was utilized in transliterating the Latin script into Cyrillic. But the monthly *Darmstädter Blätter* still looks very much as it did thirty years ago, not much different from its mimeographed version. It is a reminder of how much can be done with how little, given the devotion, the will, and the energy. Günther died in January, 1996, aged 91.

Among those who shared my interest in general system theory was Russell Ackoff, whose Doctor of Philosophy degree was actually in philosophy but whose professional activity revolved around "practical" matters such as consultation largely in the world of business. My contacts with that world have always been minimal for reasons that should be apparent in the light of this narrative. There was no room in my spheres of empathy and identification for businesses. I had no difficulty in conceiving firms or corporations as kinds of organisms. In fact the general system paradigm made this identification easy. What I found difficult was to empathize with organisms of this sort, for example to prefer seeing them survive rather than die. For in the last analysis, as it seemed to me, the prosperity of some enterprises must be associated with deterioration or demise of others. That is what "free enterprise" is all about. Helping one enterprise overcome its difficulties so that it can prosper and grow, in short "succeed" was, to my way of thinking, not unlike enhancing the efficiency of one military establishment vis-a-vis others—the impartial professional activity of military specialists who go from one country to another as consultants, advisors, or instructors. My deep aversion to competition was a source of my ambivalence about management science, operations research and related fields where a major goals of scientific analysis is to enhance the robustness and vitality of an enterprise in a competitive environment.

Russ Ackoff's activity helped me overcome this prejudice to a certain extent, largely because in academic context he emphasized the intellectual and philosophic significance of operations research and partly because his consulting was not confined to business, He was deeply committed to applying the same methods to community work.

In "sophisticated" business consultation, psychological considerations enter the design of strategies. For example knowledge of mass psychology plays an important part in the design of promotion strategies. This use of scientific knowledge is primarily exploitative to the extent that the effectiveness of a strategy is evaluated with respect to advantages accruing to the client while the effects on the target population (except those related to the aims of the adopted policy) are deemed irrelevant. In contrast, in the context of people-oriented community projects strategies are designed with the view of encouraging integrative and therapeutic social processes. It was this potential that to some extent changed my view concerning the possible role of system oriented operations research and its applications.

It was the peace movement that provided me with the most diverse contacts. During my year in Scandinavia (1968-1969), I got to know Alva Myrdal, whose experiences as Swedish ambassador to the UN provided me with rich information about the institutional obstacles to significant disarmament.

Dieter Senghaas, subsequently author of perceptive books on the problems of European integration, lived with us in Ann Arbor when he was studying there.

In Poland, my closest friends were Adam Schaff and Mieczyslaw Choynowski. I admired Adam for his valiant efforts to steer Marxism into channels of humane thought, to purge it of debilitating degeneration to which it succumbed in the Soviet Union. Mieczyslaw tried valiantly to inject rigorous theorizing and quantitative approaches into Polish psychology and enjoyed a measure of success during the Polish "thaw" of the late fifties.

I owe much to Andreas Diekmann, who improved on my rather sketchy research on experimental games by subjecting the results to refined statistical analysis, and to Rolf Ziegler, who was my academic host during my sojourn in Munich.

I think of Hiroharu Seki, Yoshida Sakamoto, and Shingo Shibata as my "sponsors" in Japan, at whose initiative I was repeatedly invited to participate in academic and peace related activates there.

In Russia I became a frequent visitor at the *Institut sistemnykh issledovaniy* (Institute of System Research) led by V.N. Sadovsky. In 1966 I translated an article on general system theory by Sadovsky and Lektorsky and published it in *General Systems*, the Yearbook of the Society for General Systems Research, which I edited. The article is an example of how Soviet scholars managed to inform their colleagues of important philosophical developments in the West, while taking necessary precautions against charges of heresy. After presenting an informative and perceptive picture of the general system approach, the authors added the usual cautionary formula to the effect that in spite of its merits, general system theory does not compare with dialectical materialism as a philosophy of cognition. Subsequently Sadovsky, Lektorsky, and I had a good laugh about it. I am grateful to them and several other colleagues at the Institute of System Research. They sustained my faith in the spiritual toughness of the Russian intelligentsia. Having survived seven decades of stifling state-imposed orthodoxy, they can probably carry on through the decades of turmoil that lie ahead.

It was also in Russia that I met Vladimir Lefebvre, a psychologist, who I think will be long remembered for bringing the psyche back into scientific psychology. That is, he developed an ingenious mathematical apparatus for dealing with introspection, the mode of cognition once central in psychology but subsequently neglected, eclipsed by the behaviorist approach and its offshoots. Subsequently Vladimir emigrated to U.S. and currently works at the University of California, Irvine. I translated his book, *Konfliktuyushchie Struktury* (*Conflicting Structures*) and wrote a preface to his *Algebra of Conscience*, in which his mathematical apparatus is ingeniously applied to the psychological dissection of several Dostoyevsky characters.

On one occasion, the validity of one implication of his model became dramatically apparent to me. In November 1991, while attending a conference in Ann Arbor, I suffered a heart attack. Lying on an operating table in Emergency, I was fascinated with the goings on: oscillographs flashing, interns and nurses presumably going through complex precisely organized procedures, etc. At one point an intern bent over me and asked, "How would you judge the intensity of your pain on a scale from 1 to 10?"

The first answer that occurred to me was, "Do you suppose I carry around an interval scale inside me?" However, in view of the gravity of the situation, I refrained from flippancy and said, "Well, I guess I would call it about 7."

He seemed satisfied and went on with whatever he was doing. After some time he asked me again, "How do you feel now? Give it a number."

"I would say between 3 and 4."

Later I realized that this apparent ability to estimate a sensation, be it pain or any other on a cardinal (not merely an ordinal) scale is implied by Lefebvre's model of the psyche. In fact, I recalled experiments in which subjects were asked to calibrate intensities of stimuli of very different modalities until they seemed equal, for instance the frequency of tactually perceived vibration and the loudness of a tone or even the bitterness of a solution and a loss of an amount of money.

I am indebted to Vladimir Lefebvre for broadening my conception of the human psyche, for polishing my Russian translation of *Peace, An Idea Whose Time Has Come* as well as the Russian translation of this book.

In Canada peace activism brought me in close contact with George Ignatieff and Leonard Johnson. Both wrote autobiographies centred on a commitment to peace. George had been one of Canada's leading diplomats. At the time I met him he was Chancellor of the University of Toronto. He succeeded me as president of Science for Peace. Leonard was the commander of the National Defence College in Kingston. In 1980 he invited me there as a visiting lecturer in a programme run by the college for both military and civilian personnel—a broadly conceived introduction to current world affairs, which included several months of globe trotting over all three worlds. General Johnson retired in 1986 and became one of Canada's leading peace activists, chair of the Canadian Pugwash group and of Project Ploughshares (peace think tanks).

I cherish the memory of Kenneth Boulding, whom I first met at CASBAH in 1954, and whom I saw last in the hospital of the University of Michigan the day after my heart attack. Last year I wrote his obituary. In some ways our world outlooks were very different, at first thought hardly compatible. Ken was a devout Christian. I had the impression that he believed in the Resurrection and in miracles. He was an economist. I am dismally ignorant of economics, but to the extent that I understand him, Ken thought along classical lines with an admixture of Keynesianism, while I have been a convinced socialist since I was fifteen. The core of our affinity was an appreciation of the poetic aspects of science and a deep hatred of war. Neither Ken nor I saw science and poetry as opposites. To our way of thinking, both reflect an appreciation of unity in diversity: science through structural analogies (what general system theory is about), poetry through the metaphor.

Closely related to the knack for metaphor, which makes Ken Boulding's poetry so deliciously witty, was his masterful encapsulation of profound ideas, especially insights that shatter conventional wisdom. One of my favourites is, "Things are as they are because they got that way." Sounds at first like an inanity, but one does a double take and sees the profundity.

For conventional wisdom has it that things are as they are because that's the way they are. Ken juxtaposes the dynamic view to the static. The whole immensely rich concept of evolution is encapsulated in that homely homily.

Or take "Everything that exists is possible!" Obvious to the point of being inane? But how frequently and how widely is this near-tautology denied! Or savour this gentle yet devastating satire on behavioursim:

In world of thought (though not in fact)
Nothing exists that doesn't act.
And that is reckoned wisdom which
Describes the scratch but not the itch.

Ken summarized all forms of social control in three words: threat, trade, and love. In a threat system, people do what is demanded to escape punishment (obedience exacted by threat). In a trade system, people do what is required in expectation of remuneration (compliance solicited by trade). In a love system people help, nurture, and care for other people who appear as extensions of their selves (family, tribe, nation, humanity). This sort of behaviour defines an integrative system—a love system for short.

To all my colleagues and friends, named and unnamed, who constantly reinforced my sense of identification and to the memory of the departed this book is gratefully dedicated.

Beyond the Sphere of Affection, Respect and Ideological Affinity

Beyond the circle of my personal contacts is "humanity." My feelings toward it are much more difficult to describe except in terms of what they are not. I cannot say I "love" humanity. In fact, I don't think it is possible to "love" more than a few persons. A minimal prerequisite of "love" seems to me to be a possibility of direct two-way communication, and while it is possible to entertain the illusion that one speaks to humanity, I can't ever imagine that it speaks to me. If I were an outside observer, the proverbial space alien, I sometimes think that I wouldn't think much of humanity or regret its apparently impending extinction. However I am not an outside observer. I am a member. In fact, I strongly *feel* I am a member and therefore am intensely concerned about the fate of our species, not only the immediate but also the ultimate fate. This is what I mean by extension of identification.

Prospects

Clearly the "prospects" with which I am concerned in my eighty-ninth year relate to a future that does not include me. I find I can't specify the limits of that imagined horizon. It surely spans at least a century, but beyond that the boundaries dissolve in a haze. I once read somewhere (I think it was in Charles Lamb's biography of Henry VIII) that in those days the end of the world was estimated to come in about 150 years. I have no way of knowing whether the concerns of Henry's contemporaries would have been very different if they saw the future stretching 150 centuries instead of years.

To my way of thinking, the demise of humanity, as of every other species, is certain. Being an atheist, I can't conceive of life after death for humanity any more than for an individual. So the only prospect I can juxtapose to the inevitable demise is analogous to the prospect that I juxtapose to my own impending demise or to the inevitable demise of any individual—the possibility of prolonging a bearable, perhaps even an enjoyable existence. This means parrying the threats.

Threats are of two kinds external (e.g., natural catastrophes) and internal, analogous to diseases of an organism. Many external threats, however, are man-made, such as the degradation of the environment resulting with attempts to change it with the view of improving human life. Advances in science may help to reduce or eliminate such threats, provided collective action can be organized on the global scale toward that end. Obstacles to this action stem from pathologies affecting humanity as a whole, such as ideologies (analogues of addictions, compulsions, or mental disorders in an individual) that may lead to self-destruction.

When I invoke a parallel between the life of humanity and the life of an individual, I think of a principle once taken rather seriously, namely, "Ontogeny recapitulates phylogeny." It refers to the apparent similarity between the development of an embryo and that of a phylum.

In some ways, the human embryo in its early stages resembles that of a fish. Even something like gills appear to start developing but are suppressed. The human infant moves at first on all fours, then assumes the erect stature, as if retelling the evolution of primates. The analogies are far fetched but may have some basis in the genetics of development. Witness the false nipples on the male breast, evidence of a suppressed "attempt" to produce a mammalian breast in the embryo of both sexes, a "reminder" that sex was "invented" long after life.

It may not be entirely farfetched to think of the life of humanity as a recapitulation of individual life—a sequence of infancy, childhood, maturity, and old age. The strongest support of this analogy is the process that Korzybski called "time binding." The accumulation of knowledge by humanity as a whole and storing it in a collective memory appears as the analogue of maturation of an individual. To imagine an "optimistic" prospect for humanity, I add an analogue of socialization carried beyond the immediate social milieu encompassing ever wider spheres of identification culminating in a loyalty to universal human values, which transcends all we-they dichotomies.

These two parallel processes—increasing cognitive sophistication and broadening spheres of identification appear (to me) to define the essence of "progress," or, if you will, of a "good life" both of the human individual and the human race. My certainties are the implications of my unshakable conviction about what the "good life" ought to mean. I know it is realizable on the level of the human individual. My doubts are about whether an analogue of a good life is realizable on the level of our species. No doubt these doubts were ignited by the general loss of faith in "progress" that marked the transition from the last century to ours (which, the reader will recall, I regard as beginning in 1914).[1]

Paradoxically, this very loss of faith in general "progress" can be interpreted as evidence of maturation of humanity. For in the light of maturing cognitive faculties of humanity the only "progress" that can be unambiguously regarded as such is in science, where it appears as the clearest manifestation of "time binding." Indeed the title of Korzybski's first book, devoted to time binding is *Manhood of Humanity*.[2] Now it appears that even growing sophistication of science (let alone burgeoning technology), is no longer universally regarded as synonymous with "progress". The most common manifestation of pessimism in our day is in the realization that "moral" progress has not kept pace with technical progress. Indeed, this realization may reflect the tragic side of maturation—the dissipation of youthful hopes. After all, in many people aging is often reflected in abrasiveness and ossification rather than in wisdom and mellowness.

In chronic arguments with people who insist that "you can't change human nature," I always agree that indeed you can't (by definition of "nature"), but neither can this "nature" be meaningfully described, for all that is human is embodied in it. Are humans cruel, cowardly, selfish, stupid, dull, treacherous? Indeed they are, and also magnanimous, courageous, altruistic, ingenious, brilliant, and faithful. Moreover, this ambiguity does not mean that some people are this, others that, not even that the same people are sometimes this, sometimes that. It means that the *potential* for everything good and everything evil is probably in all people but under certain circumstances (affecting entire cultures or societies) people in whom some of the above characteristics have a stronger potential to emerge and develop come into positions of influence of power, and then it seems as if an entire culture or society exhibits those traits. The apparent pervasiveness of evil makes it appear that human nature is "incurable". But this is because manifestations of evil traits are so much more conspicuous and dramatic than of good ones. (Similarly, we are much more keenly aware of disease than of health.)

On the other hand, the richness of our genetic heritage makes possible virtually unlimited linkages between genetically determined drives. Do all humans reaching sexual maturity experience the gratification of the sexual urge as *shared* delight? Overt, lethal sadism may be rare, but how about linkage of sex and power in men or sex and submission in women, possibly biologically inherited linkages? If so, is the suppression of power hunger and power lust on the level of society possible or stable? How "curable" are the clearly manifested, apparently widely pervasive addictions to personal gratification and power, on which the axiomatic base of respectable branches of social science (economics and political science respectively) rest?

I am certain that maturation of humanity in the "good" sense of the word is *possible*, and this certainty has fueled my appetite for actions which I believe contribute to its realization. However, the very word "possible" implies absence of certainty. Thus, the same conviction generates my doubts. So far, however, they have not ossified as despair.

In sum, my hope hinges on the integration of humanity. Integration means identification with others, and this, in turn means that sharing becomes a cardinal value. What is there to share? Three things: delight, such as sensuous experience or perception of beauty, knowledge of truth, and conceptions of good and evil. Of these, sharing delight can be confined to among only a few, in fact, in the case of the most intense delight to between only two persons. It is in this area that pervasive diversity is no obstacle to unity. Tolerance comes naturally and easily. Sharing of truth in the sense of agreement on what is true or false has been made possible by the advent of science. Here, too, tolerance (of ignorance, of preference for childhood fantasies instead of cognition rooted in universally perceivable realities) is possible. In my opinion universal sharing of distinction between truth and fantasy is highly desirable but not as imperative as the sharing of conceptions of what is evil, which entails sharing of universal values. Unfortunately this is the most problematic aspect of genuine integration.

To see this, consider what actual integration of human aggregates entailed. As noted above, the original human cooperating groups were bound by kinship. These coalesced into clans, tribes, chiefdoms, and the like. Eventually predominantly ethnically related populations were organized into states. An important factor in each expansion of integrated (or at least pacified) social entities was a perception of a common enemy. The main manifestation of cooperation was in a struggle against this common enemy. That is, integration involved both inclusion and inevitably exclusion, a crystallization of a we-they dichotomy the driving force of implacable hatred and lethal violence.

Now integration (identification with Other) inherent in shared delight is manifested in inclusion but not in explicit exclusion. The intense integration of intimacy or of shared aesthetic experience is consistent with more dilute integrative relationships, such as of friendship, collegiality, or civility. These, too are inclusive but not necessarily exclusive (that is, generating hostility toward outsiders). Likewise integration based on shared knowledge does not necessarily entail a crystallization of a sharp, hostility-ridden we-they dichotomy. Integration based on shared values, that is on a common perception of good and especially of evil usually does. People who perceive as good what we perceive as evil almost inevitably appear evil. Inclusion is tightly bound with exclusion.

It is in the area of values that my doubts concerning the eventual imminence of global integration are strongest and most disturbing. As I said, I try to dissipate them by picturing "human nature" as embodying a vast multitude of diverse potentials and by banking on enlightenment as an imminent by-product of sophisticated cognition inculcated by the spread of science. I try to picture the interaction between cognitive sophistication and moral growth as a self-reinforcing process. But in the same way I see addiction to power and degeneration of humane values as a pair of processes linked by positive feedback. And it is this tantalizing uncertainty this awareness of the instability of the system we call humanity (which way, which way?) that reinforces my conviction: action providing impulses toward survival and against premature demise of humanity makes life meaningful whether at the moment or in retrospect.

Therefore the fundamental question about the nature of human maturation (on the level of the species as well as of the individual) is not a question about what is the case but one about what ought to be the case, in short a guide to action. On this score I have no doubts.

NOTES

1. The reader may recall my acknowledgment of a "Eurocentric" bias in my thinking, which I can't help.
2. New York: G.P. Dutton & Co., 1921.

Index

About the Author

Anatol Rapoport (1911), Russian-born mathematician and biologist, is a pioneer and lead-figure of the systems sciences, studies in conflict and cooperation, and peace research.

Author of approximately 500 publications, Rapoport has spearheaded many scientific innovations, including the application of mathematical methods, first to Biology and later to the Social Sciences.

Operating from a multidimensional background of experience and studies—concert pianist, lecturer, mathematician, scientist, philosopher—embodying a deep humanistic commitment, and a profoundly systemic thinking, he is one of the rare thinkers who have contributed significantly to "marrying" philosophy and science, extending these areas into studies of psychological conflict in debates as large as world politics and disarmament.

Professor Emeritus of Psychology and Mathematics at the University of Toronto, Toronto, Canada, he has been the recipient of many awards including the Lenz International Peace Research Prize and the Harold D. Lasswell Award for Distinguished Scientific Contributions to Political Psychology; and honorary doctorates, of Human Letters (University of Western Michigan); of Laws (University of Toronto), of Science (Royal Military College); and of Sociology (University of Bern).

He is an active member of the American Academy of Arts and Sciences; the Council Study Committee on Ethics and Responsibilities of Scientists (chairman 1966-1968); the American Association for the Advancement of Science; the American Mathematical Society; the Mathematical Association of America; the Biometric Society; the Society for General Systems Research (president 1966); the International Society for General Semantics (president 1953-1955); the Canadian Peace Research and Education Association (president 1972-1975); and Science for Peace (president 1984-1986).

PUBLIC PLACE

Citizen Participation in the Neighbourhood and the City

Dimitrios I. Roussopoulos

The public square, the piazza, the agora, the public park were once meeting places not only for neighbourly nods and greetings, but where opinions could be exchanged on matters of the day, both private and public.

Drawing on his experience in community journalism, Roussopoulos writes on a broad range of issues that affect the daily life of neighbourhoods and cities, using *The Public Place* as a source of citizen participation.

The lessons to be learned from the examples are invaluable ✗ and the book acts as a manual of sorts, guiding communities by the principals of social ecology. The topics were well chosen ✗ Public Place succeeds in making citizens conscious of their role in the community, and how they too can make significant change.

—James Hörner, editor, *Canadian Content Online*

Dimitrios I. Roussopoulos is an editor, writer, and ecologist. He has written widely on international politics, democracy, and social change. His most recent books are *Dissidence: Essays Against the Mainstream* (1992), and *Political Ecology* (1993) Black Rose Books.

208 pages, bibliography, index
Paperback ISBN: 1-55164-156-9 $19.99
Hardcover ISBN: 1-55164-157-7 $48.99

MURRAY BOOKCHIN READER

Janet Biehl, editor

This collection provides an overview of the thought of the foremost social theorist and political philosopher of the libertarian left today. His writings span five decades, and subject matter of remarkable breadth.

A major American political philosopher. —San Francisco Chronicle

His books are classic statements of contemporary anarchism. —The Independent

Stands at the pinnacle of the genre of utopian social criticism. —The Village Voice

The selections in this reader constitute a sampling from the writings of one of the pivotal thinkers of our era.

Janet Biehl is also the author of *Finding Our Way: Rethinking Ecofeminist Politics*, and, with Murray Bookchin, *Politics of Social Ecology*, all published by Black Rose Books. She lectures at the Institute of Social Ecology in Plainfield, Vermont.

Murray Bookchin, Professor Emeritus at the School of Environmental Studies, Ramapo College and Director Emeritus of the Institute of Social Ecology, has authored more than a dozen books on urbanism, ecology, technology and philosophy. For those interested in exploring more deeply his ideas, Black Rose Books has published nine of these titles.

288 pages, bibliography, index
Paperback ISBN: 1-55164-118-6 $24.99
Hardcover ISBN: 1-55164-119-4 $53.99

ALSO PUBLISHED BY

EVERY LIFE IS A STORY

The Social Relations of Science, Ecology and Peace
Fred H. Knelman

The theme of globalization and the nature of global change provide the context and environment of the book's analysis.

Knelman first deals with the nature of science and the behaviour of scientists, using the decision to drop the atom bomb on Hiroshima in 1945 and its lasting legacy, as a case study. He then turns to an analysis of nuclear power, military and civil, and the fatal link between them.

A history of environmental thought precedes a shift to the global stage—the phenomenon of global change and the challenge of global governance. The last chapter describes a model of social sustainability.

An astute analysis coupled with profound understanding. Designed to provoke both conscience and intellect. —Roger Dittmann, Coordinator, United States Federation of Scholars and Scientists

For everyone concerned with creating a better future. —David Krieger, President, Nuclear Age Peace Foundation

A most definitive work destined to be the anti-nuclear classic of all time. —Ben Weintraub, United Nations Representative, Veterans Against Nuclear Arms

Especially welcome is his [Knelman's] plain, blunt language and especially enlightening his presentation of the material in a historical perspective. —Anatol Rapoport, Professor Emeritus of Psychology, University of Toronto

With his life-time commitment to the cause of peace, justice and ecology, Knelman's intellectual biography is a brilliant and provocative book permeated with knowledge, hope and inspiration. —Shreesh Juyal, Director, Institute for United Nations & International Affairs, and Professor of Political Science, University of Regina

Fred H. Knelman received his doctorate in Physics and Engineering at the University of London, UK. For almost fifty years, he has been synonymous with the anti-nuclear and peace movements in Canada and throughout the Western hemisphere. As listed in the 1997 edition of *Who's Who*, Knelman is the recipient of many awards.

256 pages
Paperback ISBN: 1-55164-136-4 $24.99
Hardcover ISBN: 1-55164-137-2 $53.99

BOOKS OF RELATED INTEREST BY

A Cure of the Mind, *by Theodore Sampson*
Bakunin, *by Brian Morris*
Beyond Boudaries, *by Barbara Noske*
Conquest of Bread, *by Peter Kropotkin*
Evolution and Environment, *by Peter Kropotkin*
Humanity, Society and Commitment, *by Kenneth McRobbie*
Humerous Sceptic, *by N.Anthony Bonaparte*
Into the European Mirror, *by Aruna Handa, John Kipphoff, editors*
Killing Hope, *by William Blum*
Manufacturing Consent, *by Mark Achbar*
Philosophy of Social Ecology, *by Murray Bookchin*
Military in Greek Politics, *by Thanos Veremis*
Mind Abuse, *by Rose Dyson*
Other Mexico, *by John Warnock*
Perspectives on Power, *by Noam Chomsky*
Pirates and Emperors, *by Noam Chomsky*
Raft of the Medusa, *by Julian Samuel*
Rethinking Camelot, *by Noam Chomsky*
Women and Religion, *by Fatmagul Berktay*
Writers and Politics, *by George Woodcock*
Women Pirates, *by Ulrike Klausmann, Marion Meinzerin, Gabriel Kuhn*
Zapata of Mexico, *by Peter Newell*

send for a free catalogue of all our titles
BLACK ROSE BOOKS
C.P. 1258, Succ. Place du Parc
Montréal, Québec
H3W 2R3 Canada

or visit our web site at: http://www.web.net/blackrosebooks

To order books in North America:
(phone) 1-800-565-9523 (fax) 1-800-221-9985
In the UK & Europe: (phone) 44 (0) 20 8986-4854 (fax) 44 (0) 20 8533-5821

Printed by the workers of
MARC VEILLEUX IMPRIMEUR INC.
Boucherville, Québec
for Black Rose Books Ltd.